Christopher Marlowe, Richard Henry Horne

The works of Christopher Marlowe

Christopher Marlowe, Richard Henry Horne

The works of Christopher Marlowe

ISBN/EAN: 9783742858252

Manufactured in Europe, USA, Canada, Australia, Japa

Cover: Foto ©Thomas Meinert / pixelio.de

Manufactured and distributed by brebook publishing software
(www.brebook.com)

Christopher Marlowe, Richard Henry Horne

The works of Christopher Marlowe

OF the *Jew of Malta* there is no earlier edition than the 4to. of 1633, which was published under the auspices of the well-known dramatist Thomas Heywood. The title is :—*The Famous Tragedy of The Rich Iew of Malta. As it was playd before the King and Queene, in His Majesties Theatre at White-Hall, by her Majesties Servants at the Cock-pit. Written by Christopher Marlo. London: Printed by I. B. for Nicholas Vavasour, and are to be sold at his Shop in the Inner-Temple, neere the Church.* 1633. No later 4to. appeared.

MY WORTHY FRIEND,

MASTER THOMAS HAMMON,

OF GRAY'S INN, &c.

THIS play, composed by so worthy an author as Mr. Marlowe, and the part of the Jew presented by so unimitable an actor as Mr. Alleyn, being in this later age commended to the stage ; as I ushered it unto the Court, and presented it to the Cock-pit, with these prologues and epilogues here inserted, so now being newly brought to the press, I was loth it should be published without the ornament of an Epistle ; making choice of you unto whom to devote it ; than whom (of all those gentlemen and acquaintance, within the compass of my long knowledge) there is none more able to tax ignorance, or attribute right to merit. Sir, you have been pleased to grace some of mine own works with your courteous patronage ; [1] I hope this will not be the worse accepted, because commended by me ; over whom, none can claim more power or privilege than yourself. I had no better a new-year's gift to present you with ; receive it therefore as a continuance of that inviolable obligement, by which, he rests still engaged ; who as he ever hath, shall always remain,

Tuissimus :

THO. HEYWOOD.

---

[1] Heywood dedicated to Thomas Hammon the *Second Part* of the *Fair Maid of the West* (1631), and the *First Part* of *The Iron Age* (1632).

THE JEW OF MALTA.

THE PROLOGUE SPOKEN AT COURT.

GRACIOUS and Great, that we so boldly dare,
('Mongst other plays that now in fashion are)
To present this, writ many years agone,
And in that age thought second unto none,
We humbly crave your pardon : We pursue
The story of a rich and famous Jew
Who lived in Malta : you shall find him still,
In all his projects, a sound Machiavill ;
And that's his character. He that hath past
So many censures, is now come at last
To have your princely ears : grace you him ; then
You crown the action, and renown the pen.

EPILOGUE.

IT is our fear (dread sovereign) we have bin
Too tedious ; neither can't be less than sin
To wrong your princely patience : If we have,
(Thus low dejected) we your pardon crave :
And if aught here offend your ear or sight,
We only act and speak what others write.

THE PROLOGUE TO THE STAGE.

WE know not how our play may pass this stage,
But by the best of poets[1] in that age
The Malta Jew had being, and was made;
And he, then by the best of actors[2] played;
In Hero and Leander, one did gain
A lasting memory: in Tamburlaine,
This Jew, with others many, th' other wan
The attribute of peerless, being a man
Whom we may rank with (doing no one wrong)
Proteus for shapes, and Roscius for a tongue,
So could he speak, so vary; nor is't hate
To merit, in him[3] who doth personate
Our Jew this day; nor is it his ambition
To exceed or equal, being of condition
More modest: this is all that he intends,
(And that too, at the urgence of some friends)
To prove his best, and, if none here gainsay it,
The part he hath studied, and intends to play it.

---

1 "Marlo." Marginal note in the old copy.

"Allin." Marginal note in the old copy. In the (old) Shakespeare Society's publications there is a memoir by J. P. Collier of the celebrated actor, the founder of Dulwich College, Edward Alleyn.

3 "Perkins." Marginal note in the old copy. Richard Perkins was an actor of great ability. At the end of the *White Devil* Webster speaks of the "well-approved industry of my friend Master Perkins," and adds that "the worth of his action did crown both the beginning and end." He took the part of Capt. Goodlack in Heywood's *Fair Maid of the West*, of Sir John Belfare in Shirley's *Wedding*, of Hanno in Nabbes' *Hannibal and Scipio*, and of Fitzwater in Davenport's *King John and Matilda*. From Wright's *Historia Histrionica* we learn that he died "some years before the Restoration."

EPILOGUE.

IN graving, with Pygmalion to contend ;
Or painting, with Apelles ; doubtless the end
Must be disgrace : our actor did not so,
He only aimed to go, but not out-go.
Nor think that this day any prize[1] was played ;
Here were no bets at all, no wagers laid ; [2]
All the ambition that his mind doth swell,
Is but to hear from you (by me), 'twas well.

---

[1] "A metaphor borrowed from the fencing-school, prizes being played for certain degrees in the schools where the Art of Defence was taught,—degrees, it appears, of Master, Provost, and Scholar."—Dyce's *Shakespeare Glossary*.

[2] A friend of Alleyn's backed him for a wager to excel George Peele in acting any part that had been sustained by Knell or Bentley. See Dyce's *Greene and Peele* (ed. 1861, pp. 330, 331). In the *Introduction* to the *Knight of the Burning Pestle* the Citizen says that his prentice Ralph "should have played Jeronimo with a shoemaker for a wager."

PERSONS REPRESENTED.

FERNEZE, *Governor of Malta.*
SELIM CALYMATH, *Son of the Grand Seignior.*
DON LODOWICK, *the Governor's Son, in love with*
    ABIGAIL.
DON MATHIAS, *also in love with her.*
MARTIN DEL BOSCO, *Vice-Admiral of Spain.*
BARABAS, *the Jew of Malta.*
ITHAMORE, *Barabas' slave.*
BARNARDINE, } *Friars.*
JACOMO, }
PILIA-BORSA, *a Bully.*
Two Merchants.
Three Jews.
Bassoes, Knights, Officers, Reader, Messengers, Slaves,
    and Carpenters.

KATHARINE, *mother of* DON MATTHIAS.
ABIGAIL, *the Jew's Daughter.*
Abbess.
Two Nuns.
BELLAMIRA, *a Courtesan.*

MACHIAVEL, *the Prologue.*

Scene—Malta.

THE JEW OF MALTA.

———o———

Enter MACHIAVEL.

Machiavel. Albeit the world thinks Machiavel is dead,
Yet was his soul but flown beyond the Alps ;
And now the Guise [1] is dead, is come from France,
To view this land, and frolic with his friends.
To some perhaps my name is odious,
But such as love me guard me from their tongues ;
And let them know that I am Machiavel,
And weigh not men, and therefore not men's words.
Admired I am of those that hate me most.
Though some speak openly against my books,   10
Yet they will read me, and thereby attain
To Peter's chair: and when they cast me off,
Are poisoned by my climbing followers.
I count religion but a childish toy,
And hold there is no sin but ignorance.
Birds of the air will tell of murders past !
I am ashamed to hear such fooleries.
Many will talk of title to a crown :

---

1 The Duc de Guise, who organised the Massacre of St. Bartholomew.
He was assassinated in 1588.

What right had Cæsar to the empery?[1]
Might first made kings, and laws were then most sure 20
When like the Draco's[2] they were writ in blood.
Hence comes it that a strong-built citadel
Commands much more than letters can import;
Which maxim had [but[3]] Phalaris observed,
He had never bellowed, in a brazen bull,
Of great one's envy.   Of the poor petty wights
Let me be envied and not pitièd!
But whither am I bound?   I come not, I,
To read a lecture hear in Britainy,[4]
But to present the tragedy of a Jew,   30
Who smiles to see how full his bags are crammed,
Which money was not got without my means.
I crave but this—grace him as he deserves,
And let him not be entertained the worse
Because he favours me.   [*Exit.*

---

[1] This is Dyce's correction for "empire."
[2] Old ed. "the Drancus."
[3] As a word is required to complete the verse, I have followed Cunningham in inserting "but."
[4] All the editions give "Britain." For the sake of the metre I read "Britainy"—a form found in *Edward II.*, ii. 2, l. 42.

ACT THE FIRST.

SCENE I.

Enter BARABAS *in his counting-house, with heaps of gold before him.*

Bar. So that of thus much that return was made :
And of the third part of the Persian ships,
There was the venture summed and satisfied.
As for those Sabans,[1] and the men of Uz,
That bought my Spanish oils and wines of Greece,
Here have I purst their paltry silverlings.[2]
Fie ; what a trouble 'tis to count this trash.
Well fare the Arabians, who so richly pay
The things they traffic for with wedge of gold,
Whereof a man may easily in a day   10
Tell that which may maintain him all his life.
The needy groom that never fingered groat,

---

[1] Old ed. "Samintes," for which the modern editors give "Samnites."
Between the "Samnites" and the "men of Uz" there can be no possible connection. My emendation suits the context. We have Saba for Sabæa in *Faustus,* xii. 25, &c.

[2] Old ed. "silverbings." Dyce observes that the word "silverling" occurs in *Isaiah* (vii. 23) :—"A thousand vines at a thousand silverlings."

Would make a miracle of thus much coin :
But he whose steel-barred coffers are crammed full,
And [he who] all his lifetime hath been tired,
Wearying his fingers' ends with telling it,
Would in his age be loth to labour so,
And for a pound to sweat himself to death.
Give me the merchants of the Indian mines,
That trade in metal of the purest mould ;   20
The wealthy Moor, that in the eastern rocks
Without control can pick his riches up,
And in his house heap pearls like pebble stones,
Receive them free, and sell them by the weight :
Bags of fiery opals, sapphires, amethysts,
Jacinths, hard topaz, grass-green emeralds,
Beauteous rubies, sparkling diamonds,
And seld-seen costly stones of so great price,
As one of them indifferently rated,
And of a carat of this quantity,   30
May serve in peril of calamity
To ransom great kings from captivity.
This is the ware wherein consists my wealth ;
And thus methinks should men of judgment frame
Their means of traffic from the vulgar trade,
And as their wealth increaseth, so inclose
Infinite riches in a little room.
But now how stands the wind?
Into what corner peers my halcyon's [1] bill ?

---

[1] It was a common belief that a stuffed halcyon (*i.e.*, kingfisher), sus-
pended by the bill, showed from what quarter the wind blew. Shakespeare alludes to the superstition in *Lear*, ii. 2,—

Ha! to the east? yes: see how stands the vanes?   40
East and by south: why then I hope my ships
I sent for Egypt and the bordering isles
Are gotten up by Nilus' winding banks:
Mine argosy from Alexandria,
Loaden with spice and silks, now under sail,
Are smoothly gliding down by Candy shore
To Malta, through our Mediterranean sea.
But who comes here?   How now.

Enter a Merchant.

Merch. Barabas, thy ships are safe,
Riding in Malta Road: and all the merchants   50
With other merchandise are safe arrived,
And have sent me to know whether yourself
Will come and custom[1] them.
  Bar. The ships are safe thou say'st, and richly fraught.
  Merch. They are.
  Bar. Why then go bid them come ashore,
And bring with them their bills of entry:
I hope our credit in the custom-house
Will serve as well as I were present there.
Go send 'em threescore camels, thirty mules,   60

  " Renege, affirm, and turn their *halcyon beaks*
    With every gale and vary of their master."
Sir Thomas Browne, who discusses the subject in *Vulgar Errors* (iii. 10),
says that " the eldest custom of hanging up these birds was founded upon
a tradition that they would renew their feathers every year as though they
were alive."
  [1] Pay the duty on them.

And twenty waggons to bring up the ware.
But art thou master in a ship of mine,
And is thy credit not enough for that?

Merch. The very custom barely comes to more
Than many merchants of the town are worth,
And therefore far exceeds my credit, sir.

Bar. Go tell 'em the Jew of Malta sent thee, man :
Tush ! who amongst 'em knows not Barabas?

Merch. I go.

Bar. So then, there's somewhat come.   70
Sirrah, which of my ships art thou master of?

Merch. Of the Speranza, sir.

Bar. And saw'st thou not
Mine argosy at Alexandria?
Thou could'st not come from Egypt, or by Caire,
But at the entry there into the sea,
Where Nilus pays his tribute to the main,
Thou needs must sail by Alexandria.

Merch. I neither saw them, nor inquired of them :
But this we heard some of our seamen say,   80
They wondered how you durst with so much wealth
Trust such a crazèd vessel, and so far.

Bar. Tush, they are wise ! I know her and her strength.
But [1] go, go thou thy ways, discharge thy ship,
And bid my factor bring his loading in.   [*Exit* Merch.
And yet I wonder at this argosy.

---

[1] Old ed. "By" (which might perhaps be defended, as meaning
"good-bye." Cf. Shirley's *Constant Maid,* i. 1,—" *Buoy,* Close, *buoy,*
honest Close : we are blanks, blanks.")

Enter a second Merchant.

2 *Merch.* Thine argosy from Alexandria,
Know, Barabas, doth ride in Malta Road,
Laden with riches, and exceeding store
Of Persian silks, of gold, and orient pearl.   90

Bar. How chance you came not with those other ships
That sailed by Eygpt?

2 *Merch.* Sir, we saw 'em not.

Bar. Belike they coasted round by Candy shore
About their oils, or other businesses.
But 'twas ill done of you to come so far
Without the aid or conduct of their ships.

2 *Merch.* Sir, we were wafted by a Spanish fleet,
That never left us till within a league,
That had the galleys of the Turk in chase.   100

Bar. O!—they were going up to Sicily :—
Well, go,
And bid the merchants and my men despatch
And come ashore, and see the fraught discharged.

2 *Merch.* I go.   [*Exit.*

Bar. Thus trowls our fortune in by land and sea,
And thus are we on every side enriched :
These are the blessings promised to the Jews,
And herein was old Abram's happiness :
What more may heaven do for earthly man   110
Than thus to pour out plenty in their laps,
Ripping the bowels of the earth for them,
Making the sea[s] their servants, and the winds
To drive their substance with successful blasts?
Who hateth me but for my happiness?

Or who is honoured now but for his wealth?
Rather had I a Jew be hated thus,
Than pitied in a Christian poverty:
For I can see no fruits in all their faith,
But malice, falsehood, and excessive pride, 120
Which methinks fits not their profession.
Haply some hapless man hath conscience,
And for his conscience lives in beggary.
They say we are a scattered nation:
I cannot tell, but we have scambled [1] up
More wealth by far than those that brag of faith.
There's Kirriah Jairim, the great Jew of Greece,
Obed in Bairseth, Nones in Portugal,
Myself in Malta, some in Italy,
Many in France, and wealthy every one; 130
I, wealthier far than any Christian.
I must confess we come not to be kings;
That's not our fault: alas, our number's few,
And crowns come either by succession,
Or urged by force; and nothing violent,
Oft have I heard tell, can be permanent.
Give us a peaceful rule, make Christians kings,
That thirst so much for principality.
I have no charge, nor many children,
But one sole daughter, whom I hold as dear 140
As Agamemnon did his Iphigene:
And all I have is hers. But who comes here?

---

[1] A recognised form of "scrambled." Cf. *Henry V.* i. 1 :—
  " But that the *scambling* and unquiet time
   Did push it out of farther question."

Enter three Jews.[1]

1 *Jew.* Tush, tell not me; 'twas done of policy.

2 *Jew.* Come, therefore, let us go to Barabas,
For he can counsel best in these affairs ;
And here he comes.

Bar. Why, how now, countrymen !
Why flock you thus to me in multitudes ?
What accident's betided to the Jews?

1 *Jew.* A fleet of warlike galleys, Barabas,　　150
Are come from Turkey, and lie in our road :
And they this day sit in the council-house
To entertain them and their embassy.

Bar. Why, let 'em come, so they come not to war ;
Or let 'em war, so we be conquerors—
Nay, let 'em combat, conquer, and kill all !
So they spare me, my daughter, and my wealth. [*Aside.*

1 *Jew.* Were it for confirmation of a league,
They would not come in warlike manner thus.

2 *Jew.* I fear their coming will afflict us all.　　160

Bar. Fond men ! what dream you of their multitudes.
What need they treat of peace that are in league ?
The Turks and those of Malta are in league.
Tut, tut, there is some other matter in't.

1 *Jew.* Why, Barabas, they come for peace or war.

Bar. Haply for neither, but to pass along
Towards Venice by the Adriatic Sea ;
With whom they have attempted many times,
But never could effect their stratagem.

---

[1] The scene is shifted to the Exchange.

3 *Jew.* And very wisely said. It may be so.   170

2 *Jew.* But there's a meeting in the senate-house,
And all the Jews in Malta must be there.

Bar. Hum : all the Jews in Malta must be there?
I, like enough, why then let every man
Provide him, and be there for fashion-sake.
If anything shall there concern our state,
Assure yourselves I'll look—unto myself.   [*Aside.*

1 *Jew.* I know you will ; well, brethren, let us go.

2 *Jew.* Let's take our leaves ; farewell, good Barabas.

Bar. Farewell,[1] Zaareth ; farewell, Temainte.   180

                      [*Exeunt Jews.*

And, Barabas, now search this secret out ;
Summon thy senses, call thy wits together :
These silly men mistake the matter clean.
Long to the Turk did Malta contribute ;
Which tribute, all in policy I fear,
The Turks have let increase to such a sum
As all the wealth in Malta cannot pay :
And now by that advantage thinks belike
To seize upon the town : I, that he seeks.
Howe'er the world go, I'll make sure for one,   190
And seek in time to intercept the worst,
Warily guarding that which I ha' got.
Ego mihimet sum semper proximus.[2]
Why, let 'em enter, let 'em take the town.   [*Exit.*

---

[1] Old ed. "*Iew.* Doe so ; Farewell, Zaareth," &c. Dyce is doubtless right in considering that " doe so " is a stage direction (= *Exeunt Merchants*), which has crept into the text.

[2] A misquotation from Terence's *Andria*, iv. 1. 12, "Proximus sum egomet mihi."

SCENE II.

Enter [1] *Governor of* Malta, Knights, *and* Officers ; *met by*
      Bassoes *of the* Turk, CALYMATH.

Gov. Now, Bassoes, what demand you at our hands?
1 *Bas.* Know, Knights of Malta, that we come from
      Rhodes,
From Cyprus, Candy, and those other Isles
That lie betwixt the Mediterranean seas.
Gov. What's Cyprus, Candy, and those other Isles
To us, or Malta ?   What at our hands demand ye ?
Cal. The ten years' tribute that remains unpaid.
Gov. Alas ! my lord, the sum is over-great,
I hope your highness will consider us.   10
Cal. I wish, grave governor,[2] 'twere in my power
To favour you, but 'tis my father's cause,
Wherein I may not, nay, I dare not dally.
Gov. Then give us leave, great Selim Calymath.
                    [*Consults apart with the* Knights.
Cal. Stand all aside, and let the Knights determine,
And send to keep our galleys under sail,
For happily we shall not tarry here ;
Now, governor,[2] [say,] how are you resolved ?
Gov. Thus : since your hard conditions are such
That you will needs have ten years' tribute past,   20
We may have time to make collection
Amongst the inhabitants of Malta for't.

---

[1] Scene : the Senate-house.
[2] Old ed. " governours."

1 *Bas.* That's more than is in our commission.

Cal. What, Callipine! a little courtesy.
Let's know their time, perhaps it is not long ;
And 'tis more kingly to obtain by peace
Than to enforce conditions by constraint.
What respite ask you, governor ?[1]

    Gov. But a month.

    Cal. We grant a month, but see you keep your pro-
        mise.

Now launch our galleys back again to sea,   30
Where we'll attend the respite you have ta'en,
And for the money send our messenger.
Farewell, great governor[1] and brave Knights of Malta.

    Gov. And all good fortune wait on Calymath !

                [*Exeunt* CALYMATH *and* Bassoes.
Go one and call those Jews of Malta hither :
Were they not summoned to appear to-day ?

    Off. They were, my lord, and here they come.

Enter BARABAS *and three* Jews.

    1 *Knight.* Have you determined what to say to them?

    Gov. Yes, give me leave :—and, Hebrews, now come
        near.
From the Emperor of Turkey is arrived   40
Great Selim Calymath, his highness' son,
To levy of us ten years' tribute past,
Now then, here know that it concerneth us—

---

[1] Old ed. ''governours.''

Bar. Then, good my lord, to keep your quiet still,
Your lordship shall do well to let them have it.

Gov. Soft, Barabas, there's more 'longs to 't than so.
To what this ten years' tribute will amount,
That we have cast, but cannot compass it
By reason of the wars that robbed our store :
And therefore are we to request your aid.   50

Bar. Alas, my lord, we are no soldiers :
And what's our aid against so great a prince ?

1 *Knight.* Tut, Jew, we know thou art no soldier :
Thou art a merchant and a moneyed man,
And 'tis thy money, Barabas, we seek.

Bar. How, my lord ! my money ?

Gov. Thine and the rest.
For, to be short, amongst you't must be had.

1 *Jew.* Alas, my lord, the most of us are poor

Gov. Then let the rich increase your portions.

Bar. Are strangers with your tribute to be taxed ? 60

2 *Knight.* Have strangers leave with us to get their
                          wealth ?
Then let them with us contribute.

Bar. How ! equally ?

Gov. No, Jew, like infidels.
For through our sufferance of your hateful lives,
Who stand accursèd in the sight of Heaven,
These taxes and afflictions are befallen,
And therefore thus we are determinèd.
Read there the articles of our decrees.

Reader. First, the tribute-money of the Turks shall all

*be levied amongst the Jews, and each of them to pay one
half of his estate.* 70

    Bar. How, half his estate? I hope you mean not
        mine.   *[Aside.*

    Gov. Read on.

    *Reader. Secondly, he that denies to pay shall straight
become a Christian.*

    Bar. How ! a Christian ? Hum, what's here to do ?
        [Aside.

    *Reader. Lastly, he that denies this shall absolutely lose
all he has.*

    All 3 *Jews.* O my lord, we will give half.

    Bar. O earth-mettled villains, and no Hebrews born !
And will you basely thus submit yourselves   80
To leave your goods to their arbitrament ?

    Gov. Why, Barabas, wilt thou be christenèd ?

    Bar. No, governor, I will be no convertite.[1]

    Gov. Then pay thy half.

    Bar. Why, know you what you did by this device?
Half of my substance is a city's wealth.
Governor, it was not got so easily ;
Nor will I part so slightly therewithal.

    Gov. Sir, half is the penalty of our decree,
Either pay that, or we will seize on all.

    Bar. Corpo di Dio ! stay! you shall have the half; 90
Let me be used but as my brethren are.

    Gov. No, Jew, thou hast denied the articles,
And now it cannot be recalled.

---

[1] Convert. The word occurs in *As You Like It, King John,* &c.

Bar. Will you then steal my goods?
Is theft the ground of your religion?
  Gov. No, Jew, we take particularly thine
To save the ruin of a multitude:
And better one want for the common good
Than many perish for a private man:
Yet, Barabas, we will not banish thee,   100
But here in Malta, where thou gott'st thy wealth,
Live still; and, if thou canst, get more.
  Bar. Christians, what or how can I multiply?
Of naught is nothing made.
  1 *Knight.* From naught at first thou cam'st to little
          wealth,
From little unto more, from more to most:
If your first curse fall heavy on thy head,
And make thee poor and scorned of all the world,
'Tis not our fault, but thy inherent sin.
  Bar. What, bring you scripture to confirm your
          wrongs?   110
Preach me not out of my possessions.
Some Jews are wicked, as all Christians are:
But say the tribe that I descended of
Were all in general cast away for sin,
Shall I be tried by their transgression?
The man that dealeth righteously shall live:
And which of you can charge me otherwise?
  Gov. Out, wretched Barabas!
Sham'st thou not thus to justify thyself,
As if we knew not thy profession?   120
If thou rely upon thy righteousness,

Be patient and thy riches will increase.
Excess of wealth is cause of covetousness :
And covetousness, O, 'tis a monstrous sin.

Bar. I, but theft is worse : tush ! take not from me then,
For that *is* theft ! and if you rob me thus,
I must be forced to steal and compass more.

1 *Knight.* Grave governor,[1] listen not to his exclaims.
Convert his mansion to a nunnery :
His house will harbour many holy nuns.   130

Gov. It shall be so.

Enter Officers.

Now, officers, have you done ?

Off. I, my lord, we have seized upon the goods
And wares of Barabas, which being valued,
Amount to more than all the wealth in Malta,
And of the other we have seizèd half.

Gov.[2] Then we'll take order for the residue.

Bar. Well then, my lord, say, are you satisfied ?
You have my goods, my money, and my wealth,
My ships, my store, and all that I enjoyed :
And, having all, you can request no more :   140
Unless your unrelenting flinty hearts
Suppress all pity in your stony breasts,
And now shall move you to bereave my life.

Gov. No, Barabas, to stain our hands with blood
Is far from us and our profession.

Bar. Why, I esteem the injury far less
To take the lives of miserable men

---

[1] Old ed. "governours."
[2] In the 4to. this line is given to the Officer.

Than be the causes of their misery.
You have my wealth, the labour of my life,
The comfort of mine age, my children's hope,   150
And therefore ne'er distinguish of the wrong.

  Gov. Content thee, Barabas, thou hast naught but right.

  Bar. Your extreme right does me exceeding wrong :
But take it to you, i' the devil's name.

  Gov. Come, let us in, and gather of these goods
The money for this tribute of the Turk.

  1 *Knight.* 'Tis necessary that be looked unto :
For if we break our day, we break the league,
And that will prove but simple policy.

              [*Exeunt, all except* BARABAS *and the* Jews.

  Bar. I, policy ! that's their profession,   160
And not simplicity, as they suggest.
The plagues of Egypt, and the curse of Heaven,
Earth's barrenness, and all men's hatred
Inflict upon them, thou great *Primus Motor !*
And here upon my knees, striking the earth,
I ban their souls to everlasting pains
And extreme tortures of the fiery deep,
That thus have dealt with me in my distress.

  1 *Jew.* O yet be patient, gentle Barabas.

  Bar. O silly brethren, born to see this day ;   170
Why stand you thus unmoved with my laments ?
Why weep ye not to think upon my wrongs ?
Why pine not I, and die in this distress ?

  1 *Jew.* Why, Barabas, as hardly can we brook
The cruel handling of ourselves in this :
Thou seest they have taken half our goods.

Bar. Why did you yield to their extortion?
You were a multitude, and I but one:
And of me only have they taken all.

    1 *Jew.* Yet, brother Barabas, remember Job.   180

    Bar. What tell you me of Job? I wot his wealth
Was written thus: he had seven thousand sheep,
Three thousand camels, and two hundred yoke
Of labouring oxen, and five hundred
She-asses: but for every one of those,
Had they been valued at indifferent rate,
I had at home, and in mine argosy,
And other ships that came from Egypt last,
As much as would have bought his beasts and him,
And yet have kept enough to live upon: 190
So that not he, but I may curse the day,
Thy fatal birth-day, forlorn Barabas:
And henceforth wish for an eternal night,
That clouds of darkness may inclose my flesh,
And hide these extreme sorrows from mine eyes:
For only I have toiled to inherit here
The months of vanity and loss of time,
And painful nights, have been appointed me.

    2 *Jew.* Good Barabas, be patient.

    Bar. I, I: pray leave me in my patience.   200
You that were [1] ne'er possessed of wealth, are pleased with
    want;
But give him liberty at least to mourn,
That in a field amidst his enemies
Doth see his soldiers slain, himself disarmed,

---

[1] Probably we should read—" You, ne'er possessed," etc.

And knows no means of his recovery :
I, let me sorrow for this sudden chance ;
'Tis in the trouble of my spirit I speak ;
Great injuries are not so soon forgot.

 1 *Jew.* Come, let us leave him ; in his ireful mood
Our words will but increase his ecstasy.   210

 2 *Jew.* On, then : but trust me 'tis a misery
To see a man in such affliction.——
Farewell, Barabas !   [*Exeunt.*

 Bar. I, fare you well.
See the simplicity of these base slaves,
Who, for the villains have no wit themselves,
Think me to be a senseless lump of clay
That will with every water wash to dirt :
No, Barabas is born to better chance,
And framed of finer mould than common men,
That measure naught but by the present time. 220
A reaching thought will search his deepest wits,
And cast with cunning for the time to come :
For evils are apt to happen every day——
But whither wends my beauteous Abigail ?

   Enter ABIGAIL, *the Jew's daughter.*

O! what has made my lovely daughter sad ?
What, woman ! moan not for a little loss :
Thy father hath enough in store for thee.

 Abig. Nor [not ?] for myself, but agèd Barabas :
Father, for thee lamenteth Abigail :
But I will learn to leave these fruitless tears, 230
And urged thereto with my afflictions,

With fierce exclaims run to the senate-house,
And in the senate reprehend them all,
And rend their hearts with tearing of my hair,
Till they reduce [1] the wrongs done to my father.

   Bar. No, Abigail, things past recovery
Are hardly cured with exclamations.
Be silent, daughter, sufferance breeds ease,
And time may yield us an occasion
Which on the sudden cannot serve the turn.   240
Besides, my girl, think me not all so fond
As negligently to forego so much
Without provision for thyself and me.
Ten thousand portagues,[2] besides great pearls,
Rich costly jewels, and stones infinite,
Fearing the worst of this before it fell,
I closely hid.

   Abig. Where, father?

   Bar. In my house, my girl.

   Abig. Then shall they ne'er be seen of Barabas: 250
For they have seized upon thy house and wares.

   Bar. But they will give me leave once more, I trow,
To go into my house.

   Abig. That may they not:
For there I left the governor placing nuns,
Displacing me; and of thy house they mean
To make a nunnery, where none but their own sect [3]
Must enter in; men generally barred.

---

   [1] Dyce proposed "redress."
   [2] Portuguese gold coins.
   [3] Steevens (on 2 *Henry IV.* ii. 4, l. 42) quotes several passages where "sect" is used for "sex."

Bar. My gold! my gold! and all my wealth is gone!
You partial heavens, have I deserved this plague?
What, will you thus oppose me, luckless stars,   260
To make me desperate in my poverty?
And knowing me impatient in distress,
Think me so mad as I will hang myself,
That I may vanish o'er the earth in air,
And leave no memory that e'er I was?
No, I will live; nor loathe I this my life:
And, since you leave me in the ocean thus
To sink or swim, and put me to my shifts,
I'll rouse my senses and awake myself.
Daughter! I have it: thou perceiv'st the plight   270
Wherein these Christians have oppressèd me:
Be ruled by me, for in extremity
We ought to make bar of no policy.

Abig. Father, whate'er it be to injure them
That have so manifestly wrongèd us,
What will not Abigail attempt?

Bar. Why, so:
Then thus, thou told'st me they have turned my house
Into a nunnery, and some nuns are there?

Abig. I did.

Bar. Then, Abigail, there must my girl
Entreat the abbess to be entertained.   280

Abig. How, as a nun?

Bar. I, daughter, for religion
Hides many mischiefs from suspicion.

Abig. I, but, father, they will suspect me there.

Bar. Let 'em suspect; but be thou so precise

As they may think it done of holiness.
Entreat 'em fair, and give them friendly speech,
And seem to them as if thy sins were great,
Till thou hast gotten to be entertained.

  Abig. Thus, father, shall I much dissemble.

  Bar. Tush!

As good dissemble that thou never mean'st,   290
As first mean truth and then dissemble it,—
A counterfeit profession is better
Than unseen [1] hypocrisy.

  Abig. Well, father, say [that] I be entertained,
What then shall follow?

  Bar. This shall follow then;
There have I hid, close underneath the plank
That runs along the upper chamber floor,
The gold and jewels which I kept for thee.
But here they come; be cunning, Abigail.

  Abig. Then, father, go with me.

  Bar. No, Abigail, in this   300
It is not necessary I be seen:
For I will seem offended with thee for 't:
Be close, my girl, for this must fetch my gold.

                  [They draw back.

    Enter Friar [2] JACOMO, Friar BERNARDINE, Abbess,
           and a Nun.

  F. Jac. Sisters, we now are almost at the new-made
     nunnery.

---

  [1] The passage is no doubt corrupt. Cunningham reads "unforeseen,"
and explains the meaning to be "a steady consistent piece of acting is
better than having to put on the hypocrite at a moment's warning."

  [2] Old ed. "Enter three Fryars and two Nuns."

Abb.[1] The better ; for we love not to be seen .
'Tis thirty winters long since some of us
Did stray so far amongst the multitude.

F. Jac. But, madam, this house
And waters [2] of this new-made nunnery
Will much delight you.   310

Abb.[3] It may be so ; but who comes here?

                    [ABIGAIL *comes forward.*

Abig. Grave abbess, and you, happy virgins' guide,
Pity the state of a distressèd maid.

Abb. What art thou, daughter?

Abig. The hopeless daughter of a hapless Jew,
The Jew of Malta, wretched Barabas ;
Sometimes [4] the owner of a goodly house,
Which they have now turned to a nunnery.

Abb. Well, daughter, say, what is thy suit with us?

Abig. Fearing the afflictions which my father feels   320
Proceed from sin, or want of faith in us,
I'd pass away my life in penitence,
And be a novice in your nunnery,
To make atonement for my labouring soul.

F. Jac. No doubt, brother, but this proceedeth of the
            spirit.

F. Barn. I, and of a moving spirit too, brother ; but
            come,
Let us intreat she may be entertained.

Abb. Well, daughter, we admit you for a nun.

---

1 Old ed. " 1 Nun."
2 Can this word be right?   Qu. " cloisters "?
3 Old ed. " *Nun.*"   4 *I.e.*, sometime.

Abig. First let me as a novice learn to frame
My solitary life to your strait laws,   330
And let me lodge where I was wont to lie,
I do not doubt, by your divine precepts
And mine own industry, but to profit much.
　　Bar. As much, I hope, as all I hid is worth.　[*Aside.*
　　Abb. Come, daughter, follow us.
　　Bar. Why, how now, Abigail,
What makest thou amongst these hateful Christians?
　　F. Jac. Hinder her not, thou man of little faith,
For she has mortified herself.
　　Bar. How! mortified?
　　F. Jac. And is admitted to the sisterhood.
　　Bar. Child of perdition, and thy father's shame!　340
What wilt thou do among these hateful fiends?
I charge thee on my blessing that thou leave
These devils, and their damnèd heresy.
　　Abig. Father, give [1] me--　　　[*She goes to him.*
　　Bar. Nay, back, Abigail,
(*And think upon the jewels and the gold,* [*Whispers to her.*
The board is markèd thus that covers it.)
Away, accursèd, from thy father's sight.
　　F. Jac. Barabas, although thou art in misbelief,
And wilt not see thine own afflictions,
Yet let thy daughter be no longer blind.   350
　　Bar. Blind friar, I reck not thy persuasions,
(*The board is markèd thus* [2] *that covers it.*)

---

[1] Dyce reads " forgive," perhaps rightly.
[2] Here the old ed. gives " +" (to indicate the notch in the plank
under which the treasure was concealed).

For I had rather die than see her thus.
Wilt thou forsake me too in my distress,
Seducèd daughter?   (*Go, forget not, go.*[1])
Becomes it Jews to be so credulous?
(*To-morrow early I'll be at the door.*)
No, come not at me ; if thou wilt be damned,
Forget me, see me not, and so be gone.
(*Farewell, remember to-morrow morning.*)   360
Out, out, thou wretch !

> [*Exeunt, on one side* Barabas, *on the other side* Friars,
> Abbess, Nun *and* Abigal ; *as they are going out,*

Enter MATHIAS.

Math. Who's this? fair Abigail, the rich Jew's daughter,
Become a nun ! her father's sudden fall
Has humbled her and brought her down to this :
Tut, she were fitter for a tale of love,
Than to be tired out with orisons :
And better would she far become a bed,
Embracèd in a friendly lover's arms,
Than rise at midnight to a solemn mass.

Enter LODOWICK.

Lod. Why, how now, Don Mathias ! in a dump?   370
Math. Believe me, noble Lodowick, I have seen
The strangest sight, in my opinion,
That ever I beheld.
Lod. What was't, I prythee?

---

[1] I have added the second "go" for the sake of the metre.

Math. A fair young maid, scarce fourteen years of age,
The sweetest flower in Cytherea's field,
Cropt from the pleasures of the fruitful earth,
And strangely metamorphos'd to a nun.

Lod. But say, what was she?

Math. Why, the rich Jew's daughter.

Lod. What, Barabas, whose goods were lately seized?
Is she so fair?

Math. And matchless beautiful;   380
As had you seen her 'twould have moved your heart,
Though countermined with walls of brass, to love,
Or at the least to pity.

Lod. And if she be so fair as you report,
'Twere time well spent to go and visit her:
How say you, shall we?

Math. I must and will, sir; there's no remedy.

Lod. And so will I too, or it shall go hard.
Farewell, Mathias.

Math. Farewell, Lodowick.   [*Exeunt severally.*

ACT THE SECOND.

SCENE I.

Enter[1] BARABAS *with a light.*

Bar. Thus,[2] like the sad presaging raven, that tolls
The sick man's passport in her hollow beak,
And in the shadow of the silent night
Doth shake contagion from her sable wings;
Vexed and tormented runs poor Barabas
With fatal curses towards these Christians
The uncertain pleasures of swift-footed time
Have ta'en their flight, and left me in despair :
And of my former riches rests no more
But bare remembrance, like a soldier's scar,   10
That has no further comfort for his maim.
O thou, that with a fiery pillar led'st
The sons of Israel through the dismal shades,
Light Abraham's offspring; and direct the hand
Of Abigail this night; or let the day
Turn to eternal darkness after this :
No sleep can fasten on my watchful eyes,

---

[1] Scene : before Barabas' house.
[2] Collier notices that ll. 1, 2, are found (with slight variation) in Guilpin's *Skialetheia*, 1598. Cf. Peele's *David and Bethsabe* :—
    "Like as the fatal raven, that in his voice
    Carries the dreadful summons of our death."

Nor quiet enter my distempered thoughts,
Till I have answer of my Abigail.

Enter ABIGAIL *above.*

Abig. Now have I happily espied a time   20
To search the plank my father did appoint;
And here behold, unseen, where I have found
The gold, the pearls, and jewels, which he hid.

Bar. Now I remember those old women's words,
Who in my wealth would tell me winter's tales,[1]
And speak of spirits and ghosts that glide by night
About the place where treasure hath been hid:[2]
And now methinks that I am one of those:
For whilst I live, here lives my soul's sole hope,
And, when I die, here shall my spirit walk.   30

Abig. Now that my father's fortune were so good
As but to be about this happy place;
'Tis not so happy: yet when we parted last,
He said he would attend me in the morn.
Then, gentle sleep, where'er his body rests,
Give charge to Morpheus that he may dream

---

[1] Cf. *Dido*, iii. 3 :—
    "Who would not undergo all kind of toil
      To be well stored with such a *winter's tale.*"
The words "in my *wealth*" have little meaning; I suspect that we should read "in my *youth.*"
[2] Cf. *Hamlet*, i. 1 :—
      "Or if thou hast uphoarded in thy life
        Extorted treasure in the womb of earth,
        For which, they say, you spirits oft walk in death,
        Speak of it."

A golden dream, and of the sudden wake,[1]
Come and receive the treasure I have found.

   Bar. Bueno para todos mi ganado no era: [2]
As good go on as sit so sadly thus.   40
But stay, what star shines yonder in the east? [3]
The loadstar of my life, if Abigail.
Who's there?

   Abig. Who's that?

   Bar. Peace, Abigail, 'tis I.

   Abig. Then, father, here receive thy happiness.

                              [Throws down bags.

   Bar. Hast thou't?

   Abig. Here, [*throws down the bags*] hast thou't?
There's more, and more, and more.

   Bar. O my girl,
My gold, my fortune, my felicity!
Strength to my soul, death to mine enemy!
Welcome the first beginner of my bliss!
O Abigail, Abigail, that I had thee here too!   50
Then my desires were fully satisfied:
But I will practise thy enlargement thence:
O girl! O gold! O beauty! O my bliss!

                              [Hugs his bags.

   Abig. Father, it draweth towards midnight now,

---

   1 Old ed. "walke."

   2 Old ed. "Birn para todos, my ganada no er." I have adopted
Dyce's reading.

   3 Dyce thinks that Shakespeare recollected this passage when he
wrote :—

       "But soft! what light through yonder window breaks?
        It is the East and Juliet is the sun."

And 'bout this time the nuns begin to wake;
To shun suspicion, therefore, let us part.

Bar. Farewell, my joy, and by my fingers take
A kiss from him that sends it from his soul.

                           [*Exit* ABIGAIL *above.*

Now Phœbus ope the eyelids [1] of the day,
And for the raven wake the morning lark,   60
That I may hover with her in the air ;
Singing o'er these, as she does o'er her young.

Hermoso [2] *Piarer de les Denirch.*   [*Exit.*

SCENE II.

Enter [3] Governor, MARTIN DEL BOSCO, *and* Knights.

Gov. Now, captain, tell us whither thou art bound ?
Whence is thy ship that anchors in our road ?
And why thou cam'st ashore without our leave ?

Bosc. Governor of Malta, hither am I bound :
My ship, the Flying Dragon, is of Spain,
And so am I : Del Bosco is my name ;
Vice-admiral unto the Catholic King.

   1 *Knight.* 'Tis true, my lord, therefore entreat him well.

Bosc. Our fraught is Grecians, Turks, and Afric Moors.

---

  [1] Cf. *Job* xli. 18 :—"By his neesings a light doth shine, and his eyes
are like the *eyelids of the morning.*" So Sophocles in the *Antigone*
speaks of the sun as ἀμέρας βλέφαρον. The reader will remember the
line in *Lycidas* :—

        "Under the opening *eyelids of the morn.*"

  [2] "Perhaps what is meant here is an exclamation on the beautiful
appearance of money, Hermoso parecer de los dinos, but it is questionable whether this would be good Spanish."—*Collier.* Dyce gives
"Hermoso Placer."

  [3] Scene : the Senate-house.

For late upon the coast of Corsica, 10
Because we vailed[1] not to the Turkish[2] fleet,
Their creeping galleys had us in the chase :
But suddenly the wind began to rise,
And then we luffed and tacked,[3] and fought at ease :
Some have we fired, and many have we sunk ;
But one amongst the rest became our prize :
The captain's slain, the rest remain our slaves,
Of whom we would make sale in Malta here.

 Gov. Martin del Bosco, I have heard of thee :
Welcome to Malta, and to all of us ; 20
But to admit a sale of these thy Turks
We may not, nay, we dare not give consent
By reason of a tributary league.

 1 *Knight.* Del Bosco, as thou lov'st and honour'st us,
Persuade our governor against the Turk ;
This truce we have is but in hope of gold,
And with that sum he craves might we wage war.

 Bosc. Will Knights of Malta be in league with
   Turks,
And buy it basely too for sums of gold ?
My lord, remember that, to Europe's shame, 30
The Christian Isle of Rhodes, from whence you came,
Was lately lost, and you were stated[4] here
To be at deadly enmity with Turks.

 Gov. Captain, we know it, but our force is small.

---

1 *I.e.*, did not lower our sails.   Cf. 1 *Tamburlaine*, i. 2, l. 193.
2 Old ed. "Spanish."
3 Old ed. "left and tooke."   The correction was made by Dyce.
4 Established.

Bosc. What is the sum that Calymath requires?

Gov. A hundred thousand crowns.

Bosc. My lord and king hath title to this isle,
And he means quickly to expel you hence ;
Therefore be ruled by me, and keep the gold :
I'll write unto his majesty for aid,   40
And not depart until I see you free.

  Gov. On this condition shall thy Turks be sold :
Go, officers, and set them straight in show.

                          [*Exeunt* Officers.

Bosco, thou shalt be Malta's general ;
We and our warlike Knights will follow thee
Against these barb'rous misbelieving Turks.

  Bosc. So shall you imitate those you succeed :
For when their hideous force environed Rhodes,
Small though the number was that kept the town,
They fought it out, and not a man survived   50
To bring the hapless news to Christendom.

  Gov. So will we fight it out : come, let's away :
Proud daring Calymath, instead of gold,
We'll send thee bullets wrapt [1] in smoke and fire :
Claim tribute where thou wilt, we are resolved,
Honour is bought with blood and not with gold.

                               [*Exeunt.*

SCENE III.

Enter [2] Officers *with* ITHAMORE *and other slaves.*

  1 *Off.* This is the market-place, here let 'em stand :
Fear not their sale, for they'll be quickly bought.

---

[1] Cf. *King John*, i. 2 :—
        " And now instead of *bullets wrapt in fire.*"
[2] Scene : the market-place.

2 *Off.* Every one's price is written on his back,
And so much must they yield or not be sold.
   1 *Off.* Here comes the Jew; had not his goods been
        seized,
He'd given us present money for them all.

Enter BARABAS.

   Bar. In spite of these swine-eating Christians,—
Unchosen nation, never circumcised,
Such[1] as (poor villains !) were ne'er thought upon
Till Titus and Vespasian conquered us,—   10
Am I become as wealthy as I was :
They hoped my daughter would ha' been a nun ;
But she's at home, and I have bought a house
As great and fair as is the Governor's ;
And there in spite of Malta will I dwell :
Having Ferneze's hand, whose heart I'll have ;
I, and his son's too, or it shall go hard.
I am not of the tribe of Levi, I,
That can so soon forget an injury.
We Jews can fawn like spaniels when we please :   20
And when we grin we bite, yet are our looks
As innocent and harmless as a lamb's.
I learned in Florence how to kiss my hand,
Heave up my shoulders when they call me dog,[2]
And duck as low as any barefoot friar ;
Hoping to see them starve upon a stall,

---

  1 The modern editors give " Poor villains, such as," &c. ; but the reading of the 4to. is quite intelligible.
  2 Cf. Shylock's " Still have I borne it with a patient shrug."

Or else be gathered for in our Synagogue,
That, when the offering-basin comes to me,
Even for charity I may spit into't.
Here comes Don Lodowick, the Governor's son,   30
One that I love for his good father's sake.

Enter LODOWICK.

Lod. I hear the wealthy Jew walkèd this way :
I'll seek him out, and so insinuate,
That I may have a sight of Abigail ;
For Don Mathias tells me she is fair.
    Bar. Now will I show myself
To have more of the serpent than the dove ;
That is—more knave than fool.
    Lod. Yond' walks the Jew ; now for fair Abigail.
    Bar. I, I, no doubt but she's at your command.   40
                                                    [*Aside.*
    Lod. Barabas, thou know'st I am the Governor's son.
    Bar. I would you were his father too, sir :
That's all the harm I wish you.—The slave looks
Like a hog's-cheek new singed.   [*Aside.*
    Lod. Whither walk'st thou, Barabas ?
    Bar. No farther : 'tis a custom held with us,
That when we speak with Gentiles like to you,
We turn into the air to purge ourselves :
For unto us the promise doth belong.
    Lod. Well, Barabas, canst help me to a diamond ?   50
    Bar. O, sir, your father had my diamonds.
Yet I have one left that will serve your turn :—
I mean my daughter : but ere he shall have her

I'll sacrifice her on a pile of wood.
I ha' the poison of the city [?] for him,
And the white leprosy.   [*Aside.*
    Lod. What sparkle does it give without a foil?
    Bar. The diamond that I talk of ne'er was foiled :—
But when he touches it, he will be foiled :—   [*Aside.*
Lord Lodowick, it sparkles bright and fair.   60
    Lod. Is it square or pointed, pray let me know.
    Bar. Pointed it is, good sir—but not for you. [*Aside.*
    Lod. I like it much the better.
    Bar. So do I too.
    Lod. How shows it by night?
    Bar. Outshines Cynthia's rays :
You'll like it better far o' nights than days.   [*Aside.*
    Lod. And what's the price?
    Bar. Your life an' if you have it. [*Aside.*] O my
        lord,
We will not jar about the price ; come to my house
And I will give 't your honour—with a vengeance. [*Aside.*
    Lod. No, Barabas, I will deserve it first.   70
    Bar. Good sir,
Your father has deserved it at my hands,
Who, of mere charity and Christian truth,
To bring me to religious purity,
And as it were in catechising sort,
To make me mindful of my mortal sins,
Against my will, and whether I would or no,
Seized all I had, and thrust me out o' doors,
And made my house a place for nuns most chaste.
    Lod. No doubt your soul shall reap the fruit of it.   80

Bar. I, but, my lord, the harvest is far off :
And yet I know the prayers of those nuns
And holy friars, having money for their pains,
Are wondrous ;—and indeed do no man good :   [*Aside.*
And seeing they are not idle, but still doing,
'Tis likely they in time may reap some fruit,
I mean in fulness of perfection.

Lod. Good Barabas, glance not at our holy nuns.

Bar. No, but I do it through a burning zeal,—
Hoping ere long to set the house afire :   90
For though they do a while increase and multiply,
I'll have a saying to[1] that nunnery.—   [*Aside.*
As for the diamond, sir, I told you of,
Come home and there's no price shall make us part,
Even for your honourable father's sake.—
It shall go hard but I will see your death.—   [*Aside.*
But now I must be gone to buy a slave.

Lod. And, Barabas, I'll bear thee company.

Bar. Come then—here's the market-place.
What's the price of this slave ?   Two hundred crowns !
Do the Turks weigh so much ?   100

1 *Off.* Sir, that's his price.

Bar. What, can he steal that you demand so much ?
Belike he has some new trick for a purse ;
And if he has, he is worth three hundred plates,[2]

---

[1] Dyce quotes from Barnabe Barnes' *Divils Charter*, 1607, " For I
must *have a saying to* those bottels."

[2] Pieces of silver. Cf. *Ant. and Cleo.* :—
" Realms and islands were
As *plates* dropt from his pocket."

So that, being bought, the town-seal might be got
To keep him for his lifetime from the gallows :
The sessions day is critical to thieves,
And few or none 'scape but by being purged.

Lod. Rat'st thou this Moor but at two hundred plates ?
1 *Off.* No more, my lord.   110
Bar. Why should this Turk be dearer than that Moor ?
1 *Off.* Because he is young and has more qualities.
Bar. What, hast the philosopher's stone ? and thou
hast, break my head with it, I'll forgive thee.
Slave.[1] No, sir ; I can cut and shave.
Bar. Let me see, sirrah, are you not an old shaver ?[2]
Slave.[3] Alas, sir ! I am a very youth.
Bar. A youth ?   I'll buy you, and marry you to Lady
Vanity,[4] if you do well.
Slave.[3] I will serve you, sir.   120
Bar. Some wicked trick or other.   It may be, under
colour of shaving, thou'lt cut my throat for my goods.
Tell me, hast thou thy health well ?
Slave.[3] I, passing well.
Bar. So much the worse ; I must have one that's
sickly, and be but for sparing victuals : 'tis not a stone of
beef a day will maintain you in these chops ; let me see
one that's somewhat leaner.

---

[1] Old ed. "*Itha.*"
[2] A cant word still in use.
[3] Old ed. "*Ith.*"
[4] An allegorical character in the old moralities.   Cf. 1 *Henry IV.* ii.
4 :—"That reverend *vice*, that grey *iniquity*, that *vanity* in years."   In
the *Devil is an Ass*, "Lady Vanity" is coupled with "Iniquity."

1 *Off.* Here's a leaner, how like you him?

Bar. Where wast thou born?   130

Itha. In Thrace; brought up in Arabia.

Bar. So much the better, thou art for my turn,
An hundred crowns, I'll have him; there's the coin.

1 *Off.* Then mark him, sir, and take him hence.

Bar. I, mark him, you were best, for this is he
That by my help shall do much villainy.   [*Aside.*
My lord, farewell: Come, sirrah, you are mine.
As for the diamond, it shall be yours:
I pray, sir, be no stranger at my house,
All that I have shall be at your command.   140

Enter MATHIAS *and his* Mother.[1]

Math. What makes the Jew and Lodowick so private?
I fear me 'tis about fair Abigail.

Bar. Yonder comes Don Mathias, let us stay;[2]

                                  [*Exit* LODOWICK.

He loves my daughter, and she holds him dear:
But I have sworn to frustrate both their hopes,
And be revenged upon the Governor.

Moth. This Moor is comeliest, is he not? speak, son.

Math. No, this is the better, mother; view this well.

Bar. Seem not to know me here before your mother,
Lest she mistrust the match that is in hand: 150
When you have brought her home, come to my house;
Think of me as thy father; son, farewell.

Math. But wherefore talked Don Lodowick with you?

---

[1] Old ed. "Mater."   [2] Stop our conversation.

Bar. Tush ! man, we talked of diamonds, not of
      Abigail.

Moth. Tell me, Mathias, is not that the Jew?

Bar. As for the comment on the Maccabees,
I have it, sir, and 'tis at your command.

Math. Yes, madam, and my talk with him was [but] [1]
About the borrowing of a book or two.

Moth. Converse not with him, he's cast off from
      heaven. 160
Thou hast thy crowns, fellow ; come, let's away.

Math. Sirrah, Jew, remember the book.

Bar. Marry will I, sir.
           [*Exeunt* MATHIAS *and his* Mother.

Off. Come, I have made
A reasonable market ; let's away.
           [*Exeunt* Officers *with slaves.*

Bar. Now let me know thy name, and therewithal
Thy birth, condition, and profession.

Itha. Faith, sir, my birth is but mean : my name's
Ithamore, my profession what you please.

Bar. Hast thou no trade? then listen to my words, 170
And I will teach [thee] that shall stick by thee :
First be thou void of these affections,
Compassion, love, vain hope, and heartless fear,
Be moved at nothing, see thou pity none,
But to thyself smile when the Christians moan.

Itha. O brave ! master, I worship your nose [2] for this

---

[1] I have followed Dyce's suggestion in adding this word.

[2] An important part in Barabas' get-up was his large nose. In
William Rowley's *Search for Money*, 1609, there is an allusion to the
"artificial Jew of Malta's nose."

Bar. As[1] for myself, I walk abroad o' nights
And kill sick people groaning under walls :
Sometimes I go about and poison wells ;
And now and then, to cherish Christian thieves,   180
I am content to lose some of my crowns,
That I may, walking in my gallery,
See 'em go pinioned along by my door.
Being young, I studied physic, and began
To practise first upon the Italian ;
There I enriched the priests with burials,
And always kept the sextons' arms in ure[2]
With digging graves and ringing dead men's knells :
And after that was I an engineer,
And in the wars 'twixt France and Germany,   190
Under pretence of helping Charles the Fifth,
Slew friend and enemy with my stratagems.
Then after that was I an usurer,
And with extorting, cozening, forfeiting,
And tricks belonging unto brokery,
I filled the jails with bankrupts in a year,
And with young orphans planted hospitals,
And every moon made some or other mad,
And now and then one hang himself for grief,
Pinning upon his breast a long great scroll   200
How I with interest tormented him.
But mark how I am blest for plaguing them ;

---

[1] In *Titus Andronicus* Aaron gives a somewhat similar catalogue of
villainies.
[2] Use.

I have as much coin as will buy the town.
But tell me now, how hast thou spent thy time?
  Itha. 'Faith, master,
In setting Christian villages on fire,
Chaining of eunuchs, binding galley-slaves.
One time I was an hostler in an inn,
And in the night time secretly would I steal
To travellers' chambers, and there cut their throats: 210
Once at Jerusalem, where the pilgrims kneeled,
I strewed powder on the marble stones,
And therewithal their knees would rankle so
That I have laughed a-good[1] to see the cripples
Go limping home to Christendom on stilts.
  Bar. Why this is something : make account of me
As of thy fellow : we are villains both :
Both circumcisèd, we hate Christians both :
Be true and secret, thou shalt want no gold.
But stand aside, here comes Don Lodowick. 220

Enter LODOWICK.

  Lod. O Barabas, well met ;
Where is the diamond you told me of?
  Bar. I have it for you, sir ; please you walk in with
      me :
What ho, Abigail![2] open the door, I say.

Enter ABIGAIL.

  Abig. In good time, father ; here are letters come
From Ormus, and the post stays here within.

---

    [1] Heartily.
    [2] The scene shifts to the front of Barabas' house.

Bar. Give me the letters.—Daughter, do you hear,
Entertain Lodowick the Governor's son
With all the courtesy you can afford ;
Provided that you keep your maidenhead.   230
Use him as if he were a Philistine.
Dissemble, swear, protest, vow love [1] to him,
He is not of the seed of Abraham.
I am a little busy, sir, pray pardon me.
Abigail, bid him welcome for my sake.   [*Aside.*
    Abig. For your sake and his own he's welcome hither.
    Bar. Daughter, a word more ; kiss him, speak him
        fair,
And like a cunning Jew so cast about,
That ye be both made sure [2] ere you come out.   [*Aside.*
    Abig. O father ! Don Mathias is my love.   240
    Bar. I know it : yet I say, make love to him ;
Do, it is requisite it should be so—
Nay, on my life, it is my factor's hand—
But go you in, I'll think upon the account.
                    [*Exeunt* ABIGAIL *and* LODOWICK.
The account is made, for Lodowick [he [3]] dies.
My factor sends me word a merchant's fled
That owes me for a hundred tun of wine :
I weigh it thus much [*snapping his fingers*]: I have
        wealth enough.

---

[1] Dyce's correction for the old copy's "vow to love him."
[2] Affianced.   "Accordailles, the betrothing or *making sure* of a man and woman together."—*Cotgrave.*
[3] The word "he" was inserted by Cunningham for the sake of the metre.

For now by this has he kissed Abigail:
And she vows love to him, and he to her.   250
As sure as heaven rained manna for the Jews,
So sure shall he and Don Mathias die:
His father was my chiefest enemy.

Enter MATHIAS.

Whither goes Don Mathias? stay awhile.
 Math. Whither, but to my fair love Abigail?
 Bar. Thou know'st, and Heaven can witness this is
    true,
That I intend my daughter shall be thine.
 Math. I, Barabas, or else thou wrong'st me much.
 Bar. O, Heaven forbid I should have such a thought.
Pardon me though I weep: the Governor's son   260
Will, whether I will or no, have Abigail:
He sends her letters, bracelets, jewels, rings.
 Math. Does she receive them?
 Bar. She? No, Mathias, no, but sends them back,
And when he comes, she locks herself up fast;
Yet through the keyhole will he talk to her,
While she runs to the window looking out,
When you should come and hale him from the door.
 Math. O treacherous Lodowick!
 Bar. Even now as I came home, he slipt me in,   270
And I am sure he is with Abigail.
 Math. I'll rouse him thence.
 Bar. Not for all Malta, therefore sheathe your sword;
If you love me, no quarrels in my house;
But steal you in, and seem to see him not;

I'll give him such a warning ere he goes
As he shall have small hopes of Abigail.
Away, for here they come.

       Enter LODOWICK *and* ABIGAIL.

Math. What, hand in hand !   I cannot suffer this.
Bar. Mathias, as thou lovest me, not a word.   280
Math. Well, let it pass, another time shall serve.
                                            [*Exit.*

Lod. Barabas, is not that the widow's son ?
Bar. I, and take heed, for he hath sworn your death.
Lod. My death ? what, is the base-born peasant mad ?
Bar. No, no, but happily he stands in fear
Of that which you, I think, ne'er dream upon,
My daughter here, a paltry silly girl.
Lod. Why, loves she Don Mathias ?
Bar. Doth she not with her smiling answer you ?
Abig. He has my heart : I smile against my will.   290
                                          [*Aside.*

Lod. Barabas, thou know'st I've loved thy daughter long.
Bar. And so has she done you, even from a child.
Lod. And now I can no longer hold my mind.
Bar. Nor I the affection that I bear to you.
Lod. This is thy diamond, tell me shall I have it ?
Bar. Win it, and wear it, it is yet unsoiled.
O : but I know your lordship would disdain
To marry with the daughter of a Jew ;
And yet I'll give her many a golden cross [1]
With Christian posies round about the ring.   300

---

[1] A piece of money marked on one side with a cross.

Lod. 'Tis not thy wealth, but her that I esteem.
Yet crave I thy consent.

Bar. And mine you have, yet let me talk to her.—
This offspring of Cain, this Jebusite,
That never tasted of the Passover,
Nor e'er shall see the land of Canaan,
Nor our Messias that is yet to come ;
This gentle maggot, Lodowick, I mean,
Must be deluded : let him have thy hand,
But keep thy heart till Don Mathias comes.   [*Aside.* 310

Abig. What, shall I be betrothed to Lodowick ?

Bar. It's no sin to deceive a Christian :
For they themselves hold it a principle,
Faith is not to be held with heretics :
But all are heretics that are not Jews;
This follows well, and therefore, daughter, fear not.

[*Aside.*

I have entreated her, and she will grant.

Lod. Then, gentle Abigail, plight thy faith to me.

Abig. I cannot chuse, seeing my father bids.—
Nothing but death shall part my love and me. [*Aside.* 320

Lod. Now have I that for which my soul hath longed.

Bar. So have not I, but yet I hope I shall.   [*Aside.*

Abig. O wretched Abigail, what hast thou [1] done ?

[*Aside.*

Lod. Why on the sudden is your colour changed ?

Abig. I know not, but farewell, I must be gone.

Bar. Stay her, but let her not speak one word more.

---

[1] Old ed. " thee."

Lod. Mute o' the sudden : here's a sudden change.

Bar. O, muse not at it, 'tis the Hebrew's guise,
That maidens new betrothed should weep awhile :
Trouble her not ; sweet Lodowick, depart :   330
She is thy wife, and thou shalt be mine heir.

Lod. O, is't the custom ? then I am resolved :
But rather let the brightsome heavens be dim,
And nature's beauty choke with stifling clouds,
Than my fair Abigail should frown on me.—
There comes the villain, now I'll be revenged.

Enter MATHIAS.

Bar. Be quiet, Lodowick, it is enough
That I have made thee sure to Abigail.

Lod. Well, let him go.   [*Exit.*

Bar. Well, but for me, as you went in at doors   340
You had been stabbed, but not a word on't now ;
Here must no speeches pass, nor swords be drawn.

Math. Suffer me, Barabas, but to follow him.

Bar. No ; so shall I, if any hurt be done,
Be made an accessary of your deeds :
Revenge it on him when you meet him next.

Math. For this I'll have his heart.

Bar. Do so ; lo here I give thee Abigail.

Math. What greater gift can poor Mathias have ?
Shall Lodowick rob me of so fair a love ?   350
My life is not so dear as Abigail.

Bar. My heart misgives me, that, to cross your love,
He's with your mother, therefore after him.

Math. What, is he gone unto my mother ?

Bar. Nay, if you will, stay till she comes herself.

Math. I cannot stay ; for if my mother come,
She'll die with grief.   [*Exit.*

Abig. I cannot take my leave of him for tears :
Father, why have you thus incensed them both ?

Bar. What's that to thee ?   360

Abig. I'll make 'em friends again.

Bar. You'll make 'em friends !
Are there not Jews enough in Malta,
But thou must doat upon a Christian ?

Abig. I will have Don Mathias, he is my love.

Bar. Yes, you shall have him : go put her in.

Itha. I, I'll put her in.   [*Puts her in.*

Bar. Now tell me, Ithamore, how lik'st thou this ?

Itha. Faith, master, I think by this
You purchase both their lives ; is it not so ?   370

Bar. True ; and it shall be cunningly performed.

Itha. O master, that I might have a hand in this.

Bar. I, so thou shalt, 'tis thou must do the deed :
Take this, and bear it to Mathias straight,

[*Gives a letter.*

And tell him that it comes from Lodowick.

Itha. 'Tis poisoned, is it not ?

Bar. No, no, and yet it might be done that way :
It is a challenge feigned from Lodowick.

Itha. Fear not : I will so set his heart afire,
That he shall verily think it comes from him.   380

Bar. I cannot choose but like thy readiness :
Yet be not rash, but do it cunningly.

Itha. As I behave myself in this, employ me here-
after.

Bar. Away then. [*Exit.*

So, now will I go in to Lodowick,
And, like a cunning spirit, feign some lie,
Till I have set 'em both at enmity. [*Exit.*

ACT THE THIRD.

SCENE I.

Enter [1] BELLAMIRA, *a courtesan.*

Bell. Since this town was besieged, my gain grows
      cold :
The time has been that, but for one bare night,
A hundred ducats have been freely given :
But now against my will I must be chaste ;
And yet I know my beauty doth not fail.
From Venice merchants, and from Padua
Were wont to come rare-witted gentlemen,
Scholars I mean, learnèd and liberal ;
And now, save Pilia-Borza, comes there none,
And he is very seldom from my house ;   10
And here he comes.

Enter PILIA-BORZA.

Pilia. Hold thee, wench, there's something for thee
to spend.

---

[1] Bellamira displays herself on a balcony. Cf. a stage-direction in
Brome's *Covent Garden Weeded* :—"Enter Dorcas above on a Bell-
conie. Gabriel gazes at her. Dorcas is habited like a curtizan of
Venice."

Bell. 'Tis silver.   I disdain it.

Pilia. I, but the Jew has gold,
And I will have it, or it shall go hard.

Court. Tell me, how cam'st thou by this?

Pilia. 'Faith, walking the back lanes, through the gardens, I chanced to cast mine eye up to the Jew's counting-house, where I saw some bags of money, and in the night I clambered up with my hooks, and, as I was taking my choice, I heard a rumbling in the house; so I took only this, and run my way: but here's the Jew's man.   24

Bell. Hide the bag.

Enter ITHAMORE.

Pilia. Look not towards him, let's away: zoon's, what a looking thou keep'st; thou'lt betray 's anon.

[*Exeunt* Courtesan *and* PILIA-BORZA.

Itha. O the sweetest face that ever I beheld: I know she is a courtesan by her attire: now would I give a hundred of the Jew's crowns that I had such a concubine. Well,   31
I have delivered the challenge in such sort,
As meet they will, and fighting die; brave sport. [*Exit.*

SCENE II.

Enter MATHIAS.[1]

Math. This is the place, now Abigail shall see
Whether Mathias holds her dear or no.

: Scene : a street.

Enter LODOWICK.[1]

What, dares the villain write in such base terms?

[*Reading a letter.*

Lod. I did it : and revenge it if thou dar'st.

[*They fight.*

Enter BARABAS, *above.*[2]

Bar. O ! bravely fought ; and yet they thrust not
home.

Now, Lodowick ! now, Mathias ! So——   [*Both fall.*

So now they have showed themselves to be tall [3] fellows.

[*Cries within.*] Part 'em, part 'em.

Bar. I, part 'em now they are dead. Farewell, farewell.

[*Exit.*

Enter Governor *and* MATHIAS'S Mother.

Gov. What sight is this?—my Lodowick [4] slain :   10
These arms of mine shall be thy sepulchre.[5]

Mother. Who is this ? my son Mathias slain !

Gov. O Lodowick : had'st thou perished by the
Turk,

Wretched Ferneze might have 'venged thy death.

---

[1] Old ed.—

"*Enter Lodow. reading.*

"*Math.* What dares the villain," &c. The challenge was "feign'd
from Lodowick."

[2] On the upper-stage, a raised platform.

[3] Bold.

[4] Here and elsewhere, for the sake of the metre, Dyce prints "Lodovico." Perhaps he is right, for the name may have been contracted into
"Lod." or "Lodo." in the MS. from which the play was printed.

[5] Dyce compares 3 *Henry VI.* ii. 5 :—

"*These arms of mine* shall be thy winding sheet ;
My heart, sweet boy, *shall be thy supulchre.*"

Mother. Thy son slew mine, and I'll revenge his
  death.

Gov. Look, Katherine, look!—thy son gave mine
  these wounds.

Mother. O leave to grieve me, I am grieved enough.

Gov. O! that my sighs could turn to lively breath :
And these my tears to blood, that he might live.

Mother. Who made them enemies ?   20

Gov. I know not, and that grieves me most of all.

Mother. My son loved thine.

Gov. And so did Lodowick him.

Mother. Lend me that weapon that did kill my son,
And it shall murder me.

Gov. Nay, madam, stay : that weapon was my son's,
And on that rather should Ferneze die.

Mother. Hold, let's inquire the causers of their deaths,
That we may 'venge their blood upon their heads.

Gov. Then take them up, and let them be interred 30
Within one sacred monument of stone :
Upon which altar [1] I will offer up
My daily sacrifice of sighs and tears,
And with my prayers pierce impartial [2] heavens,

---

[1] Cf. *Two Gentlemen of Verona*, iii. 2 :—
    "Say that upon the altar of her beauty
     You sacrifice your tears."

[2] "Impartial" is occasionally used by old writers in the sense of
"unkindly." Cf. Prologue to Peele's *Arraignment of Paris* :—
    "Th' *unpartial* daughters of Necessity
     Bin aiders in her suit."
So in William Smith's *Chloris* (Sonnet 11) :—
    "No, it was not Nature's ornament
     But wingèd love's *unpartial* cruel wound."

Till they [reveal] the causers of our smarts,
Which forced their hands divide united hearts :
Come, Katherine, our losses equal are,
Then of true grief let us take equal share.

[Exeunt with the bodies.

SCENE III.

Enter ITHAMORE.[1]

Itha. Why, was there ever seen such villainy,
So neatly plotted, and so well performed?
Both held in hand,[2] and flatly both beguiled?

Enter ABIGAIL.

Abig. Why, how now, Ithamore, why laugh'st thou so?
Itha. O mistress, ha! ha! ha!
Abig. Why, what ail'st thou?
Itha. O my master!
Abig. Ha!
Itha. O mistress ˙ I have the bravest, gravest, secret, subtle, bottle-nosed knave to my master, that ever gentleman had.

11

Abig. Say, knave, why rail'st upon my father thus?
Itha. O, my master has the bravest policy.
Abig. Wherein?
Itha. Why, know you not?
Abig. Why, no.
Itha. Know you not of Mathia[s'] and Don Lodowick['s] disaster?

---

1 Scene : a room in Barabas' house.
2 " Kept in expectation, having their hopes flattered."—*Dyce.*

Abig. No, what was it?

Itha. Why, the devil invented a challenge, my master
writ it, and I carried it, first to Lodowick, and *imprimis*
to Mathia[s].   22
And then they met, [and,] as the story says,
In doleful wise they ended both their days.

Abig. And was my father furtherer of their deaths?

Itha. Am I Ithamore?

Abig. Yes.

Itha. So sure did your father write, and I carry the
challenge.

Abig. Well, Ithamore, let me request thee this,   30
Go to the new-made nunnery, and inquire
For any of the Friars of St. Jaques,[1]
And say, I pray them come and speak with me.

Itha. I pray, mistress, will you answer me but one
question?

Abig. Well, sirrah, what is't?

Itha. A very feeling one : have not the nuns fine sport
with the friars now and then?

Abig. Go to, sirrah sauce, is this your question? get
ye gone.   40

Itha. I will, forsooth, mistress.   [*Exit.*

Abig. Hard-hearted father, unkind Barabas,
Was this the pursuit of thy policy !
To make me show them favour severally,
That by my favour they should both be slain?
Admit thou lov'dst not Lodowick for his sire,[2]

---

1 Old ed. "Jaynes."
2 Dyce's correction : old ed. "sinne."

Yet Don Mathias ne'er offended thee :
But thou wert set upon extreme revenge,
Because the Prior [1] dispossessed thee once,
And could'st not 'venge it, but upon his son :   50
Nor on his son, but by Mathias' means ;
Nor on Mathias, but by murdering me.
But I perceive there is no love on earth,
Pity in Jews, or piety in Turks.
But here comes cursed Ithamore, with the friar.

Enter ITHAMORE *and* FRIAR JACOMO.

F. Jac. Virgo, salve.
Itha. When ! duck you ! [2]
Abig. Welcome, grave friar ; Ithamore begone.

[*Exit* ITHAMORE.

Know, holy sir, I am bold to solicit thee.
   F. Jac. Wherein ?   60
   Abig. To get me be admitted for a nun.
   F. Jac. Why, Abigail, it is not yet long since
That I did labour thy admission,
And then thou did'st not like that holy life.
   Abig. Then were my thoughts so frail and unconfirmed,
And I was chained to follies of the world :
But now experience, purchasèd with grief,
Has made me see the difference of things.
My sinful soul, alas, hath paced too long

---

1 So the old ed. Cunningham boldly reads "Governor," which is
certainly the word we should have expected.

2 Dyce and the other editors give "When duck you?" I take
"when" to be an abrupt exclamation denoting impatience, in which
sense the word is often found (see Dyce's *Shakespeare Glossary*).

The fatal labyrinth of misbelief,   70
Far from the sun that gives eternal life.

  F. Jac. Who taught thee this?

  Abig. The abbess of the house,
Whose zealous admonition I embrace:
O, therefore, Jacomo, let me be one,
Although unworthy, of that sisterhood.

  F. Jac. Abigail, I will, but see thou change no more,
For that will be most heavy to thy soul.

  Abig. That was my father's fault.

  F. Jac. Thy father's! how?   80

  Abig. Nay, you shall pardon me.—O Barabas,
Though thou deservest hardly at my hands,
Yet never shall these lips bewray thy life.   [*Aside.*

  F. Jac. Come, shall we go?

  Abig. My duty waits on you.   [*Exeunt.*

SCENE IV.

Enter[1] BARABAS, *reading a letter.*

  Bar. What, Abigail become a nun again!
False and unkind; what, hast thou lost thy father?
And all unknown, and unconstrained of me,
Art thou again got to the nunnery?
Now here she writes, and wills me to repent.
Repentance! *Spurca!* what pretendeth[2] this?

---

[1] Scene: a room in Barabas' house.
[2] *I.e.* portendeth.

I fear she knows—'tis so—of my device
In Don Mathias' and Lodovico's deaths :
If so, 'tis time that it be seen into :
For she that varies from me in belief   10
Gives great presumption that she loves me not :
Or loving, doth dislike of something done.
But who comes here?

Enter ITHAMORE.

O Ithamore, come near ;
Come near, my love ; come near, thy master's life,
My trusty servant, nay, my second self : [1]
For I have now no hope but even in thee :
And on that hope my happiness is built ;
When saw'st thou Abigail?

Itha. To-day.
Bar. With whom?   20
Itha. A friar.
Bar. A friar ! false villain, he hath done the deed.
Itha. How, sir?
Bar. Why, made mine Abigail a nun.
Itha. That's no lie, for she sent me for him.
Bar. O unhappy day !
False, credulous, inconstant Abigail !
But let 'em go : and, Ithamore, from hence
Ne'er shall she grieve me more with her disgrace ;
Ne'er shall she live to inherit aught of mine,   30
Be blest of me, nor come within my gates,

---

[1] Old ed. "life."

But perish underneath my bitter curse,
Like Cain by Adam, for his brother's death.

　Itha. O master!

　Bar. Ithamore, entreat not for her, I am moved,
And she is hateful to my soul and me:
And 'less [1] thou yield to this that I entreat,
I cannot think but that thou hat'st my life.

　Itha. Who, I, master? Why, I'll run to some rock,
And throw myself headlong into the sea; 　　　　40
Why, I'll do anything for your sweet sake.

　Bar. O trusty Ithamore, no servant, but my friend:
I here adopt thee for mine only heir,
All that I have is thine when I am dead,
And whilst I live use half; spend as myself:
Here take my keys, I'll give 'em thee anon:
Go buy thee garments: but thou shall not want:
Only know this, that thus thou art to do:
But first go fetch me in the pot of rice
That for our supper stands upon the fire. 　　　　50

　Itha. I hold my head my master's hungry. I go, sir.
　　　　　　　　　　　　　　　　　　　　[*Exit.*

　Bar. Thus every villain ambles after wealth,
Although he ne'er be richer than in hope:
But, husht!

　　　　Enter ITHAMORE *with the pot.*

　Itha. Here 'tis, master.

　Bar. Well said, Ithamore; what, hast thou brought
The ladle with thee too?

---

[1] Old ed. "least."

Itha. Yes, sir, the proverb says he that eats with the devil had need of a long spoon.[1] I have brought you a ladle.   60

Bar. Very well, Ithamore, then now be secret;
And for thy sake, whom I so dearly love,
Now shalt thou see the death of Abigail,
That thou may'st freely live to be my heir.

Itha. Why, master, will you poison her with a mess of rice porridge? that will preserve life, make her round and plump, and batten more than you are aware.

Bar. I, but, Ithamore, seest thou this?
It is a precious powder that I bought
Of an Italian, in Ancona, once,   70
Whose operation is to bind, infect,
And poison deeply, yet not appear
In forty hours after it is ta'en.

Itha. How, master?

Bar. Thus, Ithamore.
This even they use in Malta here,—'tis called
Saint Jacques' Even,—and then I say they use
To send their alms unto the nunneries:
Among the rest bear this, and set it there;
There's a dark entry where they take it in,   80
Where they must neither see the messenger,
Nor make inquiry who hath sent it them.

Itha. How so?

Bar. Belike there is some ceremony in't.

---

[1] A very old proverb; it is found in Chaucer's *Squieres Tale,* John Heywood's *Proverbs, Comedy of Errors,* &c.

There, Ithamore, must thou go place this pot![1]
Stay, let me spice it first.

Itha. Pray do, and let me help you, master.   Pray let
me taste first.

Bar. Prythee do : what say'st thou now?

Itha. Troth, master, I'm loth such a pot of pottage
should be spoiled.   90

Bar. Peace, Ithamore, 'tis better so than spared.
Assure thyself thou shalt have broth by the eye.[2]
My purse, my coffer, and myself is thine.

Itha. Well, master, I go.

Bar. Stay, first let me stir it, Ithamore.
As fatal be it to her as the draught
Of which great Alexander drunk and died :
And with her let it work like Borgia's wine,
Whereof his sire, the Pope, was poisoned.
In few,[3] the blood of Hydra, Lerna's bane :   100
The juice of hebon,[4] and Cocytus' breath,
And all the poisons of the Stygian pool
Break from the fiery kingdom ; and in this
Vomit your venom and invenom her
That like a fiend hath left her father thus.

---

[1] Old ed. "plot."

[2] *I.e.* in abundance. Dyce compares Beaumont and Fletcher's *Knight of the Burning Pestle*, ii. 2 :—"Here's money and gold *by th' eye*, my boy."

[3] Briefly.

[4] The juice of ebony (variously written "hebon" or "hebenon") was thought to be a strong poison. Cf. *Hamlet*, i. 5 :—

> "Upon my secure hour thy uncle stole
> With juice of cursed *hebenon* in a vial."

Itha. What a blessing has he given 't! was ever pot of
rice porridge so sauced! What shall I do with it?

Bar. O, my sweet Ithamore, go set it down,
And come again so soon as thou hast done,
For I have other business for thee.   110

Itha. Here's a drench to poison a whole stable of
Flanders mares: I'll carry 't to the nuns with a powder.

Bar. And the horse pestilence to boot; away.

Itha. I am gone.
Pay me my wages, for my work is done.   [*Exit.*

Bar. I'll pay thee with a vengeance, Ithamore. [*Exit.*

SCENE V.

Enter [1] Governor, DEL BOSCO, Knights, Basso.

Gov. Welcome, great Basso; [2] how fares Calymath,
What wind thus drives you into Malta Road?

Bas. The wind that bloweth all the world besides,
Desire of gold.

Gov. Desire of gold, great sir?
That's to be gotten in the Western Ind:
In Malta are no golden minerals.

Bas. To you of Malta thus saith Calymath:
The time you took for respite is at hand,
For the performance of your promise passed,
And for the tribute-money I am sent.   10

---

[1] Scene: the Senate-house.
[2] Old ed. "Bashaws." (I have kept the spelling "Basso" throughout.)

Gov. Basso, in brief, 'shalt have no tribute here,
Nor shall the heathens live upon our spoil :
First will we raze the city walls ourselves,
Lay waste the island, hew the temples down,
And, shipping off our goods to Sicily,
Open an entrance for the wasteful sea,
Whose billows beating the resistless banks,
Shall overflow it with their refluence.

   Bas. Well, Governor, since thou hast broke the league
By flat denial of the promised tribute,   20
Talk not of razing down your city walls,
You shall not need trouble yourselves so far,
For Selim Calymath shall come himself,
And with brass bullets batter down your towers,
And turn proud Malta to a wilderness
For these intolerable wrongs of yours ;
And so farewell.

   Gov. Farewell :
And now, ye men of Malta, look about,
And let's provide to welcome Calymath :   30
Close your portcullis, charge your basilisks,
And as you profitably take up arms,
So now courageously encounter them ;
For by this answer, broken is the league,
And naught is to be looked for now but wars,
And naught to us more welcome is than wars.

                               [Exeunt.

SCENE VI.

Enter[1] Friar JACOMO *and* Friar BARNARDINE.

F. Jac. O brother, brother, all the nuns are sick,
And physic will not help them : they must die.

F. Barn. The abbess sent for me to be confessed :
O, what a sad confession will there be !

F. Jac. And so did fair Maria send for me :
I'll to her lodging : hereabouts she lies.   [*Exit.*

Enter ABIGAIL.

F. Barn. What, all dead, save only Abigail ?

Abig. And I shall die too, for I feel death coming.
Where is the friar that conversed with me.

F. Barn. O, he is gone to see the other nuns.   10

Abig. I sent for him, but seeing you are come,
Be you my ghostly father : and first know,
That in this house I lived religiously,
Chaste, and devout, much sorrowing for my sins,
But ere I came——

F. Barn. What then ?

Abig. I did offend high Heaven so grievously,
As I am almost desperate for my sins :
And one offence torments me more than all.
You knew Mathias and Don Lodowick ?   20

F. Barn. Yes, what of them ?

Abig. My father did contract me to 'em both :

---

1 Scene: a room in the convent.—The stage direction in the 4to. is
" *Enter two Friars and Abigail.*"

First to Don Lodowick; him I never loved :
Mathias was the man that I held dear,
And for his sake did I become a nun.

F. Barn. So, say how was their end?

Abig. Both jealous of my love, envied each other,
And by my father's practice, which is there

[*Gives a paper.*

Set down at large, the gallants were both slain.

F. Barn. O monstrous villainy !   30

Abig. To work my peace, this I confess to thee ;
Reveal it not, for then my father dies.

F. Barn. Know that confession must not be revealed,
The canon law forbids it, and the priest
That makes it known, being degraded first,
Shall be condemned, and then sent to the fire.

Abig. So I have heard ; pray, therefore keep it close.
Death seizeth on my heart, ah gentle friar !
Convert my father that he may be saved,
And witness that I die a Christian.   [*Dies.* 40

F. Barn. I, and a virgin too : that grieves me
              most :
But I must to the Jew and exclaim on him,
And make him stand in fear of me.

Enter Friar JACOMO.

F. Jac. O brother, all the nuns are dead, let's bury
              them.

F. Barn. First help to bury this, then go with me
And help me to exclaim against the Jew.

F. Jac. Why, what has he done?

F. Barn. A thing that makes me tremble to unfold.

F. Jac. What, has he crucified a child?

F. Barn. No, but a worse thing: 'twas told me in
    shrift,   50

Thou know'st 'tis death an if it be revealed.

Come, let's away.   [*Exeunt.*

ACT THE FOURTH.

SCENE I.

Enter[1] B\RABAS *and* ITHAMORE.   *Bells within.*

Bar. There is no music to[2] a Christian's knell :
How sweet the bells ring now the nuns are dead,
That sound at other times like tinkers' pans?
I was afraid the poison had not wrought ;
Or, though it wrought, it would have done no good,
For every year they swell, and yet they live ;
Now all are dead, not one remains alive.
  Iath. That's brave, master, but think you it will not
      be known?
  Bar. How can it, if we two be secret?
  Itha. For my part fear you not.   10
  Bar. I'd cut thy throat if I did.
  Itha. And reason too.
But here's a royal monastery hard by ;
Good master, let me poison all the monks.
  Bar. Thou shalt not need, for now the nuns are dead
They'll die with grief.

---

[1] Scene : a street.   [2] *I.e.* compared to.

Itha. Do you not sorrow for your daughter's death?

Bar. No, but I grieve because she lived so long.
An Hebrew born, and would become a Christian!
Cazzo,[1] *diabolo.* 20

Enter the two Friars.

Itha. Look, look, master, here come two religious
caterpillars.

Bar. I smelt 'em ere they came.

Itha. God-a-mercy, nose; come, let's begone.

F. Barn. Stay, wicked Jew, repent, I say, and stay.

F. Jac. Thou hast offended, therefore must be damned.

Bar. I fear they know we sent the poisoned broth.

Itha. And so do I, master, therefore speak 'em fair.

F. Barn. Barabas, thou hast——

F. Jac. I, that thou hast—— 30

Bar. True, I have money, what though I have?

F. Barn. Thou art a——

F. Jac. I, that thou art a——

Bar. What needs all this? I know I am a Jew.

F. Barn. Thy daughter——

F. Jac. I, thy daughter——

Bar. O speak not of her, then I die with grief.

F. Barn. Remember that——

F. Jac. I, remember that—— 40

Bar. I must needs say that I have been a great usurer.

F. Barn. Thou hast committed——

Bar. Fornication—but that

---

1 A vulgar Italian oath. (Old ed. "*Catho diabola.*")

Was in another country : and besides,
The wench is dead.

 F. Barn. I, but, Barabas,
Remember Mathias and Don Lodowick.

 Bar. Why, what of them ?

 F. Barn. I will not say that by a forged challenge they
   met.

 Bar. She has confest, and we are both undone,   50
My bosom inmate ![1] but I must dissemble.— [*Aside.*
O holy friars, the burthen of my sins
Lie heavy on my soul; then pray you tell me.
Is't not too late now to turn Christian ?
I have been zealous in the Jewish faith,
Hard-hearted to the poor, a covetous wretch,
That would for lucre's sake have sold my soul.
A hundred for a hundred I have ta'en ;
And now for store of wealth may I compare
With all the Jews in Malta ; but what is wealth ?   60
I am a Jew, and therefore am I lost.
Would penance serve for this my sin,
I could afford to whip myself to death——

 Itha. And so could I ; but penance will not serve.

 Bar. To fast, to pray, and wear a shirt of hair,
And on my knees creep to Jerusalem.
Cellars of wine, and sollers [2] full of wheat,
Warehouses stuft with spices and with drugs,
Whole chests of gold, in bullion, and in coin,

---

[1] Old ed. "inmates."

[2] Upper rooms ; lofts. The word is still used in some parts of the country.

Besides I know not how much weight in pearl,　　70
Orient and round, have I within my house;
At Alexandria, merchandise unsold :[1]
But yesterday two ships went from this town,
Their voyage will be worth ten thousand crowns.
In Florence, Venice, Antwerp, London, Seville,
Frankfort, Lubeck, Moscow, and where not,
Have I debts owing; and in most of these,
Great sums of money lying in the banco;
All this I'll give to some religious house
So I may be baptized, and live therein.　　80

 F. Jac. O good Barabas, come to our house.

 F. Barn. O no, good Barabas, come to our house;
And, Barabas, you know——

 Bar. I know that I have highly sinned.
You shall convert me, you shall have all my wealth.

 F. Jac. O Barabas, their laws are strict.

 Bar. I know they are, and I will be with you.
         [*To* F. JAC.

 F. Barn. They wear no shirts, and they go barefoot too.

 Bar. Then 'tis not for me; and I am resolved
         [*To* F. BARN.

You shall confess me, and have all my goods.　　90

 F. Jac. Good Barabas, come to me.

 Bar. You see I answer him, and yet he stays;
         [*To* F. BARN.

Rid him away, and go you home with me.

 F. Jac. I'll be with you to-night.

---

[1] Dyce reads " untold."

Bar. Come to my house at one o'clock this night.

[*To* F. JAC.

F. Jac. You hear your answer, and you may be gone.

F. Barn. Why, go get you away.

F. Jac. I will not go for thee.

F. Barn. Not! then I'll make thee go.

F. Jac. How, dost call me rogue?   [*They fight.* 100

Itha. Part 'em, master, part 'em.

Bar. This is mere frailty, brethren, be content.
Friar Barnardine, go you with Ithamore:
You[1] know my mind, let me alone with him.

[*Aside to* F. BARN.

F. Jac. Why does he go to thy house; let him begone.

Bar. I'll give him something and so stop his mouth.

[*Exit* ITHAMORE *with* F. BARN.

I never heard of any man but he
Maligned the order of the Jacobins:
But do you think that I believe his words?
Why, brother, you converted Abigail: 110
And I am bound in charity to requite it,
And so I will.   O Jacomo, fail not, but come.

F. Jac. But, Barabas, who shall be your godfathers,
For presently you shall be shrived.

Bar. Marry, the Turk[2] shall be one of my godfathers,
But not a word to any of your covent.[3]

F. Jac. I warrant thee, Barabas.   [*Exit.*

Bar. So, now the fear is past, and I am safe:

---

[1] This line and the next are given to Ithamore in the old copy.
[2] Ithamore.
[3] The old form (preserved in "Covent Garden") of "convent.

For he that shrived her is within my house,
What if I murdered him ere Jacomo comes? 120
Now I have such a plot for both their lives
As never Jew nor Christian knew the like;
One turned my daughter, therefore he shall die :
The other knows enough to have my life,
Therefore 'tis not requisite he should live.
But are not both these wise men to suppose
That I will leave my house, my goods, and all
To fast and be well whipt ? I'll none of that.
Now Friar Barnardine I come to you,
I'll feast you, lodge you, give you fair words, 130
And after that, I and my trusty Turk—
No more but so : it must and shall be done.   *[Exit.*

SCENE II.

Enter[1] BARABAS *and* ITHAMORE.

Bar. Ithamore, tell me, is the friar asleep ?
Itha. Yes ; and I know not what the reason is,
Do what I can he will not strip himself,
Nor go to bed, but sleeps in his own clothes ;
I fear me he mistrusts what we intend.
Bar. No, 'tis an order which the friars use :
Yet, if he knew our meanings, could he 'scape ?
Itha. No, none can hear him, cry he ne'er so loud.
Bar. Why true, therefore did I place him there :
The other chambers open towards the street. 10

---

[1] Scene : a room in Barabas' house.   In the 4to. this scene is a con-
tinuation of the former.

Itha. You loiter, master, wherefore stay we thus?
O how I long to see him shake his heels.

Bar. Come on, sirrah.
Off with your girdle, make a handsome noose;

> [ITHAMORE *makes a noose in his girdle. They put it round the* Friar's *neck.*

Friar, awake!

F. Barn. What, do you mean to strangle me?

Itha. Yes, 'cause you use to confess.

Bar. Blame not us but the proverb, confess and be hanged; pull hard.

F. Barn. What, will you have[1] my life?   20

Bar. Pull hard, I say; you would have had my goods.

Itha. I, and our lives too, therefore pull amain.

> [*They strangle him.*

'Tis neatly done, sir, here's no print at all.

Bar. Then it is as it should be; take him up.

Itha. Nay, master, be ruled by me a little [*Stands up the body*]; so, let him lean upon his staff; excellent! he stands as if he were begging of bacon.

Bar. Who would not think but that this friar lived? What time o' night is't now, sweet Ithamore?

Itha. Towards one.   30

Bar. Then will not Jacomo be long from hence.

> [*Exeunt.*

Old ed. "save." Perhaps we should read:—"What will you? save my life!"

SCENE III.

Enter[1] Friar JACOMO.

F. Jac. This is the hour wherein I shall proceed;
O happy hour,[2] wherein I shall convert
An infidel, and bring his gold into our treasury!
But soft, is not this Barnardine? it is;
And, understanding I should come this way,
Stands here a purpose, meaning me some wrong,
And intercept my going to the Jew.
Barnardine!
Wilt thou not speak? thou think'st I see thee not:
Away, I'd wish thee, and let me go by: 10
No, wilt thou not? nay, then, I'll force my way;
And see, a staff stands ready for the purpose:
As thou lik'st that, stop me another time.

> [*Strikes him and he falls.*

Enter BARABAS *and* ITHAMORE.

Bar. Why, how now, Jacomo, what hast thou done?
F. Jac. Why, stricken him that would have struck at me.
Bar. Who is it?
Barnardine? now out, alas! he's slain.
Itha. I, master, he's slain: look how his brains drop
out on's nose.

---

1 Scene : the front of Barabas' house.
2 I am tempted to arrange the verse thus :—
    "O happy hour,
      Wherein I shall convert an infidel,
      And bring his gold into our treasury!"

F. Jac. Good sirs, I have done't, but nobody knows it
but you two—I may escape.   21

Bar. So might my man and I hang with you for
company.

Itha. No, let us bear him to the magistrates.

F. Jac. Good Barabas, let me go.

Bar. No, pardon me; the law must have its course.
I must be forced to give in evidence,
That being importuned by this Barnardine
To be a Christian, I shut him out,
And there he sat: now I, to keep my word,   30
And give my goods and substance to your house,
Was up thus early; with intent to go
Unto your friary, because you stayed.

Itha. Fie upon 'em, master; will you turn Christian
when holy friars turn devils and murder one another?

Bar. No, for this example I'll remain a Jew:
Heaven bless me: what! a friar a murderer?
When shall you see a Jew commit the like?

Itha. Why, a Turk could ha' done no more.

Bar. To-morrow is the sessions; you shall to it.   40
Come, Ithamore, let's help to take him hence.

F. Jac. Villains, I am a sacred person; touch me not.

Bar. The law shall touch you, we'll but lead you, we:
'Las I could weep at your calamity.
Take in the staff too, for that must be shown:
Law wills that each particular be known.   [*Exeunt.*

SCENE IV.

Enter [1] BELLAMIRA *and* PILIA-BORSA.

Bell. Pilia-Borsa, did'st thou meet with Ithamore?

Pilia. I did.

Bell. And didst thou deliver my letter?

Pilia. I did.

Bell. And what think'st thou? will he come?

Pilia. I think so, but yet I cannot tell; for at the reading of the letter he look'd like a man of another world.

Bell. Why so?

Pilia. That such a base slave as he should be saluted by such a tall man as I am, from such a beautiful dame as you.   12

Bell. And what said he?

Pilia. Not a wise word, only gave me a nod, as who should say, "Is it even so;" and so I left him, being driven to a non-plus at the critical aspect of my terrible countenance.

Bell. And where didst meet him?

Pilia. Upon mine own freehold, within forty feet of the gallows, conning his neck-verse,[2] I take it, looking of a friar's execution, whom I saluted with an old hempen proverb, *Hodie tibi, cras mihi,* and so I left him to the

---

[1] Scene : a balcony of Bellamira's house.

[2] The verse read by criminals to entitle them to "benefit of clergy." The first words of the 51st Psalm were commonly chosen.

mercy of the hangman : but the exercise[1] being done, see where he comes. 24

Enter ITHAMORE.

Itha. I never knew a man take his death so patiently as this friar ; he was ready to leap off ere the halter was about his neck ; and when the hangman had put on his hempen tippet, he made such haste to his prayers, as if he had had another cure to serve ; well, go whither he will, I'll be none of his followers in haste : And, now I think on't, going to the execution, a fellow met me with a muschatoes[2] like a raven's wing, and a dagger with a hilt like a warming-pan, and he gave me a letter from one Madam Bellamira, saluting me in such sort as if he had meant to make clean my boots with his lips ; the effect was, that I should come to her house. I wonder what the reason is ; it may be she sees more in me than I can find in myself : for she writes further, that she loves me ever since she saw me, and who would not requite such love ? Here's her house, and here she comes, and now would I were gone : I am not worthy to look upon her. 41

Pilia. This is the gentleman you writ to.

Itha. Gentleman ! he flouts me ; what gentry can be in a poor Turk of tenpence ?[3] I'll be gone. [*Aside.*

---

[1] Sermon. Cf. *Richard III.* iii. 2 :—
  " I thank thee, good Sir John, with all my heart ;
  I am in debt for your last *exercise.*"
[2] *I.e.*, a pair of mustachios.
[3] The contemptuous expression "Turk of tenpence " is found in Dekker's *Satiromastix,* &c.

Bell. Is't not a sweet-faced youth, Pilia?

Itha. Again, "sweet youth;" [*Aside*]—did not you, sir, bring the sweet youth a letter?

Pilia. I did, sir, and from this gentlewoman, who, as myself, and the rest of the family, stand or fall at your service.   50

Bell. Though woman's modesty should hale me back, I can withhold no longer: welcome, sweet love.

Itha. Now am I clean, or rather foully out of the way.
                                                                                             [*Aside.*

Bell. Whither so soon?

Itha. I'll go steal some money from my master to make me handsome [*Aside*]: Pray pardon me, I must go and see a ship discharged.

Bell. Canst thou be so unkind to leave me thus?

Pilia. And ye did but know how she loves you, sir.

Itha. Nay, I care not how much she loves me.   Sweet Bellamira, would I had my master's wealth for thy sake.

Pilia. And you can have it, sir, an if you please.   62

Itha. If 'twere above ground I could and would have it; but he hides and buries it up, as partridges do their eggs, under the earth.

Pilia. And is't not possible to find it out?

Itha. By no means possible.

Bell. What shall we do with this base villain then?
                                                                      [*Aside to* PILIA-BORSA.

Pilia. Let me alone; do you but speak him fair:
                                                                             [*Aside to her.*

But [sir] you know some secrets of the Jew,   70
Which, if they were revealed, would do him harm.

Itha. I, and such as—Go to, no more. I'll make him send me half he has, and glad he scapes so too.

[*Pen and ink.*[1]

I'll write unto him; we'll have money straight.

Pilia. Send for a hundred crowns at least.

Itha. Ten hundred thousand crowns—*Master Bara-*
   bas.   [*Writing.*

Pilia. Write not so submissively, but threatening him.

Itha. Sirrah, Barabas, send me a hundred crowns.

Pilia. Put in two hundred at least.

Itha. I charge thee send me three hundred by this bearer, and this shall be your warrant; if you do not, no more, but so.   82

Pilia. Tell him you will confess.

Itha. Otherwise I'll confess all—Vanish, and return in a twinkle.

Pilia. Let me alone; I'll use him in his kind.

[*Exit* PILIA-BORSA.

Itha. Hang him, Jew.

Bell. Now, gentle Ithamore, lie in my lap.
Where are my maids? provide a running [2] banquet;
Send to the merchant, bid him bring me silks, 90
Shall Ithamore, my love, go in such rags?

Itha. And bid the jeweller come hither too.

Bell. I have no husband, sweet; I'll marry thee.

Itha. Content, but we will leave this paltry land,

---

[1] In old ed. these words are printed as part of the text. I have followed Dyce in printing them as a stage-direction.

[2] So the old ed.—Dyce and Cunningham read "cunning;" but the expression "running banquet" (akin to our "hasty meal") occurs in *Henry VIII.* i. 4, l. 13.

And sail from hence to Greece, to lovely Greece.
I'll be thy Jason, thou my golden fleece;
Where painted carpets o'er the meads are hurled,
And Bacchus' vineyards overspread the world;
Where woods and forests go in goodly green,
I'll be Adonis, thou shalt be Love's Queen.   100
The meads, the orchards, and the primrose lanes,
Instead of sedge and reed, bear sugar-canes:
Thou in those groves, by Dis above,
Shalt live with me and be my love.

    Bell. Whither will I not go with gentle Ithamore?

Enter PILIA-BORSA.

    Itha. How now! hast thou the gold?

    Pilia. Yes.

    Itha. But came it freely? did the cow give down her milk freely?

    Pilia. At reading of the letter, he stared and stamped and turned aside. I took him by the beard,[1] and looked upon him thus: told him he were best to send it; then he hugged and embraced me.   113

    Itha. Rather for fear than love.

    Pilia. Then, like a Jew, he laughed and jeered, and told me he loved me for your sake, and said what a faithful servant you had been.

    Itha. The more villain he to keep me thus: here's goodly 'parel, is there not?

    Pilia. To conclude, he gave me ten crowns.   120

    Itha. But ten? I'll not leave him worth a grey groat.

---

    1 So modern editors. Old ed. "steed."

Give me a ream[1] of paper; we'll have a kingdom of gold for 't.

Pilia. Write for five hundred crowns.

Itha. [*Writing.*] *Sirrah, Jew, as you love your life send me five hundred crowns, and give the bearer one hundred.* Tell him I must have 't.

Pilia. I warrant your worship shall have 't.

Itha. And if he ask why I demand so much, tell him I scorn to write a line under a hundred crowns.　　　130

Pilia. You'd make a rich poet, sir. I am gone. [*Exit.*

Itha. Take thou the money : spend it for my sake.

Bell. 'Tis not thy money, but thyself I weigh :
Thus Bellamira esteems of gold. [*Throws it on the floor.*
But thus of thee.　　　　　　　　　　[*Kisses him.*

Itha. That kiss again : she runs division[2] of my lips.
What an eye she casts on me? It twinkles like a star.

Bell. Come, my dear love, let's in and sleep together.

Itha. O, that ten thousand nights were put in one,
that we might sleep seven years together afore we wake.

Bell. Come, amorous wag, first banquet, and then
　　　sleep.　　　　　　　　　　　　[*Exeunt.* 141

SCENE V.

Enter[3] BARABAS, *reading a letter.*

Bar. "Barabas, send me three hundred crowns."
Plain Barabas : O, that wicked courtesan!

---

[1] Dyce observes that "realm" was often written "ream." Marlowe was not much addicted to quibbling.

[2] A musical term.

[3] Scene : a room in Barabas' house.

He was not wont to call me Barabas.
"Or else I will confess:" I, there it goes:
But if I get him, *coupe de gorge*, for that.
He sent a shaggy tottered [1] staring slave,
That when he speaks draws out his grisly beard,
And winds it twice or thrice about his ear; [2]
Whose face has been a grindstone for men's swords;
His hands are hacked, some fingers cut quite off;　　　10
Who, when he speaks, grunts like a hog, and looks
Like one that is employed in catzerie [3]
And crossbiting,[4]—such a rogue
As is the husband to a hundred whores:
And I by him must send three hundred crowns!
Well, my hope is, he will not stay there still;
And when he comes: O, that he were but here!

Enter PILIA-BORSA.

Pilia. Jew, I must have more gold.
Bar. Why, want'st thou any of thy tale?
Pilia. No; but three hundred will not serve his turn. 20
Bar. Not serve his turn, sir?

---

1 "Tottered" and "tattered" are used indifferently by old writers.
2 Cf. a somewhat similar description of a ruffian in *Arden of Fever-sham*:—
　　　　"A lean-faced writhen knave,
　　　　Hawk-nosed and very hollow-eyed,
　　　　With mighty furrows in his stormy brows;
　　　　Long hair down his shoulders curled;
　　　　His chin was bare, but on his upper lip
　　　　A mutchado which he *wound about his ear.*"
3 A word formed from "catso."
4 Swindling.

Pilia. No, sir; and, therefore, I must have five hundred more.

Bar. I'll rather——

Pilia. O good words, sir, and send it you were best; see, there's his letter.   [*Gives letter.*

Bar. Might he not as well come as send; pray bid him come and fetch it; what he writes for you, ye shall have straight.

Pilia. I, and the rest too, or else——   30

Bar. I must make this villain away.   [*Aside.* Please you dine with me, sir;—and you shall be most heartily poisoned.   [*Aside.*

Pilia. No, God-a-mercy.   Shall I have these crowns?

Bar. I cannot do it, I have lost my keys.

Pilia. O, if that be all, I can pick ope your locks.

Bar. Or climb up to my counting-house window: you know my meaning.

Pilia. I know enough, and therefore talk not to me of your counting-house.   The gold, or know, Jew, it is in my power to hang thee.   41

Bar. I am betrayed.   [*Aside.*
'Tis not five hundred crowns that I esteem,
I am not moved at that: this angers me,
That he who knows I love him as myself,
Should write in this imperious vein.   Why, sir,
You know I have no child, and unto whom
Should I leave all but unto Ithamore?

Pilia. Here's many words, but no crowns: the
          crowns!

Bar. Commend me to him, sir, most humbly,   50
And unto your good mistress, as unknown.

Pilia. Speak, shall I have 'em, sir?

Bar. Sir, here they are.

O, that I should part with so much gold!   [*Aside.*

Here, take 'em, fellow, with as good a will——

As I would see thee hang'd [*Aside*]: O, love stops my
    breath:

Never loved man servant as I do Ithamore.

Pilia. I know it, sir.

Bar. Pray, when, sir, shall I see you at my house?

Pilia. Soon enough, to your cost, sir. Fare you well. 60
                                           [*Exit.*

Bar. Nay, to thine own cost, villain, if thou com'st.
Was ever Jew tormented as I am?
To have a shag-rag knave to come,—
Three hundred crowns,—and then five hundred crowns!
Well, I must seek a means to rid 'em all,
And presently; for in his villainy
He will tell all he knows, and I shall die for it.
I have it:
I will in some disguise go see the slave,
And how the villain revels with my gold.   70
                                           [*Exit.*

SCENE VI.

Enter[1] BELLAMIRA, ITHAMORE, *and* PILIA-BORSA.

Bell. I'll pledge thee, love, and therefore drink it off.

---

1 Scene: the balcony of Bellamira's house.

Itha. Say'st thou me so? have at it; and do you
    hear?   [*Whispers.*

Bell. Go to, it shall be so.

Itha. Of that condition I will drink it up.
Here's to thee

Bell.[1] Nay, I'll have all or none.

Itha. There, if thou lov'st me do not leave a drop.

Bell. Love thee! fill me three glasses.

Itha. Three and fifty dozen, I'll pledge thee.

Pilia. Knavely spoke, and like a knight at arms.

Itha. Hey, *Rivo*[2] *Castiliano!* a man's a man.   10

Bell. Now to the Jew.

Itha. Ha! to the Jew, and send me money he were
    best.

Pilia. What would'st thou do if he should send thee
    none?

Itha. Do nothing : but I know what I know; he's a
murderer.

Bell. I had not thought he had been so brave a man.

Itha. You knew Mathias and the Governor's son; he
and I killed 'em both, and yet never touched 'em.

Pilia. O, bravely done.

Itha. I carried the broth that poisoned the nuns; and
he and I, snickle hand too fast,[3] strangled a friar.   20

---

[1] Old ed. *Pil.*

[2] The origin of this boisterous exclamation is uncertain. Gifford
suggested that it was corrupted from the Spanish *rio*, which is figura-
tively used for a large quantity of liquor." Dyce quotes from the
anonymous comedy, *Look about you* :—
        "And *Ryvo* will he cry and *Castile* too."

[3] A corrupt passage.   "Snickle" is a North-country word for
"noose."   Cunningham proposed "snickle *hard and fast.*"

Bell. You two alone!

Itha. We two, and 'twas never known, nor never shall be for me.

Pilia. This shall with me unto the Governor.

[*Aside to* BELLAMIRA.

Bell. And fit it should : but first let's ha' more gold.

[*Aside.*

Come, gentle Ithamore, lie in my lap.

Itha. Love me little, love me long ; let music rumble Whilst I in thy incony [1] lap do tumble.

Enter BARABAS, *with a lute, disguised.*

Bell. A French musician : come, let's hear your skill ?

Bar. Must tuna my lute for sound, *twang, twang* first.   31

Itha. Wilt drink, Frenchman ? here's to thee with a——Pox on this drunken hiccup !

Bar. Gramercy, monsieur.

Bell. Prythee, Pilia-Borsa, bid the fiddler give me the posy in his hat there.

Pilia. Sirrah, you must give my mistress your posy.

Bar. *A votre commandment, madame.*

Bell. How sweet, my Ithamore, the flowers smell.

Itha. Like thy breath, sweetheart, no violet like 'em. 40

Pilia. Foh : methinks they stink like a hollyhock.

---

[1] Old ed. "*incoomy.*" The word "incony" (which is found in *Love's Labour's Lost,* &c.) means "delicate, dainty." It has been doubtfully derived from the North-country "canny" or "conny" (in the sense of pretty), the prefix "in" having an intensive force.

Bar. So, now I am revenged upon 'em all.
The scent thereof was death ; I poisoned it.   [*Aside.*

Itha. Play, fiddler, or I'll cut your cat's guts into chitterlings.

Bar. Pardonnez moi, be no in tune yet : so now, now all be in.

Itha. Give him a crown, and fill me out more wine.

Pilia. There's two crowns for thee, play.

Bar. How liberally the villain gives me mine own gold.   [*Aside.* 51

Pilia. Methinks he fingers very well.

Bar. So did you when you stole my gold.   [*Aside.*

Pilia. How swift he runs.

Bar. You ran swifter when you threw my gold out of my window.   [*Aside.*

Bell. Musician, hast been in Malta long?

Bar. Two, three, four month, madam.

Itha. Dost not know a Jew, one Barabas?

Bar. Very mush ; monsieur, you no be his man?   60

Pilia. His man?

Itha. I scorn the peasant : tell him so.

Bar. He knows it already.   [*Aside.*

Itha. 'Tis a strange thing of that Jew, he lives upon pickled grasshoppers and sauced mushrooms.

Bar. What a slave's this? the Governor feeds not as I do.   [*Aside.*

Itha. He never put on clean shirt since he was circumcised.

Bar. O rascal! I change myself twice a day.   70
    [*Aside.*

Itha. The hat he wears, Judas left under the elder [1] when he hanged himself.

Bar. 'Twas sent me for a present from the great
　　　Cham. 　　　　　　　　　　　　　　　　[*Aside.*

Pilia. A musty [2] slave he is ; whither now, fiddler ?

Bar. Pardonnez moi, monsieur, me [3] be no well. [*Exit.*

Pilia. Farewell, fiddler : one letter more to the Jew.

Bell. Prythee, sweet love, one more, and write it sharp.

Itha. No, I'll send by word of mouth now; bid him deliver thee a thousand crowns, by the same token, that the nuns loved rice,—that Friar Barnardine slept in his own clothes ; any of 'em will do it. 　　　　　　81

Pilia. Let me alone to urge it, now I know the meaning.

Itha. The meaning has a meaning ; come let's in :
To undo a Jew is charity, and not sin. 　　　　[*Exeunt.*

---

1 Dyce quotes from Sir John Mandeville :—" And fast by is zit the tree of Eldre that Judas henge him self upon for despeyt that he hadde when he solde and betrayed our Lorde."—*Voiage and Travell,* &c., p. 112, ed. 1725. "That Judas hanged himself," says Sir Thomas Browne, "much more that he perished thereby, we shall not raise a doubt. Although Jansenius, discoursing the point, produceth the testimony of Theophylact and Euthymius that he died not by the gallows but under a cart-wheel ; and Baronius also delivereth, this was the opinion of the Greeks and derived as high as Papias one of the disciples of John. Although, also, how hardly the expression of Matthew is reconcileable unto that of Peter, and that he plainly hanged himself, with that, that falling headlong he burst asunder in the midst—with many other the learned Grotius plainly doth acknowledge."—*Vulgar Errors,* vii. 11.

2 Old ed. " masty." Dyce " nasty."

3 Old ed. " we."

ACT THE FIFTH.

SCENE I.

Enter [1] Governor, Knights, *and* MARTIN DEL BOSCO.

Gov. Now, gentlemen, betake you to your arms,
And see that Malta be well fortified;
And it behoves you to be resolute;
For Calymath, having hovered here so long,
Will win the town or die before the walls.
    Knights. And die he shall, for we will never yield.

Enter BELLAMIRA *and* PILIA-BORSA.

    Bell. O, bring us to the Governor.
    Gov. Away with her; she is a courtesan.
    Bell. Whate'er I am, yet, Governor, hear me speak;
I bring thee news by whom thy son was slain: 10
Mathias did it not; it was the Jew.
    Pilia. Who, besides the slaughter of these gentlemen,
Poisoned his own daughter and the nuns,
Strangled a friar, and I know not what
Mischief besides.

---

[1] Scene: the Senate-house.

Gov. Had we but proof of this——

Bell. Strong proof, my lord; his man's now at my
　　　lodging,

That was his agent; he'll confess it all.

Gov. Go fetch him straight [*Exeunt* Officers]; I
　　　always feared that Jew.　　　　　　　　20

Enter Officers *with* BARABAS *and* ITHAMORE.

Bar. I'll go alone; dogs, do not hale me thus.

Itha. Nor me neither, I cannot outrun you, constable :
O my belly!

Bar. One dram of powder more had made all sure;
What a damned slave was I!　　　　　　　[*Aside.*

Gov. Make fires, heat irons, let the rack be fetched.

Knights. Nay, stay, my lord, 't may be he will confess?

Bar. Confess! what mean you, lords, who should
　　　confess?

Gov. Thou and thy Turk; 'twas you that slew my son.

Itha. Guilty, my lord, I confess : your son and Mathias
were both contracted unto Abigail; [he] forged a counterfeit challenge.　　　　　　　　　　　　31

Bar. Who carried that challenge?

Itha. I carried it, I confess; but who writ it? Marry,
even he that strangled Barnardine, poisoned the nuns,
and his own daughter.

Gov. Away with him, his sight is death to me.

Bar. For what, you men of Malta? hear me speak :
She is a courtesan, and he a thief,
And he my bondman. Let me have law,
For none of this can prejudice my life.　　　　40

Gov. Once more, away with him ; you shall have law.

Bar. Devils, do your worst, I live in spite of you. [*Aside.*
As these have spoke, so be it to their souls !—
I hope the poisoned flowers will work anon.   [*Aside.*
                                                      [*Exeunt.*

Enter the Mother *of* MATHIAS.

Mother. Was my Mathias murdered by the Jew?
Ferneze, 'twas thy son that murdered him.

Gov. Be patient, gentle madam, it was he.
He forged the daring challenge made them fight.

Mother. Where is the Jew? where is that murderer?

Gov. In prison till the law has past on him.   50

Enter Officer.

Off. My lord, the courtesan and her man are dead :
So is the Turk and Barabas the Jew.

Gov. Dead !

Off. Dead, my lord, and here they bring his body.

Bosco. This sudden death of his is very strange.

Re-enter Officers *carrying* BARABAS *as dead.*

Gov. Wonder not at it, sir, the heavens are just ;
Their deaths were like their lives, then think not of 'em :
Since they are dead, let them be buried.
For the Jew's body, throw that o'er the walls,
To be a prey for vultures and wild beasts.   60
So now away, and fortify the town.

[*Exeunt all, leaving* BARABAS *on the floor.*[1]

---

[1] We are to suppose that Barabas' body had been thrown "o'er the
walls," according to the Governor's order. The scene is now changed
from the Senate-house to the outside of the city.

Bar. [*Rising.*] What, all alone? well fare, sleepy drink.
I'll be revenged on this accursèd town;
For by my means Calymath shall enter in.
I'll help to slay their children and their wives,
To fire the churches, pull their houses down,
Take my goods too, and seize upon my lands:
I hope to see the Governor a slave,
And, rowing in a galley, whipt to death.

Enter CALYMATH, Bassoes, *and* Turks.

Caly. Whom have we here, a spy?   70
Bar. Yes, my good lord, one that can spy a place
Where you may enter, and surprise the town:
My name is Barabas: I am a Jew.
Caly. Art thou that Jew whose goods we heard were
            sold
For tribute-money?
Bar. The very same, my lord:
And since that time they have hired a slave, my man,
To accuse me of a thousand villanies:
I was imprisoned, but escaped their hands.
Caly. Did'st break prison?   80
Bar. No, no;
I drank of poppy and cold mandrake juice:[1]

---

[1] A herb of powerful soporific qualities. Shakespeare couples it with
"poppy" in *Othello*:—
            " Not poppy nor *mandragora*,
            Nor all the powerful syrups of the world,
            Shall ever medicine thee to that sweet sleep
            Which thou ow'dst yesterday."

And being asleep, belike they thought me dead,
And threw me o'er the walls : so, or how else,
The Jew is here, and rests at your command.

   Caly. 'Twas bravely done : but tell me, Barabas,
Canst thou, as thou report'st, make Malta ours ?

   Bar. Fear not, my lord, for here against the sluice,[1]
The rock is hollow, and of purpose digged,
To make a passage for the running streams   90
And common channels of the city.
Now, whilst you give assault unto the walls,
I'll lead five hundred soldiers through the vault,
And rise with them i' the middle of the town,
Open the gates for you to enter in,
And by this means the city is your own.

   Caly. If this be true, I'll make thee governor.

   Bar. And if it be not true, then let me die.

   Caly. Thou'st doomed thyself.   Assault it presently.

                      [Exeunt.

SCENE II.

Alarms.   *Enter*[2] Turks, BARABAS, *&c. :* Governor *and*
Knights *prisoners.*

   Caly. Now vail[3] your pride, you captive Christians,
And kneel for mercy to your conquering foe :
Now where's the hope you had of haughty Spain ?

---

[1] Old ed. "truce." The correction is Collier's. Dyce reads "trench."
[2] Scene : a square in the city.
[3] Lower.

Ferneze, speak, had it not been much better
T'have [1] kept thy promise than be thus surprised?
   Gov. What should I say? We are captives and must
       yield.
   Caly. I, villains, you must yield, and under Turkish
       yokes
Shall groaning bear the burden of our ire;
And, Barabas, as erst we promised thee,
For thy desert we make thee governor;   10
Use them at thy discretion.
   Bar. Thanks, my lord.
   Gov. O fatal day, to fall into the hand
Of such a traitor and unhallowed Jew!
What greater misery could Heaven inflict?
   Caly. 'Tis our command: and, Barabas, we give
To guard thy person these our Janizaries:
Intreat them well, as we have uséd thee.
And now, brave bassoes, come, we'll walk about
The ruined town, and see the wreck we made: 20
Farewell, brave Jew; farewell, great Barabas!
               [*Exeunt* CALYMATH *and* Bassoes.
   Bar. May all good fortune follow Calymath.
And now, as entrance to our safety,
To prison with the Governor and these
Captains, his consorts and confederates.
   Gov. O villain, Heaven will be revenged on thee.
                   [*Exeunt.*
   Bar. Away, no more, let him not trouble me.

---

1 Old ed. "to kept."

Thus[1] hast thou gotten, by thy policy,
No simple place, no small authority,
I now am governor of Malta ; true,   30
But Malta hates me, and in hating me
My life's in danger, and what boots it thee,
Poor Barabas, to be the governor,
Whenas thy life shall be at their command?
No, Barabas, this must be looked into ;
And since by wrong thou got'st authority,
Maintain it bravely by firm policy.
At least unprofitably lose it not :
For he that liveth in authority,
And neither gets him friends, nor fills his bags,   40
Lives like the ass that Æsop speaketh of,
That labours with a load of bread and wine,
And leaves it off to snap on thistle tops :
But Barabas will be more circumspect.
Begin betimes : occasion's bald behind,
Slip not thine opportunity, for fear too late
Thou seek'st for much, but canst not compass it.
Within here !

Enter Governor, *with a* Guard.

  Gov. My lord?
  Bar. I, *lord ;* thus slaves will learn.   50
Now, Governor, stand by there :—wait within.

                            [*Exit* Guard.
This is the reason that I sent for thee ;

---

[1] The scene shifts to the Governor's house.

Thou seest thy life and Malta's happiness
Are at my arbitrement ; and Barabas
At his discretion may dispose of both :
Now tell me, Governor, and plainly too,
What think'st thou shall become of it and thee ?

   Gov. This, Barabas : since things are in thy power,
I see no reason but of Malta's wreck,
Nor hope of thee but extreme cruelty ;   60
Nor fear I death, nor will I flatter thee.

   Bar. Governor, good words ; be not so furious.
'Tis not thy life which can avail me aught,
Yet you do live, and live for me you shall :
And, as for Malta's ruin, think you not
'Twere slender policy for Barabas
To dispossess himself of such a place ?
For sith, as once you said, 'tis in this isle,
In Malta here, that I have got my goods,
And in this city still have had success,   70
And now at length am grown your governor,
Yourselves shall see it shall not be forgot :
For as a friend not known, but in distress,
I'll rear up Malta, now remediless.

   Gov. Will Barabas recover Malta's loss ?
Will Barabas be good to Christians ?

   Bar. What wilt thou give me, Governor, to procure
A dissolution of the slavish bands
Wherein the Turk hath yoked your lands and you ?
What will you give me if I render you   80
The life of Calymath, surprise his men
And in an outhouse of the city shut

His soldiers, till I have consumed 'em all with fire?
What will you give him that procureth this?

Gov. Do but bring this to pass which thou pretend'st,[1]
Deal truly with us as thou intimatest,
And I will send amongst the citizens;
And by my letters privately procure
Great sums of money for thy recompense:
Nay more, do this, and live thou governor still.   90

Bar. Nay, do thou this, Ferneze, and be free;
Governor, I enlarge thee; live with me,
Go walk about the city, see thy friends:
Tush, send not letters to 'em, go thyself,
And let me see what money thou canst make;
Here is my hand that I'll set Malta free:
And thus we cast it: To a solemn feast
I will invite young Selim Calymath,
Where be thou present only to perform
One stratagem that I'll impart to thee,   100
Wherein no danger shall betide thy life,
And I will warrant Malta free for ever.

Gov. Here is my hand, believe me, Barabas,
I will be there, and do as thou desirest;
When is the time?

Bar. Governor, presently.
For Calymath, when he hath viewed the town,
Will take his leave and sail towards Ottoman.

Gov. Then will I, Barabas, about this coin,
And bring it with me to thee in the evening.   110

---

[1] *I.e.* "intend'st."

Bar. Do so, but fail not; now farewell, Ferneze:

[Exit Governor.

And thus far roundly goes the business:
Thus loving neither, will I live with both,
Making a profit of my policy;
And he from whom my most advantage comes'
Shall be my friend.
This is the life we Jews are used to lead;
And reason too, for Christians do the like.
Well, now about effecting this device:
First to surprise great Selim's soldiers,   120
And then to make provision for the feast,
That at one instant all things may be done:
My policy detests prevention:
To what event my secret purpose drives,
I know; and they shall witness with their lives.   [*Exit.*

SCENE III.

Enter CALYMATH *and* Bassoes.

Caly. Thus have we viewed the city, seen the sack,
And caused the ruins to be new repaired,
Which with our bombards'[1] shot and basilisk[s][2]
We rent in sunder at our entry:
And now I see the situation,
And how secure this conquered island stands
Environed with the Mediterranean sea,
Strong countermined with other petty isles;

---

[1] Large cannons.   [2] See vol. 1, p. 67, note 2.

And,[1] toward Calabria, backed by Sicily,
(Where Syracusian Dionysius reigned,)   10
Two lofty turrets that command the town ;
I wonder how it could be conquered thus ?

Enter a Messenger.

Mess. From Barabas, Malta's governor. I bring
A message unto mighty Calymath ;
Hearing his sovereign was bound for sea,
To sail to Turkey, to great Ottoman,
He humbly would entreat your majesty
To come and see his homely citadel,
And banquet with him ere thou leav'st the isle.

Caly. To banquet with him in his citadel?   20
I fear me, messenger, to feast my train
Within a town of war so lately pillaged,
Will be too costly and too troublesome :
Yet would I gladly visit Barabas,
For well has Barabas deserved of us.

Mess. Selim, for that, thus saith the Governor,
That he hath in [his] store a pearl so big,
So precious, and withal so orient,
As, be it valued but indifferently,
The price thereof will serve to entertain   30
Selim and all his soldiers for a month ;

---

[1] Old ed.—
        " And toward Calabria back'd by Sicily,
            Two lofty Turrets that command the Towne.
            When Siracusian Dionisius reign'd ;
            I wonder how it could be conquer'd thus."
    The correction was made by the editor of 1826.

Therefore he humbly would entreat your highness
Not to depart till he has feasted you.

Caly. I cannot feast my men in Malta walls,
Except he place his tables in the streets.

Mess. Know, Selim, that there is a monastery
Which standeth as an outhouse to the town :
There will he banquet them, but thee at home,
With all thy bassoes and brave followers.

Caly. Well, tell the Governor we grant his suit,   40
We'll in this summer evening feast with him.

Mess. I shall, my lord.   [*Exit.*

Caly. And now, bold bassoes, let us to our tents,
And meditate how we may grace us best
To solemise our Governor's great feast.   [*Exeunt.*

SCENE IV.

Enter[1] Governor, Knights, *and* DEL BOSCO.

Gov. In this, my countrymen, be ruled by me,
Have special care that no man sally forth
Till you shall hear a culverin discharged
By him that bears the linstock,[2] kindled thus ;
Then issue out and come to rescue me,
For happily I shall be in distress,
Or you released of this servitude.

Knight. Rather than thus to live as Turkish thralls
What will we not adventure ?

---

1 Scene : a street.
2 The stick that held the gunner's match.

Gov. On then, begone.

Knight, Farewell, grave Governor ! [*Exeunt.* 11

SCENE V.

Enter,[1] *above,* BARABAS, *with a hammer, very busy ;*
and Carpenters.

Bar. How stand the cords ? How hang these hinges ?
fast ?
Are all the cranes and pulleys sure ?

First Carp.[2] All fast.

Bar. Leave nothing loose, all levelled to my mind.
Why now I see that you have art indeed.
There, carpenters, divide that gold amongst you :
Go swill in bowls of sack and muscadine !
Down to the cellar, taste of all my wines.

Carp. We shall, my lord, and thank you. [*Exeunt.*

Bar. And, if you like them, drink your fill and die : 10
For so I live, perish may all the world.
Now Selim Calymath return me word
That thou wilt come, and I am satisfied.
Now, sirrah, what, will he come ?

Enter Messenger.

Mess. He will ; and has commanded all his men
To come ashore, and march through Malta streets,
That thou mayest feast them in thy citadel.

Bar. Then now are all things as my wish would have
'em,

---

[1] Scene : the hall of the Governor's house. Barabas is in the gallery.
[2] Old ed. "Serv."

There wanteth nothing but the Governor's pelf,
And see, he brings it.   20

Enter Governor.

Now, Governor, the sum.
  Gov. With free consent, a hundred thousand pounds.
  Bar. Pounds say'st thou, Governor? well, since it is
      no more,
I'll satisfy myself with that; nay, keep it still,
For if I keep not promise, trust not me.
And, Governor, now take my policy :
First, for his army, they are sent before,
Entered the monastery, and underneath
In several places are field-pieces pitched,
Bombards, whole barrels full of gunpowder,   30
That on the sudden shall dissever it,
And batter all the stones about their ears,
Whence none can possibly escape alive :
Now as for Calymath and his consorts,
Here have I made a dainty gallery,
The floor whereof, this cable being cut,
Doth fall asunder; so that it doth sink
Into a deep pit past recovery.
Here, hold that knife, and when thou seest he comes,
And with his bassoes shall be blithely set,   40
A warning-piece shall be shot off from the tower,
To give thee knowledge when to cut the cord
And fire the house : say, will not this be brave ?
  Gov. O excellent ! here, hold thee, Barabas,
I trust thy word, take what I promised thee.

Bar. No, Governor, I'll satisfy thee first,
Thou shalt not live in doubt of anything.
Stand close, for here they come [Governor *retires*].   Why,
  is not this
A kingly kind of trade to purchase towns
By treachery and sell 'em by deceit?   50
Now tell me, worldlings, underneath the sun [1]
If greater falsehood ever has been done?

    Enter CALYMATH *and* Bassoes.

Caly. Come, my companion bassoes : see, I pray,
How busy Barabas is there above
To entertain us in his gallery ;
Let us salute him. Save thee, Barabas !
 Bar. Welcome, great Calymath !
 Gov. How the slave jeers at him.   [*Aside.*
 Bar. Will 't please thee, mighty Selim Calymath,
To ascend our homely stairs?   60
 Caly. I, Barabas ;
Come, bassoes, attend.[2]
 Gov. Stay, Calymath !
For I will show thee greater courtesy
Than Barabas would have afforded thee.
 Knight [*within*]. Sound a charge there !
  [*A charge; the cable cut.* BARABAS *falls into a cal-*
   dron.   Enter MARTIN DEL BOSCO *and* Knights.[3]

---

 [1] Old ed. "summe."
 [2] Dyce reads "ascend."
 [3] The stage-direction in old ed. is "A charge, the cable cut.   A caldron
discovered."   In Scene 4 the Governor had directed the Knights and
Del Bosco to issue out at the discharge of the culverin.

Caly. How now, what means this!

Bar. Help, help me, Christians, help.

Gov. See, Calymath, this was devised for thee.

Caly. Treason! treason! bassoes, fly!   70

Gov. No, Selim, do not fly;

See his end first, and fly then if thou canst.

Bar. O help me, Selim, help me, Christians!

Governor, why stand you all so pitiless?

Gov. Should I in pity of thy plaints or thee,

Accursèd Barabas, base Jew, relent?

No, thus I'll see thy treachery repaid,

But wish thou hadst behaved thee otherwise.

Bar. You will not help me, then?

Gov. No, villain, no.   80

Bar. And, villains, know you cannot help me
      now—

Then, Barabas, breathe forth thy latest hate,[1]

And in the fury of thy torments strive

To end thy life with resolution:

Know, Governor, 'twas I that slew thy son;

I framed the challenge that did make them meet:

Know, Calymath, I aimed thy overthrow,

And had I but escaped this stratagem,

I would have brought confusion on you all,

Damned Christians! dogs . and Turkish infidels!   90

But now begins the extremity of heat

To pinch me with intolerable pangs:

Die life, fly soul, tongue curse thy fill, and die!   [*Dies.*

---

[1] Cunningham's correction for the old eds. "fate."

Caly. Tell me, you Christians, what doth this por-
　　tend?

Gov. This train he laid to have entrapped thy life;
Now, Selim, note the unhallowed deeds of Jews:
Thus he determined to have handled thee,
But I have rather chose to save thy life.

Caly. Was this the banquet he prepared for us?
Let's hence, lest further mischief be pretended.[1]　　　100

Gov. Nay, Selim, stay, for since we have thee
　　here,
We will not let thee part so suddenly;
Besides, if we should let thee go, all's one,
For with thy galleys could'st thou not get hence,
Without fresh men to rig and furnish them.

Caly. Tush, Governor, take thou no care for
　　that,
My men are all aboard.
And do attend my coming there by this.

Gov. Why, heard'st thou not the trumpet sound a
　　charge?

Caly. Yes, what of that?　　　110

Gov. Why then the house was fired,
Blown up, and all thy soldiers massacred.

Caly. O monstrous treason!

Gov. A Jew's courtesy:
For he that did by treason work our fall,
By treason hath delivered thee to us:
Know, therefore, till thy father hath made good

---

[1] Intended.

The ruins done to Malta and to us,
Thou canst not part: for Malta shall be freed,
Or Selim ne'er return to Ottoman.   120
    Caly. Nay, rather, Christians, let me go to Turkey,
In person there to mediate [1] your peace;
To keep me here will not advantage you.
    Gov. Content thee, Calymath, here thou must stay,
And live in Malta prisoner; for come all [2] the world
To rescue thee, so will we guard us now,
As sooner shall they drink the ocean dry
Than conquer Malta, or endanger us.
So march away, and let due praise be given
Neither to fate nor fortune, but to Heaven.   [*Exeunt.*

---

[1] Old ed. "meditate."   [2] Old ed. "call."

EDWARD THE SECOND.

EDWARD II. was entered in the Stationers' Books 6th July 1593. In the Dyce Library at South Kensington there is a 4to. with a MS. title-page (in a hand of the late seventeenth century) dated 1593. Without doubt the date 1593 is a copyist's mistake for 1598. In the first leaf, which is in MS., there are a few textual differences, due to the copyist's carelessness; but the printed matter throughout (A. 3—K. 2) exhibits the text of ed. 1598.

In 1876 an edition of *Edward II.* in 8vo., dated 1594, was discovered in the library at Cassel. The title is:—*The troublesome raigne and lamentable death of Edward the second, King of England: with the tragicall fall of proud Mortimer. As it was sundrie times publiquely acted in the honourable citie of London, by the right honourable the Earl of Pembroke his servants. Written by Chri. Marlow Gent. Imprinted at London for William Jones, dwelling neare Holborne conduit at the Signe of the Gunne, 1594.*

The title of the 4to. of 1598 runs as follows:—*The troublesome raigne and lamentable death of Edward the second, King of England: with the tragicall fall of proud Mortimer: And also the life and death of Peirs Gaueston, the great Earle of Cornewall, and mighty favorite of king Edward the second, as it was publiquely acted by the right honorable the Earle of Pembrooke his seruauntes. Written by Chri. Marlow Gent. Imprinted at London by Richard Bradocke, for William Jones, dwelling neere Holbourne conduit, at the signe of the Gunne, 1598.*

Another edition (in 4to.) appeared in 1612, with the following title:—*The troublesome raigne and lamentable death of Edward the second, King of England: with the tragicall fall of proud Mortimer. And also the life and death of Peirs Gaueston, the great Earle of Cornewall, and mighty fauorite of King Edward the second, as it was publiquely acted by the right honorable the Earle of Pembrooke his seruants. Written by Christopher Marlow Gent. Printed at London for Roger Barnes, and are to be sould at his shop in Chauncerie Lane ouer against the Rolles,* 1612.

The last of the old editions is dated 1622 :—*The troublesome raigne and lamentable death of Edward the second, King of England: with the tragicall fall of proud Mortimer. And also the life and death of Peirs Gauestone, the great Earle of Cornewall, and mighty Fauorite of King Edward the second. As it was publikely Acted by the late Queenes Maiesties Seruants at the Red Bull in S. Johns streete. Written by Christopher Marlow Gent. London, Printed for Henry Bell, and are to be sold at his Shop at the Lame-hospitall Gate, neere Smithfield,* 1622.

The text of the 1598 4to., which is fairly free from corruptions, differs but slightly from the texts of the two later 4tos. I have not had an opportunity of inspecting the 8vo. of 1594; but I suspect that it agrees very closely with the later copies.

PERSONS REPRESENTED.

EDWARD II.
PRINCE EDWARD, *his son, afterwards* Edward III.
GAVESTON.
OLD SPENCER.
YOUNG SPENCER.
EARL MORTIMER.
YOUNG MORTIMER.
BERKELEY.
LANCASTER.
LEICESTER.
EDMUND, *Earl of Kent.*
ARUNDEL.
WARWICK.
PEMBROKE.
ARCHBISHOP OF CANTERBURY.
BISHOP OF WINCHESTER.
BISHOP OF COVENTRY.
BEAUMONT.
TRUSSEL.
Sir JOHN HAINAULT.
LEVUNE.
BALDOCK.
MATREVIS.
GURNEY.
RICE AP HOWEL.
LIGHTBORN.
Abbot.
Lords, Messengers, Monks, James, &c., &c.

QUEEN ISABELLA.
Niece *to* Edward II.
Ladies.

EDWARD THE SECOND.

—o—

ACT THE FIRST.

SCENE I.

Enter [1] GAVESTON, *reading a letter from the* King.

Gav. My father is deceased! Come, Gaveston,
And share the kingdom with thy dearest friend.
Ah! words that make me surfeit with delight!
What greater bliss can hap to Gaveston
Than live and be the favourite of a king!
Sweet prince, I come; these, these thy amorous lines
Might have enforced me to have swum from France,
And, like Leander, gasped upon the sand,
So thou would'st smile, and take me in thine arms.
The sight of London to my exiled eyes   10
Is as Elysium to a new-come soul;
Not that I love the city, or the men,
But that it harbours him I hold so dear—
The king, upon whose bosom let me die,[2]

---

[1] Scene : a street in London.
[2] So 4tos.—Dyce gives " lie ; " but " die " may perhaps be interpreted
as " swoon."

And with the world be still at enmity.
What need the arctic people love starlight,
To whom the sun shines both by day and night?
Farewell base stooping to the lordly peers!
My knee shall bow to none but to the king.
As for the multitude, that are but sparks,   20
Raked up in embers of their poverty;—
Tanti;[1] I'll fawn[2] first on the wind
That glanceth at my lips, and flieth away.
But how now, what are these?

Enter three poor Men.

Men. Such as desire your worship's service.
Gav. What canst thou do?
1 *Man.* I can ride.
Gav. But I have no horse.   What art thou?
2 *Man.* A traveller.
Gav. Let me see—thou would'st do well
To wait at my trencher and tell me lies at dinner-time;   30
And as I like your discoursing, I'll have you.
And what art thou?
3 *Man.* A soldier, that hath served against the Scot.

---

[1] Cf. Day's *Parliament of Bees* :—
        " Yet if you meet a tart antagonist,
          Or discontented rugged satirist,
          That slights your errant or his art that penned it,
          Cry *Tanti !*"
So in the Prologue to Day's *Isle of Gulls* :—
        " Detraction he scorns, honours the best :
          Tanti for hate, thus low for all the rest."
[2] So Dyce,—4tos. "fanne."

Gav. Why, there are hospitals for such as you;
I have no war, and therefore, sir, begone.

   3 *Man.* Farewell, and perish by a soldier's hand,
That would'st reward them with an hospital.

   Gav. I, I, these words of his move me as much
As if a goose would play the porcupine,
And dart her plumes,[1] thinking to pierce my breast.   40
But yet it is no pain to speak men fair;
I'll flatter these, and make them live in hope.   [*Aside.*
You know that I came lately out of France,
And yet I have not viewed my lord the king;
If I speed well, I'll entertain you all.

   Omnes. We thank your worship.

   Gav. I have some business.   Leave me to myself.

   Omnes. We will wait here about the court.   [*Exeunt*

   Gav. Do; these are not men for me;
I must have wanton poets, pleasant wits,   50
Musicians, that with touching of a string
May draw the pliant king which way I please.
Music and poetry is his delight;
Therefore I'll have Italian masks by night,
Sweet speeches, comedies, and pleasing shows;
And in the day, when he shall walk abroad,
Like silvian[2] nymphs my pages shall be clad;
My men, like satyrs grazing on the lawns,

---

   [1] Mr. Tancock quotes from Pliny's *Natural History:*—" Hystrici
longiores aculei et cum intendit cutem missiles.   Ora urgentium figit
canum et paulo longius jaculatur."
   [2] So the 4tos.—Dyce reads " sylvan."

Shall with their goat-feet dance the antic hay.[1]
Sometime a lovely boy in Dian's shape,   60
With hair that gilds the water as it glides,
Crownets of pearl about his naked arms,
And in his sportful hands an olive-tree,
To hide those parts which men delight to see,
Shall bathe him in a spring; and there hard by,
One like Actæon peeping through the grove,
Shall by the angry goddess be transformed,
And running in the likeness of an hart
By yelping hounds pulled down, and [2] seem to die ;—
Such things as these best please his majesty.   70
Here comes my lord [3] the king, and [here] the nobles
From the parliament.   I'll stand aside.

Enter the KING, LANCASTER, OLD MORTIMER, YOUNG
    MORTIMER, EDMUND, *Earl of Kent,* GUY, *Earl of
    Warwick, &c.*

   Edw. Lancaster !
   Lan. My lord.
   Gav. That Earl of Lancaster do I abhor.   [*Aside.*
   Edw. Will you not grant me this?   In spite of them

---

  [1] The name of a rustic dance.
  [2] So the 4tos.—Dyce reads " shall."
  [3] The 4tos. read, " My lord, here comes the king and the nobles."
Dyce gives, " Here comes my lord the king and the nobles."   Mr.
Fleay arranges the passage thus :—
     " Here comes my lord
       The king and th' nobles from the parliament.
       I'll stand aside."

I'll have my will ; and these two Mortimers,
That cross me thus, shall know I am displeased.

   E. Mor. If you love us, my lord, hate Gaveston.

   Gav. That villain Mortimer, I'll be his death ! [*Aside.*

   Y. Mor. Mine uncle here, this earl, and I myself, 81
Were sworn [1] to your father at his death,
That he should ne'er return into the realm :
And know, my lord, ere I will break my oath,
This sword of mine, that should offend your foes,
Shall sleep within the scabbard at thy need,
And underneath thy banners march who will,
For Mortimer will hang his armour up.

   Gav. Mort dieu !   [*Aside.*

   Edw. Well, Mortimer, I'll make thee rue these words.
Beseems it thee to contradict thy king ?   91
Frown'st thou thereat, aspiring Lancaster ? [2]
The sword shall plane the furrows of thy brows,
And hew these knees that now are grown so stiff.
I will have Gaveston ; and you shall know
What danger 'tis to stand against your king.

   Gav. Well done, Ned !   [*Aside.*

   Lan. My lord, why do you thus incense your peers,
That naturally would love and honour you
But for that base and obscure Gaveston ?   100
Four earldoms have I, besides Lancaster—
Derby, Salisbury, Lincoln, Leicester,
These will I sell, to give my soldiers pay,

---

[1] Equivalent to a dissyllable.
[2] Cf. 3 *Henry VI.* v. 6, " *aspiring* blood of Lancaster."

Ere Gaveston shall stay within the realm;
Therefore, if he be come, expel him straight.
  Edw. Barons and earls, your pride hath made me
       mute;
But now I'll speak, and to the proof, I hope.
I do remember, in my father's days,
Lord Percy of the north, being highly moved,
Braved Moubery [1] in presence of the king;   110
For which, had not his highness loved him well,
He should have lost his head; but with his look
The undaunted spirit of Percy was appeased,
And Moubery and he were reconciled.
Yet dare you brave the king unto his face;
Brother, revenge it, and let these their heads
Preach upon poles, for trespass of their tongues.
  War. O, our heads!
  Edw. I, yours; and therefore I would wish you
       grant—
  War. Bridle thy anger, gentle Mortimer.   120
  Y. Mor. I cannot, nor I will not; I must speak.
Cousin, our hands I hope shall fence our heads,
And strike off his that makes you threaten us.
Come, uncle, let us leave the brainsick king,
And henceforth parley with our naked swords.
  E. Mor. Wiltshire hath men enough to save our heads.
  War. All Warwickshire will love [2] him for my sake.

---

  [1] I have kept the form found in ed. 1598, as a trisyllable is here required.
  [2] Dyce's correction "leave" seems unnecessary. Warwick is speaking ironically.

Lan. And northward Gaveston [1] hath many friends.
Adieu, my lord ; and either change your mind,
Or look to see the throne, where you should sit,   130
To float in blood ; and at thy wanton head,
The glozing head of thy base minion thrown.

[*Exeunt* Nobles.

Edw. I cannot brook these haughty menaces;
Am I a king, and must be overruled?
Brother, display my ensigns in the field ;
I'll bandy [2] with the barons and the earls,
And either die or live with Gaveston.

Gav. I can no longer keep me from my lord.

[*Comes forward.*

Edw. What, Gaveston! welcome.—Kiss not my hand—
Embrace me, Gaveston, as I do thee.   140
Why should'st thou kneel? know'st thou not who I
     am?
Thy friend, thyself, another Gaveston !
Not Hylas was more mourned of [3] Hercules,
Than thou hast been of me since thy exile.

Gav. And since I went from hence, no soul in hell
Hath felt more torment than poor Gaveston.

Edw. I know it.—Brother, welcome home my friend.
Now let the treacherous Mortimers conspire,
And that high-minded Earl of Lancaster :

---

[1] Dyce altered "Gaveston" to "Lancaster;" but the language is
ironical.
[2] Fight, contend.   The word is borrowed from the game of tennis.
[3] Ed. 1598, "mourned *for* Hercules." Eds. 1612, 1622, "mourned *for*
of Hercules"—and so Dyce.

I have my wish, in that I joy thy sight;   150
And sooner shall the sea o'erwhelm my land,
Than bear the ship that shall transport thee hence.
I here create thee Lord High Chamberlain,
Chief Secretary to the state and me,
Earl of Cornwall, King and Lord of Man.
 Gav. My lord, these titles far exceed my worth.
 Kent. Brother, the least of these may well suffice
For one of greater birth than Gaveston.
 Edw. Cease, brother : for I cannot brook these words.
Thy worth, sweet friend, is far above my gifts,   160
Therefore, to equal it, receive my heart ;
If for these dignities thou be envied,
I'll give thee more ; for, but to honour thee,
Is Edward pleased with kingly regiment.[1]
Fear'st thou thy person ? thou shalt have a guard.
Wantest thou gold ? go to my treasury.
Wouldst thou be loved and feared ? receive my seal ;
Save or condemn, and in our name command
Whatso thy mind affects, or fancy likes.
 Gav. It shall suffice me to enjoy your love,   170
Which whiles I have, I think myself as great
As Cæsar riding in the Roman street,
With captive kings at his triumphant car.

Enter the BISHOP OF COVENTRY.

 Edw. Whither goes my lord of Coventry so fast ?

---

[1] Rule.   Cf. 1 *Tamburlaine*, i. 1, l. 119.

Bish. To celebrate your father's exequies.
But is that wicked Gaveston returned?

Edw. I, priest, and lives to be revenged on thee,
That wert the only cause of his exile.

Gav. 'Tis true; and but for reverence of these robes,
Thou should'st not plod one foot beyond this place. 180

Bish. I did no more than I was bound to do;
And, Gaveston, unless thou be reclaimed,
As then I did incense the parliament,
So will I now, and thou shalt back to France.

Gav. Saving your reverence, you must pardon me.

Edw. Throw off his golden mitre, rend his stole,
And in the channel[1] christen him anew.

Kent. Ah, brother, lay not violent hands on him,
For he'll complain unto the see of Rome.

Gav. Let him complain unto the see of hell, 190
I'll be revenged on him for my exile.

Edw. No, spare his life, but seize upon his goods:
Be thou lord bishop and receive his rents,
And make him serve thee as thy chaplain:
I give him thee—here, use him as thou wilt.

Gav. He shall to prison, and there die in bolts.

Edw. I, to the Tower, the Fleet, or where thou wilt.

Bish. For this offence, be thou accurst of God!

Edw. Who's there? Convey this priest to the Tower.

Bish. True, true.[2] 200

---

[1] Kennel, gutter. Cf. *Jew of Malta*, v. 1, l. 91.
[2] Dyce proposed to read "Prut prut!" others suppose that the

Edw. But in the meantime, Gaveston, away,
And take possession of his house and goods.
Come, follow me, and thou shalt have my guard
To see it done, and bring thee safe again.
　Gav. What should a priest do with so fair a house?
A prison may best [1] beseem his holiness.

[*Exeunt.*

SCENE II.

Enter [1] *both the* MORTIMERS, WARWICK, *and* LANCASTER.

War. 'Tis true, the bishop is in the Tower,
And goods and body given to Gaveston.
　Lan. What! will they tyrannise upon the church?
Ah, wicked king! accursed Gaveston!
This ground, which is corrupted with their steps,
Shall be their timeless [3] sepulchre or mine.
　Y. Mor. Well, let that peevish Frenchman guard him
　　　　　　sure;
Unless his breast be sword-proof he shall die.
　E. Mor. How now, why droops the Earl of Lancaster?
　Y. Mor. Wherefore is Guy of Warwick discontent? 10
　Lan. That villain Gaveston is made an earl.
　E. Mor. An earl!

---

bishop is playing on the word "convey," which was a cant term for
"steal." Cf. *Richard II.* iv. 1, l. 113 :—
　　　"*Bol.* Go, some of you, convey him to the Tower.
　　　King. O good! convey! conveyers are you all."
　[1] So eds. 1612, 1622.—Ed. 1598 omits "best."
　[2] Scene : Westminster.
　[3] Untimely.

War. I, and besides Lord Chamberlain of the realm,
And Secretary too, and Lord of Man.

E. Mor. We may not, nor we will not suffer this.

Y. Mor. Why post we not from hence to levy men?

Lan. "My Lord of Cornwall," now at every word!
And happy is the man whom he vouchsafes,
For vailing of his bonnet, one good look.
Thus, arm in arm, the king and he doth march: 20
Nay more, the guard upon his lordship waits;
And all the court begins to flatter him.

War. Thus leaning on the shoulder of the king,
He nods and scorns, and smiles at those that pass.

E. Mor. Doth no man take exceptions at the slave?

Lan. All stomach[1] him, but none dare speak a word.

Y. Mor. Ah, that bewrays their baseness, Lancaster.
Were all the earls and barons of my mind,
We'd[2] hale him from the bosom of the king,
And at the court-gate hang the peasant up;   30
Who, swoln with venom of ambitious pride,
Will be the ruin of the realm and us.

Enter the ARCHBISHOP *of* CANTERBURY *and a*
Messenger.

War. Here comes my Lord of Canterbury's grace.

Lan. His countenance bewrays he is displeased.

Archbish. First were his sacred garments rent and torn,
Then laid they violent hands upon him : next

---

[1] Are angry at him. We have the word again later in the play—
    "I know, my lord, many will *stomach* me."
[2] Old eds. "Weele."

Himself imprisoned, and his goods asseized :
This certify the pope ;—away, take horse.

> [*Exit* Messenger.

Lan. My lord, will you take arms against the king ?

Archbish. What need I ? God himself is up in arms, 40
When violence is offered to the church.

Y. Mor. Then will you join with us, that be his peers,
To banish or behead that Gaveston ?

Archbish. What else, my lords ? for it concerns me
>   near ;—

The bishoprick of Coventry is his.

Enter QUEEN ISABELLA.

Y. Mor. Madam, whither walks your majesty so fast ?

Queen. Unto the forest,[1] gentle Mortimer,
To live in grief and baleful discontent ;
For now, my lord, the king regards me not,
But doats upon the love of Gaveston.   50
He claps his cheek, and hangs about his neck,
Smiles in his face, and whispers in his ears ;
And when I come he frowns, as who should say,
" Go whither thou wilt, seeing I have Gaveston."

E. Mor. Is it not strange, that he is thus bewitched ?

Y. Mor. Madam, return unto the court again :
That sly inveigling Frenchman we'll exile,
Or lose our lives ; and yet ere that day come

---

[1] It is not absolutely necessary to suppose that there is an allusion to any particular forest. What the queen means is that she is seeking solitude.

The king shall lose his crown ; for we have power,
And courage too, to be revenged at full.   60
   Archbish. But yet lift not your swords against the king.
   Lan. No ; but we will lift Gaveston from hence.
   War. And war must be the means, or he'll stay still.
   Queen. Then let him stay : for rather than my lord
Shall be oppressed with civil mutinies,
I will endure a melancholy life,
And let him frolic with his minion.
   Archbish. My lords, to ease all this, but hear me
          speak :—
We and the rest, that are his counsellors,
Will meet, and with a general consent   70
Confirm his banishment with our hands and seals.
   Lan. What we confirm the king will frustrate.
   Y. Mor. Then may we lawfully revolt from him.
   War. But say, my lord, where shall this meeting be ?
   Archbish. At the New Temple.
   Y. Mor. Content.
   [*Archbish.*] And, in the meantime, I'll entreat you all
To cross to Lambeth, and there stay with me.
   Lan. Come then, let's away.
   Y. Mor. Madam, farewell !   80
   Queen. Farewell, sweet Mortimer ; and, for my sake,
Forbear to levy arms against the king.
   Y. Mor. I, if words will serve ; if not, I must.
                          [*Exeunt.*

SCENE III.

Enter [1] GAVESTON *and the* EARL *of* KENT.

Gav. Edmund, the mighty prince of Lancaster,
That hath more earldoms than an ass can bear,
And both the Mortimers, two goodly men,
With Guy of Warwick, that redoubted knight,
Are gone toward Lambeth—there let them remain.

                          [*Exeunt.*

SCENE IV.

Enter [2] NOBLES *and the* ARCHBISHOP *of* CANTERBURY.

Lan. Here is the form of Gaveston's exile :
May it please your lordship to subscribe your name.
Archbish. Give me the paper.

                [*He subscribes, as the others do after him.*
Lan. Quick, quick, my lord ; I long to write my name.
War. But I long more to see him banished hence.
Y. Mor. The name of Mortimer shall fright the king,
Unless he be declined from that base peasant.

        Enter the KING, GAVESTON, *and* KENT.

Edw. What, are you moved that Gaveston sits here ?
It is our pleasure, and we will have it so.

---

[1] Scene : a street.
[2] Scene : the New Temple (cf. ll. 74–5 of scene ii.).　At the entrance
of the king we are to suppose a change of scene.

Lan. Your grace doth well to place him by your side, 10
For nowhere else the new earl is so safe.

E. Mor. What man of noble birth can brook this
　　　　sight?

Quam male conveniunt ! [1]
See what a scornful look the peasant casts!

Pem. Can kingly lions fawn on creeping ants?

War. Ignoble vassal, that like Phaeton
Aspir'st unto the guidance of the sun.

Y. Mor. Their downfall is at hand, their forces down:
We will not thus be faced and over-peered.

Edw. Lay hands on [2] that traitor Mortimer!　　　20

E. Mor. Lay hands on that traitor Gaveston!

Kent. Is this the duty that you owe your king?

War. We know our duties—let him know his peers.

Edw. Whither will you bear him? Stay, or ye shall
　　　　die.

E. Mor. We are no traitors; therefore threaten not.

Gav. No, threaten not, my lord, but pay them home!
Were I a king——

Y. Mor. Thou villain, wherefore talk'st thou of a king,
That hardly art a gentleman by birth?

Edw. Were he a peasant, being my minion,　　　30
I'll make the proudest of you stoop to him.

Lan. My lord, you may not thus disparage us.
Away, I say, with hateful Gaveston.

---

1 "Was the poet thinking of Ovid, 'Non bene conveniunt,' &c. Met.
ii. 846?"—*Dyce.*

2 Perhaps we should read "upon": but "traitor" may be pronounced as a trisyllable by inserting a vowel sound before the first *r.*

E. Mor. And with the Earl of Kent that favours him.

    [Attendants *remove* KENT *and* GAVESTON.

Edw. Nay, then, lay violent hands upon your king,
Here, Mortimer, sit thou in Edward's throne:
Warwick and Lancaster, wear you my crown:
Was ever king thus over-ruled as I?

Lan. Learn then to rule us better, and the realm.

Y. Mor. What we have done, our heart-blood shall
    maintain.   40

War. Think you that we can brook this upstart pride?

Edw. Anger and wrathful fury stops my speech.

Archbish. Why are you moved? be patient, my lord,
And see what we your counsellors have done.

Y. Mor. My lords, now let us all be resolute,
And either have our wills or lose our lives.

Edw. Meet you for this? proud overbearing peers!
Ere my sweet Gaveston shall part from me,
This isle shall fleet [1] upon the ocean,
And wander to the unfrequented Inde.   50

Archbish. You know that I am legate to the pope;
On your allegiance to the see of Rome,
Subscribe, as we have done, to his exile.

Y. Mor. Curse him, if he refuse; and then may we
Depose him and elect another king.

Edw. I, there it goes—but yet I will not yield:
Curse me, depose me, do the worst you can.

Lan. Then linger not, my lord, but do it straight.

Archbish. Remember how the bishop was abused!

---

[1] Float.

Either banish him that was the cause thereof,   60
Or I will presently discharge these lords [1]
Of duty and allegiance due to thee.

   Edw. It boots me not to threat—I must speak fair :
                                                      [*Aside.*

The legate of the pope will be obeyed.
My lord, you shall be Chancellor of the realm ;
Thou, Lancaster, High Admiral of the fleet ;
Young Mortimer and his uncle shall be earls ;
And you, Lord Warwick, President of the North ;
And thou of Wales.   If this content you not,
Make several kingdoms of this monarchy,   70
And share it equally amongst you all,
So I may have some nook or corner left,
To frolic with my dearest Gaveston.

   Archbish. Nothing shall alter us—we are resolved.

   Lan. Come, come, subscribe.

   Y. Mor. Why should you love him whom the world
         hates so ?

   Edw. Because he loves me more than all the world.
Ah, none but rude and savage-minded men
Would seek the ruin of my Gaveston ;
You that be [2] noble born should pity him.   80

   War. You that are princely born should shake him
        off :
For shame subscribe, and let the lown [3] depart.

---

[1] So ed. 1612.—Ed. 1598 "lord."
[2] So ed. 1598.—Ed. 1612 "are."
[3] Loon, worthless fellow.

E. Mor. Urge him, my lord.

Archbish. Are you content to banish him the realm?

Edw. I see I must, and therefore am content:
Instead of ink I'll write it with my tears.   [*Subscribes.*

Y. Mor. The king is love-sick for his minion.

Edw. 'Tis done—and now, accursed hand, fall off!

Lan. Give it me—I'll have it published in the streets.

Y. Mor. I'll see him presently despatched away.   90

Archbish. Now is my heart at ease.

War. And so is mine.

Pem. This will be good news to the common sort.

E. Mor. Be it or no, he shall not linger here.

[*Exeunt* Nobles.

Edw. How fast they run to banish him I love!
They would not stir, were it to do me good.
Why should a king be subject to a priest?
Proud Rome! that hatchest such imperial grooms,
For [1] these thy superstitious taper-lights,
Wherewith thy antichristian churches blaze,
I'll fire thy crazèd buildings, and enforce   100
The papal towers to kiss the lowly ground! [2]
With slaughtered priests make [3] Tiber's channel swell,
And banks raised higher with their sepulchres!

---

[1] So ed. 1598.—Dyce prints "with," and neglects—contrary to his custom—to record the reading of the earlier copies.

[2] This line and the preceding occur with slight alteration in the *Massacre of Paris* :—

    " I'll fire his crazèd buildings and incense
        The papal towers to kiss the holy [sic] earth."

[3] 4tos. "may."

As for the peers, that back the clergy thus,
If I be king, not one of them shall live.

Enter GAVESTON.

Gav. My lord, I hear it whispered everywhere,
That I am banished, and must fly the land.
　Edw. 'Tis true, sweet Gaveston—O ! were it false !
The legate of the Pope will have it so,
And thou must hence, or I shall be deposed.　　110
But I will reign to be revenged of them ;
And therefore, sweet friend, take it patiently.
Live where thou wilt, I'll send thee gold enough ;
And long thou shalt not stay, or if thou dost,
I'll come to thee ; my love shall ne'er decline.
　Gav. Is all my hope turned to this hell of grief?
　Edw. Rend not my heart with thy too-piercing words :
Thou from this land, I from myself am banished.
　Gav. To go from hence grieves not poor Gaveston ;
But to forsake you, in whose gracious looks　　120
The blessedness of Gaveston remains :
For nowhere else seeks he felicity.
　Edw. And only this torments my wretched soul,
That, whether I will or no, thou must depart.
Be governor of Ireland in my stead,
And there abide till fortune call thee home.
Here take my picture, and let me wear thine ;
　　　　　　　　　　[*They exchange pictures.*
O, might I keep thee here as I do this,
Happy were I ! but now most miserable !
　Gav. 'Tis something to be pitied of a king.　　130

Edw. Thou shalt not hence—I'll hide thee, Gaveston.

Gav. I shall be found, and then 'twill grieve me more.

Edw. Kind words, and mutual talk makes our grief
        greater :

Therefore, with dumb embracement, let us part—

Stay, Gaveston, I cannot leave thee thus.

Gav. For every look, my lord [1] drops down a tear :

Seeing I must go, do not renew my sorrow.

Edw. The time is little that thou hast to stay,

And therefore, give me leave to look my fill :

But come, sweet friend, I'll bear thee on thy way.   140

Gav. The peers will frown.

Edw. I pass [2] not for their anger—Come, let's go ;

O that we might as well return as go.

Enter KENT [3] *and* QUEEN ISABEL.

Queen. Whither goes my lord ?

Edw. Fawn not on me, French strumpet ! get thee
        gone.

Queen. On whom but on my husband should I fawn ?

Gav. On Mortimer ! with whom, ungentle queen—

I say no more—judge you the rest, my lord.

Queen. In saying this, thou wrong'st me, Gaveston ;

Is't not enough that thou corrupt'st my lord,   150

And art a bawd to his affections,

But thou must call mine honour thus in question ?

---

[1] So the old copies.—Dyce reads " My *love* drops down a tear."

[2] Care.

[3] "The entrance of Kent seems to have been marked here by mistake."—*Dyce.*

Gav. I mean not so; your grace must pardon me.

Edw. Thou art too familiar with that Mortimer,
And by thy means is Gaveston exiled;
But I would wish thee reconcile the lords,
Or thou shalt ne'er be reconciled to me.

Queen. Your highness knows it lies not in my power.

Edw. Away then! touch me not—Come, Gaveston.

Queen. Villain! 'tis thou that robb'st me of my lord. 160

Gav. Madam, 'tis you that rob me of my lord.

Edw. Speak not unto her; let her droop and pine.

Queen. Wherein, my lord, have I deserved these
                words?
Witness the tears that Isabella sheds,
Witness this heart, that sighing for thee, breaks,
How dear my lord is to poor Isabel.

Edw. And witness heaven how dear thou art to me:
There weep: for till my Gaveston be repealed,
Assure thyself thou com'st not in my sight.

                    [*Exeunt* EDWARD *and* GAVESTON.

Queen. O miserable and distressèd queen!   170
Would, when I left sweet France and was embarked,
That charming Circe[1] walking on the waves,
Had changed my shape, or at[2] the marriage-day
The cup of Hymen had been full of poison,
Or with those arms that twined about my neck
I had been stifled, and not lived to see
The king my lord thus to abandon me!

---

[1] 4tos. "Circes."
[2] So ed. 1598.—Ed. 1612 "that."

Like frantic Juno will I fill the earth
With ghastly murmur of my sighs and cries;
For never doated Jove on Ganymede   180
So much as he on cursed Gaveston:
But that will more exasperate his wrath:
I must entreat him, I must speak him fair,
And be a means to call home Gaveston:
And yet he'll ever doat on Gaveston:
And so am I for ever miserable.

Enter the Nobles.

Lan. Look where the sister of the king of France
Sits wringing of her hands, and beats her breast!
War. The king, I fear, hath ill-entreated her.
Pem. Hard is the heart that injuries[1] such a saint. 190
Y. Mor. I know 'tis 'long of Gavestone she weeps.
E. Mor. Why, he is gone.
Y. Mor. Madam, how fares your grace?
Queen. Ah, Mortimer! now breaks the king's hate forth,
And he confesseth that he loves me not.
Y. Mor. Cry quittance, madam, then; and love not
              him.
Queen. No, rather will I die a thousand deaths:
And yet I love in vain—he'll ne'er love me.
Lan. Fear ye not, madam; now his minion's gone,
His wanton humour will be quickly left.
Queen. O never, Lancaster! I am enjoined   200
To sue upon you all for his repeal;

---

[1] So ed. 1598.—Dyce (who retains the verb "injury" in 1 *Tambur-laine*, 1, i.) prints silently "injures."

This wills my lord, and this must I perform,
Or else be banished from his highness' presence.

Lan. For his repeal, madam! he comes not back,
Unless the sea cast up his shipwrecked body.

War. And to behold so sweet a sight as that,
There's none here but would run his horse to death.

Y. Mor. But, madam, would you have us call him
    home?

Queen. I, Mortimer, for till he be restored,
The angry king hath banished me the court;   210
And, therefore, as thou lov'st and tender'st me,
Be thou my advocate upon the peers.

Y. Mor. What! would you have me plead for Gave-
    ston?

E. Mor. Plead for him that will, I am resolved.

Lan. And so am I, my lord! dissuade the queen.

Queen. O Lancaster! let him dissuade the king,
For 'tis against my will he should return.

War. Then speak not for him, let the peasant go.

Queen. 'Tis for myself I speak, and not for him.

Pem. No speaking will prevail,[1] and therefore cease. 220

Y. Mor. Fair queen, forbear to angle for the fish
Which, being caught, strikes him that takes it dead;
I mean that vile torpedo, Gaveston,
That now I hope floats on the Irish seas.

Queen. Sweet Mortimer, sit down by me awhile,
And I will tell thee reasons of such weight
As thou wilt soon subscribe to his repeal.

Y. Mor. It is impossible; but speak your mind.

---

[1] Avail.

Queen. Then thus, but none shall hear it but ourselves.

         [Talks to Y. MOR. *apart.*

Lan. My lords, albeit the queen win Mortimer, 230

Will you be resolute, and hold with me?

E. Mor. Not I, against my nephew.

Pem. Fear not, the queen's words cannot alter him.

War. No, do but mark how earnestly she pleads.

Lan. And see how coldly his looks make denial.

War. She smiles; now for my life his mind is changed.

Lan. I'll rather lose his friendship, I, than grant.

Y. Mor. Well, of necessity it must be so.

My lords, that I abhor base Gaveston,

I hope your honours take no question,   240

And therefore, though I plead for his repeal,

'Tis not for his sake, but for our avail!

Nay for the realm's behoof, and for the king's.

 Lan. Fie, Mortimer, dishonour not thyself!

Can this be true, 'twas good to banish him?

And is this true, to call him home again?

Such reasons make white black, and dark night day.

 Y. Mor. My lord of Lancaster, mark the respect.[1]

 Lan. In no respect can contraries be true.

 Queen. Yet, good my lord, here what he can allege. 250

War. All that he speaks is nothing, we are resolved.

 Y. Mor. Do you not wish that Gaveston were dead?

 Pem. I would he were.

 Y. Mor. Why then, my lord, give me but leave to speak

---

[1] Regard, consideration, Cf. *Hamlet*—

    '' There's the *respect*

That makes calamity of so long life.''

E. Mor. But, nephew, do not play the sophister.

Y. Mor. This which I urge is of a burning zeal
To mend the king, and do our country good,
Know you not Gaveston hath store of gold,
Which may in Ireland purchase him such friends,
As he will front the mightiest of us all?   260
And whereas he shall live and be beloved,
'Tis hard for us to work his overthrow.

War. Mark you but that, my lord of Lancaster.

Y. Mor. But were he here, detested as he is,
How easily might some base slave be suborned
To greet his lordship with a poniard,
And none so much as blame the murderer,
But rather praise him for that brave attempt,
And in the chronicle enrol his name
For purging of the realm of such a plague?   270

Pem. He saith true.

Lan. I, but how chance this was not done before?

Y. Mor. Because, my lords, it was not thought upon;
Nay, more, when he shall know it lies in us
To banish him, and then to call him home,
'Twill make him vail[1] the top-flag of his pride,
And fear to offend the meanest nobleman.

E. Mor. But how if he do not, nephew?

Y. Mor. Then may we with some colour rise in arms?
For howsoever we have borne it out,   280
'Tis treason to be up against the king;
So we shall have the people of our side,

---

[1] Lower.

Which for his father's sake lean to the king,
But cannot brook a night-grown mushroom,
Such a one as my lord of Cornwall is,
Should bear us down of the nobility.
And when the commons and the nobles join,
'Tis not the king can buckler Gaveston ;
We'll pull him from the strongest hold he hath.
My lords, if to perform this I be slack,   290
Think me as base a groom as Gaveston.

   Lan. On that condition, Lancaster will grant.
   War. And so will Pembroke and I.
   E. Mor. And I.
   Y. Mor. In this I count me highly gratified,
And Mortimer will rest at your command.
   Queen. And when this favour Isabel forgets,
Then let her live abandoned and forlorn.
But see, in happy time, my lord the king,
Having brought the Earl of Cornwall on his way,   300
Is new returned : this news will glad him much ;
Yet not so much as me ; I love him more
Than he can Gaveston ; would he loved me
But half so much, then were I treble-blessed !

        Enter KING EDWARD, *mourning.*

   Edw. He's gone, and for his absence thus I mourn.
Did ever sorrow go so near my heart,
As doth the want of my sweet Gaveston !
And could my crown's revenue bring him back,
I would freely give it to his enemies,
And think I gained, having bought so dear a friend. 310

Queen. Hark! how he harps upon his minion.

Edw. My heart is as an anvil unto sorrow,
Which beats upon it like the Cyclops' hammers,
And with the noise turns up my giddy brain,
And makes me frantic for my Gaveston.
Ah! had some bloodless fury rose from hell,
And with my kingly sceptre struck me dead,
When I was forced to leave my Gaveston!

Lan. Diablo! what passions call you these?

Queen. My gracious lord, I come to bring you news. 320

Edw. That you have parled with your Mortimer?

Queen. That Gaveston, my lord, shall be repealed.

Edw. Repealed! the news is too sweet to be true!

Queen. But will you love me, if you find it so?

Edw. If it be so, what will not Edward do?

Queen. For Gaveston, but not for Isabel.

Edw. For thee, fair queen, if thou lov'st Gaveston,
I'll hang a golden tongue about thy neck,
Seeing thou hast pleaded with so good success.

Queen. No other jewels hang about my neck   330
Than these, my lord; nor let me have more wealth
Than I may fetch from this rich treasury—
O how a kiss revives poor Isabel!

Edw. Once more receive my hand; and let this be
A second marriage 'twixt thyself and me.

Queen. And may it prove more happy than the first!
My gentle lord, bespeak these nobles fair,
That wait attendance for a gracious look,
And on their knees salute your majesty.

Edw. Courageous Lancaster, embrace thy king; 340

And, as gross vapours perish by the sun,
Even so let hatred with thy sovereign's[1] smile.
Live thou with me as my companion.

Lan. This salutation overjoys my heart.

Edw. Warwick shall be my chiefest counsellor:
These silver hairs will more adorn my court
Than gaudy silks, or rich embroidery.
Chide me, sweet Warwick, if I go astray.

War. Slay me, my lord, when I offend your grace.

Edw. In solemn triumphs, and in public shows, 350
Pembroke shall bear the sword before the king.

Pem. And with this sword Pembroke will fight for
you.

Edw. But wherefore walks young Mortimer aside?
Be thou commander of our royal fleet;
Or, if that lofty office like thee not,
I make thee here Lord Marshal of the realm.

Y. Mor. My lord, I'll marshal so your enemies,
As England shall be quiet, and you safe.

Edw. And as for you, Lord Mortimer of Chirke,
Whose great achievements in our foreign war 360
Deserves no common place, nor mean reward;
Be you the general of the levied troops,
That now are ready to assail the Scots.

E. Mor. In this your grace hath highly honoured me,
For with my nature war doth best agree.

Queen. Now is the king of England rich and strong,
Having the love of his renownéd peers.

---

[1] So ed. 1612.—ed. 1598 "soueraigne."

Edw. I, Isabel, ne'er was my heart so light.
Clerk of the crown, direct our warrant forth
For Gaveston to Ireland : [*Enter* Beaumont *with war-*
     rant.] Beaumont, fly,   370
As fast as Iris, or Jove's Mercury.
     Bea. It shall be done, my gracious lord.
     Edw. Lord Mortimer, we leave you to your charge.
Now let us in, and feast it royally.
Against our friend the Earl of Cornwall comes,
We'll have a general tilt and tournament ;
And then his marriage shall be solemnised.
For wot you not that I have made him sure [1]
Unto our cousin, the earl of Gloucester's heir?
     Lan. Such news we hear, my lord.   380
     Edw. That day, if not for him, yet for my sake,
Who in the triumph will be challenger,
Spare for no cost ; we will requite your love.
     War. In this, or aught your highness shall command
          us.
     Edw. Thanks, gentle Warwick : come, let's in and
          revel.   [*Exeunt. Manent the* MORTIMERS.
     E. Mor. Nephew, I must to Scotland ; thou stayest
          here.
Leave now t'oppose thyself against the king.
Thou seest by nature he is mild and calm,
And, seeing his mind so doats on Gaveston,
Let him without controulment have his will.   390
The mightiest kings have had their minions :

---

[1] Affianced him.

Great Alexander loved Hephestion ;
The conquering Hercules [1] for his Hylas wept ;
And for Patroclus stern Achilles drooped.
And not kings only, but the wisest men :
The Roman Tully loved Octavius ;
Grave Socrates wild Alcibiades.
Then let his grace, whose youth is flexible,
And promiseth as much as we can wish,
Freely enjoy that vain, light-headed earl ;   400
For riper years will wean him from such toys.

    Y. Mor. Uncle, his wanton humour grieves not me ;
But this I scorn, that one so basely born
Should by his sovereign's favour grow so pert,
And riot it with the treasure of the realm.
While soldiers mutiny for want of pay,
He wears a lord's revenue on his back,[2]
And Midas-like, he jets it in the court,
With base outlandish cullions at his heels,
Whose proud fantastic liveries make such show,   410
As if that Proteus, god of shapes, appeared.
I have not seen a dapper Jack so brisk ;
He wears a short Italian hooded cloak,
Larded with pearl, and, in his Tuscan cap,
A jewel of more value than the crown.
While other [4] walk below, the king and he

---

[1] Eds. 1598, 1612, "Hector." Ed. 1622 "The conquering *Hector did* for Hilas weepe."

[2] Cf. 2 *Henry VI.* i. 3 :—
        "She bears a *duke's revenue on her back.*"

[3] Worthless fellows.

[4] So ed. 1598.—Later eds. "others."

From out a window laugh at such as we,
And flout our train, and jest at our attire.
Uncle, 'tis this makes me impatient.   419
    E. Mor. But, nephew, now you see the king is changed.
    Y. Mor. Then so am I, and live to do him service:
But whilst I have a sword, a hand, a heart,
I will not yield to any such upstart.
You know my mind; come, uncle, let's away. [*Exeunt.*

ACT THE SECOND.

SCENE I.

Enter [1] YOUNG SPENCER *and* BALDOCK.

Bald. Spencer,
Seeing that our lord the Earl of Gloucester's dead,
Which of the nobles dost thou mean to serve?

Y. Spen. Not Mortimer, nor any of his side;
Because the king and he are enemies.
Baldock, learn this of me, a factious lord
Shall hardly do himself good, much less us;
But he that hath the favour of a king,
May with one word advance us while we live:
The liberal Earl of Cornwall is the man   10
On whose good fortune Spencer's hope depends.

Bald. What, mean you then to be his follower?

Y. Spen. No, his companion; for he loves me well,
And would have once preferred me to the king.

Bald. But he is banished; there's small hope of him.

Y. Spen. I, for a while: but, Baldock, mark the end.
A friend of mine told me in secresy

---

[1] Scene: a hall in Gloucester's mansion.

That he's repealed, and sent for back again ;
And even now a post came from the court
With letters to our lady from the king ;　　　　20
And as she read she smiled, which makes me think
It is about her lover Gaveston.

　　Bald. 'Tis like enough ; for since he was exiled
She neither walks abroad, nor comes in sight.
But I had thought the match had been broke off,
And that his banishment had changed her mind.

　　Y. Spen. Our lady's first love is not wavering ;
My life for thine she will have Gaveston.

　　Bald. Then hope I by her means to be preferred,
Having read unto her since she was a child.　　30

　　Y. Spen. Then, Baldock, you must cast the scholar off,
And learn to court it like a gentleman.
'Tis not a black coat and a little band,
A velvet caped cloak, faced before with serge,
And smelling to a nosegay all the day,
Or holding of a napkin in your hand,
Or saying a long grace at a table's end,
Or making low legs to a nobleman,
Or looking downward with your eyelids close,
And saying, "Truly, an't may please your honour,"　　40
Can get you any favour with great men ;
You must be proud, bold, pleasant, resolute,
And now and then stab, as occasion serves.

　　Bald. Spencer, thou know'st I hate such formal toys,
And use them but of mere hypocrisy.
Mine old lord while he lived was so precise,
That he would take exceptions at my buttons,

And being like pins' heads, blame me for the bigness;
Which made me curate-like in mine attire,
Though inwardly licentious enough,   50
And apt for any kind of villainy.
I am none of these common pedants, I,
That cannot speak without *propterea quod*.
    Y. Spen. But one of those that saith, *quandoquidem*,
And hath a special gift to form a verb.
    Bald. Leave off this jesting, here my lady comes.

Enter the Lady.

    Lady. The grief for his exile was not so much,
As is the joy of his returning home.
This letter came from my sweet Gaveston:
What need'st thou, love, thus to excuse thyself?   60
I know thou could'st not come and visit me:
I will not long be from thee, though I die.   [*Reads.*
This argues the entire love of my lord;
When I forsake thee, death seize on my heart: [*Reads.*
But stay[1] thee here where Gaveston shall sleep.
Now to the letter of my lord the king.—
He wills me to repair unto the court,
And meet my Gaveston? why do I stay,
Seeing that he talks thus of my marriage-day?
Who's there? Baldock!   70
See that my coach be ready, I must hence.
    Bald. It shall be done, madam.   *Exit.*
    Lady. And meet me at the park-pale presently.

---

[1] So ed. 1612.—Omitted in ed. 1598.

Spencer, stay you and bear me company,
For I have joyful news to tell thee of;
My lord of Cornwall is a coming over,
And will be at the court as soon as we.

 Spen. I knew the king would have him home again.

 Lady. If all things sort out, as I hope they will,
Thy service, Spencer, shall be thought upon.   80

 Spen. I humbly thank your ladyship.

 Lady. Come, lead the way; I long till I am there.
             [*Exeunt.*

SCENE II.

Enter[1] EDWARD, *the* QUEEN, LANCASTER, YOUNG MOR-
TIMER, WARWICK, PEMBROKE, KENT, *and* Attendants.

 Edw. The wind is good, I wonder why he stays;
I fear me he is wrecked upon the sea.

 Queen. Look, Lancaster, how passionate he is,
And still his mind runs on his minion!

 Lan. My lord.

 Edw. How now! what news? is Gaveston arrived?

 Y. Mor. Nothing but Gaveston! what means your
    grace?
You have matters of more weight to think upon;
The King of France sets foot in Normandy.

 Edw. A trifle: we'll expel him when we please. 10
But tell me, Mortimer, what's thy device
Against the stately triumph we decreed?

---

1 Scene: before Tynemouth Castle.

Y. Mor. A homely one, my lord, not worth the telling.

Edw. Pray thee let me know it.

Y. Mor. But, seeing you are so desirous, thus it is:
A lofty cedar-tree, fair flourishing,
On whose top-branches kingly eagles perch,
And by the bark a canker creeps me up,
And gets into the highest bough of all:
The motto, *Æque tandem.*   20

Edw. And what is yours, my lord of Lancaster?

Lan. My lord, mine's more obscure than Mortimer's.
Pliny[1] reports there is a[2] flying fish
Which all the other fishes deadly hate,
And therefore, being pursued, it takes the air:
No sooner is it up, but there's a fowl
That seizeth it: this fish, my lord, I bear,
The motto this: *Undique mors est.*

Kent.[3] Proud Mortimer! ungentle Lancaster!
Is this the love you bear your sovereign?   30
Is this the fruit your reconcilement bears?

---

[1] Reed refers to Pliny's *Nat. Hist.*, ix. 19; but Pliny merely says that the exocœtus would leap on to a rocky ledge in warm weather and there bask in the sun. It is curious that Dyce, who was such an enthusiast for Athenæus, did not refer his readers to the account of the exocœtus quoted from Clearchus in *Deipnos.* viii. 5. According to this authority the fish, when basking on the ledge, has to be constantly on his guard against king-fishers and the like, and when he sees them afar, flies leaping and gasping until he dives under the water. Perhaps Marlowe had in his mind some embellished account that he had found in Gesner or Bellonius.

[2] So ed. 1612.—Omitted in ed. 1598.

[3] Old eds. "*Edw.*" (a misprint for "*Edm.*"—the prefix in the 4tos. to Kent's speeches.)

Can you in words make show of amity,
And in your shields display your rancorous minds !
What call you this but private libelling
Against the Earl of Cornwall and my brother?
   Queen. Sweet husband, be content, they all love you.
   Edw. They love me not that hate my Gaveston.
I am that cedar, shake me not too much ;
And you the eagles ; soar ye ne'er so high,
I have the jesses [1] that will pull you down ;   40
And *Æque tandem* shall that canker cry
Unto the proudest peer of Britainy.
Though thou compar'st him to a flying fish,
And threatenest death whether he rise or fall,
'Tis not the hugest monster of the sea,
Nor foulest harpy that shall swallow him.
   Y. Mor. If in his absence thus he favours him,
What will he do whenas he shall be present?
   Lan. That shall we see ; look where his lordship comes.

Enter GAVESTON.

   Edw. My Gaveston !   50
Welcome to Tynemouth ! welcome to thy friend !
Thy absence made me droop and pine away ;
For, as the lovers of fair Danae,
When she was locked up in a brazen tower,
Desired her more, and waxed outrageous,
So did it fare [2] with me : and now thy sight

---

[1] Old eds. "gresses" (for "gesses.")—"Jesses" were the straps round
a hawk's legs, with rings (called "varvels,") to which the falconer's leash
was attached.
  [2] So ed. 1622.—Eds. 1598, 1612, "sure."

Is sweeter far than was thy parting hence
Bitter and irksome to my sobbing heart.

Gav. Sweet lord and king, your speech preventeth mine,
Yet have I words left to express my joy: 60
The shepherd nipt with biting winter's rage
Frolics not more to see the painted spring,
Than I do to behold your majesty.

Edw. Will none of you salute my Gaveston?

Lan. Salute him? yes; welcome, Lord Chamberlain :

Y. Mor. Welcome is the good Earl of Cornwall!

War. Welcome, Lord Governor of the Isle of Man!

Pem. Welcome, Master Secretary!

Kent. Brother, do you hear them?

Edw. Still will these earls and barons use me thus.   70

Gav. My lord, I cannot brook these injuries.

Queen. Aye me, poor soul, when these begin to jar.

                                              [*Aside.*

Edw. Return it to their throats, I'll be thy warrant.

Gav. Base, leaden earls, that glory in your birth,
Go sit at home and eat your tenants' beef;
And come not here to scoff at Gaveston,
Whose mounting thoughts did never creep so low
As to bestow a look on such as you.

Lan. Yet I disdain not to do this for you.   [*Draws.*

Edw. Treason! treason! where's the traitor?   80

Pem. Here! here! king.[1]

---

[1] Old eds. read:—

"*Pem.* Here, here, king: convey hence Gaveston, thaiie murder
       him."

I have followed Dyce in giving the line "Convey hence Gaveston,

[*Edw.*] Convey hence Gaveston; they'll murder him.

Gav. The life of thee shall salve this foul disgrace.

Y. Mor. Villain! thy life, unless I miss mine aim.

[*Offers to stab him.*

Queen. Ah! furious Mortimer, what hast thou done?

Y. Mor. No more than I would answer, were he slain.

[*Exit* GAVESTON *with Attendants.*

Edw. Yes, more than thou canst answer, though he live;
Dear shall you both abide this riotous deed.
Out of my presence! come not near the court.

Y. Mor. I'll not be barred the court for Gaveston. 90

Lan. We'll hale him by the ears unto the block.

Edw. Look to your own heads; his is sure enough.

War. Look to your own crown, if you back him thus.

Kent. Warwick, these words do ill beseem thy years.

Edw. Nay, all of them conspire to cross me thus;
But if I live, I'll tread upon their heads
That think with high looks thus to tread me down.
Come, Edmund, let's away and levy men,
'Tis war that must abate these barons' pride.

[*Exeunt the* KING, QUEEN, *and* KENT.

War. Let's to our castles, for the king is moved. 100

Y. Mor. Moved may he be, and perish in his wrath!

Lan. Cousin, it is no dealing with him now,
He means to make us stoop by force of arms;
And therefore let us jointly here protest,
To prosecute that Gaveston to the death.

&c.," to the king; but I do not agree with him in regarding "king" as
a prefix (for in the old copies "*Edw.*" is always the prefix to the king's
speeches.)

Y. Mor. By heaven, the abject villain shall not live!
War. I'll have his blood, or die in seeking it.
Pem. The like oath Pembroke takes.
Lan. And so doth Lancaster.
Now send our heralds to defy the king;
And make the people swear to put him down.   110

Enter Messenger.

Y. Mor. Letters! from whence?
Mess. From Scotland, My lord.
                              [*Giving letters to* MORTIMER.
Lan. Why, how now, cousin, how fares all our friends?
Y. Mor. My uncle's taken prisoner by the Scots.
Lan. We'll have him ransomed, man; be of good cheer.
Y. Mor. They rate his ransom at five thousand pound.
Who should defray the money but the king,
Seeing he is taken prisoner in his wars?
I'll to the king.
      Lan. Do, cousin, and I'll bear thee company.
War. Meantime, my lord of Pembroke and myself   120
Will to Newcastle here, and gather head.
Y. Mor. About it then, and we will follow you.
Lan. Be resolute and full of secrecy.
War. I warrant you.   [*Exit with* PEMBROKE.
Y. Mor. Cousin, and if he will not ransom him,
I'll thunder such a peal into his ears,
As never subject did unto his king.[1]

---

[1] The reader cannot fail to be reminded of Hotspur:—
      " But I will find him when he lies asleep,
         And in his ear I'll holla 'Mortimer!'"

Lan. Content, I'll bear my part—Holla! whose there?

[Guard *appears.*

Enter Guard.

Y. Mor. I, marry, such a guard as thus doth well.

Lan. Lead on the way.   130

Guard. Whither will your lordships?

Y. Mor. Whither else but to the king.

Guard. His highness is disposed to be alone.

Lan. Why, so he may, but we will speak to him.

Guard. You may not in, my lord.

Y. Mor. May we not?

Enter [1] EDWARD *and* KENT.

Edw. How now! what noise is this?

Who have we there, is't you?   [*Going.*

Y. Mor. Nay, stay, my lord, I come to bring you news:

Mine uncle's taken prisoner by the Scots.   140

Edw. Then ransom him.

Lan. 'Twas in your wars; you should ransom him.

Y. Mor. And you shall ransom him, or else——

Kent. What! Mortimer, you will not threaten him?

Edw. Quiet yourself, you shall have the broad seal,

To gather for him th[o]roughout the realm.

Lan. Your minion Gaveston hath taught you this.

Y. Mor. My lord, the family of the Mortimers

Are not so poor, but, would they sell their land,

'Twould [2] levy men enough to anger you.   150

We never beg, but use such prayers as these.

---

[1] The scene shifts to the interior of Tynemouth Castle.

[2] So ed. 1612.—Ed. 1598 "would."

Edw. Shall I still be haunted thus?

Y. Mor. Nay, now you're here alone, I'll speak my mind.

Lan. And so will I, and then, my lord, farewell.

Y. Mor. The idle triumphs, masks, lascivious shows,
And prodigal gifts bestowed on Gaveston,
Have drawn thy treasury [1] dry, and made thee weak;
The murmuring commons, overstretchèd, break. [2]

Lan. Look for rebellion, look to be deposed;
Thy garrisons are beaten out of France,   160
And, lame and poor, lie groaning at the gates.
The wild Oneyl, with swarms of Irish kerns, [3]
Lives uncontrolled within the English pale.
Unto the walls of York the Scots make [4] road,
And unresisted drive [5] away rich spoils.

Y. Mor. The haughty Dane commands the narrow seas, [6]
While in the harbour ride thy ships unrigged.

Lan. What foreign prince sends thee ambassadors?

Y. Mor. Who loves thee, but a sort of flatterers?

Lan. Thy gentle queen, sole sister to Valois,   170
Complains that thou hast left her all forlorn.

Y. Mor. Thy court is naked, being bereft of those
That make a king seem glorious to the world;
I mean the peers, whom thou should'st dearly love:

---

[1] So ed. 1612.—Ed. 1598 "thy *treasure* drie and made *the* weake."

[2] So modern editors.—Old eds. "hath."

[3] Light-armed foot soldiers, poor and undisciplined.—Compare a passage in the *Contention of York and Lancaster:*—

> "The wild Onele, my lord, is up in arms,
> With troops of Irish kernes that uncontroll'd
> Doth plant themselves within the English pale."

[4] Old eds. "made."—"Road,"="Inroad."   [5] Old eds. "Drave."

[6] Cf. 3 *Henry VI.* i. 1:—"Stern Faulconbridge *commands the narrow seas.*"

Libels are cast again [1] thee in the street :
Ballads and rhymes made of thy overthrow.

Lan. The Northern borderers seeing their houses
      burnt,
Their wives and children slain, run up and down,
Cursing the name of thee and Gaveston.

Y. Mor. When wert thou in the field with banner
      spread,   180
But once? and then thy soldiers marched like players,
With garish robes, not armour; and thyself,
Bedaubed with gold, rode laughing at the rest,
Nodding and shaking of thy spangled crest,
Where women's favours hung like labels down.

Lan. And thereof came it, that the fleering [2] Scots,
To England's high disgrace, have made this jig :
Maids [3] of England, sore may you mourn,
For your lemans you have lost at Bannocksbourn,
With a heave and a ho.   190
What weeneth the King of England,
So soon to have won Scotland ?
With a rombelow ? [4]

---

1 Against.   2 Jeering.

3 This jig (ballad) is taken with slight alteration from Fabyan's
"Chronicle," ii. 169 (ed. 1559).—"The battle of Bannockburn," says
Mr. Fleay, "was fought in 1314, yet is here alluded to in a scene which
is made up from narratives of events which occurred between 1309 and
1311. This is a striking instance of Marlowe's carelessness in such
matters."

4 "Common burdens to songs : see Skelton's *Works*, ii. 110, ed.
Dyce."—*Dyce*.

Y. Mor. Wigmore [1] shall fly, to set my uncle free.

Lan. And when 'tis gone, our swords shall purchase
    more.
If ye be moved, revenge it if you can ;
Look next to see us with our ensigns spread.
                      [Exeunt Nobles.

Edw. My swelling heart for very anger breaks !
How oft have I been baited by these peers,
And dare not be revenged, for their power is great ! 200
Yet, shall the crowing of these cockerels
Affright a lion?   Edward, unfold thy paws,
And let their lives' blood slake thy fury's hunger.
If I be cruel and grow tyrannous,
Now let them thank themselves, and rue too late.

Kent. My lord, I see your love to Gaveston
Will be the ruin of the realm and you,
For now the wrathful nobles theaten wars,
And therefore, brother, banish him for ever.

Edw. Art thou an enemy to my Gaveston?   210

Kent. I, and it grieves me that I favoured him.

Edw. Traitor, begone ! whine thou with Mortimer.

Kent. So will I, rather than with Gaveston.

Edw. Out of my sight, and trouble me no more !

Kent. No marvel though thou scorn thy noble peers,
When I thy brother am rejected thus.   *[Exit.*

Edw. Away !

---

[1] " Ralph de Wigmore, who came into England with the Conqueror,
obtained the Castle of Wigmore, Co. Hereford, and the Roger Mortimer of this play was summoned to Parliament as 'de Wigmore.' "
—*Cunningham.*

Poor Gaveston, that has no friend but me,
Do what they can, we'll live in Tynemouth here,
And, so I walk with him about the walls, 220
What care I though the Earls begirt us round—
Here cometh she that's cause of all these jars.

Enter the QUEEN, *with* King's Niece, *two* Ladies,
GAVESTON, BALDOCK, *and* YOUNG SPENCER.

Queen. My lord, 'tis thought the Earls are up in arms.
Edw. I, and 'tis likewise thought you favour 'em.[1]
Queen. Thus do you still suspect me without cause?
Lady. Sweet uncle! speak more kindly to the queen.
Gav. My lord, dissemble with her, speak her fair.
Edw. Pardon me, sweet, I forgot myself.
Queen. Your pardon is quickly got of Isabel.
Edw. The younger Mortimer is grown so brave, 230
That to my face he threatens civil wars.
Gav. Why do you not commit him to the Tower?
Edw. I dare not, for the people love him well.
Gav. Why then we'll have him privily made away.
Edw. Would Lancaster and he had both caroused
A bowl of poison to each other's health!
But let them go, and tell me what are these.
Lady. Two of my father's servants whilst he liv'd,—
May't please your grace to entertain them now.
Edw. Tell me, where wast thou born? what is thine
          arms? 240
Bald. My name is Baldock, and my gentry
I fetch from Oxford, not from heraldry.

---

[1] Old eds. "him."

Edw. The fitter art thou, Baldock, for my turn.
Wait on me, and I'll see thou shall not want.

Bald. I humbly thank your majesty.

Edw. Knowest thou him, Gaveston?

Gav. I, my lord;
His name is Spencer, he is well allied;
For my sake, let him wait upon your grace;
Scarce shall you find a man of more desert.

Edw. Then, Spencer, wait upon me, for his sake   250
I'll grace thee with a higher style ere long.

Y. Spen. No greater titles happen unto me,
Than to be favoured of your majesty.

Edw. Cousin, this day shall be your marriage feast.
And, Gaveston, think that I love thee well,
To wed thee to our niece, the only heir
Unto the Earl of Gloucester late deceased.

Gav I know. my lord, many will stomach me,
But I respect neither their love nor hate.

Edw. The headstrong barons shall not limit me;   260
He that I list to favour shall be great.
Come, let's away; and when the marriage ends,
Have at the rebels, and their 'complices!

[Exeunt omnes.

SCENE III.

Enter [1] LANCASTER, YOUNG MORTIMER, WARWICK,
PEMBROKE, *and* KENT.

Kent. My lords, of love to this our native land
I come to join with you and leave the king:

---

[1] Scene : the neighbourhood of Tynemouth.

And in your quarrel and the realm's behoof
Will be the first that shall adventure life.

Lan. I fear me, you are sent of policy,
To undermine us with a show of love.

War. He is your brother, therefore have we cause
To cast [1] the worst, and doubt of your revolt.

Kent. Mine honour shall be hostage of my truth :
If that will not suffice, farewell, my lords.   10

Y. Mor. Stay, Edmund ; never was Plantagenet
False of his word, and therefore trust we thee.

Pem. But what's the reason you should leave him
         now?

Kent. I have informed the Earl of Lancaster.

Lan. And it sufficeth.   Now, my lords, know this,
That Gaveston is secretly arrived,
And here in Tynemouth frolics with the king.
Let us with these our followers scale the walls,
And suddenly surprise them unawares.

Y. Mor. I'll give the onset.

War. And I'll follow thee.   20

Y. Mor. This tottered [2] ensign of my ancestors,
Which swept the desert shore of that dead [3] sea
Whereof we got the name of Mortimer,
Will I advance upon this castle['s] walls.
Drums, strike alarum, raise them from their sport,
And ring aloud the knell of Gaveston !

---

[1] Surmise.   [2] Tattered.
[3] " In all Latin deeds the Mortimers are called ' de Mortuo mari.' "
Cunningham.

Lan. None be so hardy as [to] touch the king :
But neither spare you Gaveston nor his friends. [*Exeunt.*

SCENE IV.

Enter [1] *the* KING *and* YOUNG SPENCER.

Edw. O tell me, Spencer, where is Gaveston ?
Spen. I fear me, he is slain, my gracious lord.
Edw. No, here he comes ; now let them spoil and
    kill.

Enter QUEEN, King's Niece, GAVESTON, *and* Nobles.

Fly, fly, my lords, the earls have got the hold ;
Take shipping and away to Scarborough ;
Spencer and I will post away by land.
    Gav. O stay, my lord, they will not injure you.
    Edw. I will not trust them ; Gaveston, away !
    Gav. Farewell, my lord.
    Edw. Lady, farewell.
    Lady. Farewell, sweet uncle, till we meet again.   10
    Edw. Farewell, sweet Gaveston : and farewell, niece.
    Queen. No farewell to poor Isabel thy queen ?
    Edw. Yes, yes, for Mortimer, your lover's sake.
                  [*Exeunt all but* ISABEL.
    Queen. Heaven can witness I love none but you :
From my embracements thus he breaks away.
O that mine arms could close this isle about,
That I might pull him to me where I would :

---

[1] Scene : the interior of Tynemouth Castle.

Or that these tears, that drizzle from mine eyes,
Had power to mollify his stony heart,
That when I had him we might never part.   20

Enter the Barons.   *Alarums.*

Lan. I wonder how he scaped !

Y. Mor. Who's this, the queen ?

Queen. I, Mortimer, the miserable queen,
Whose pining heart her inward sighs have blasted,
And body with continual mourning wasted :
These hands are tired with haling of my lord
From Gaveston, from wicked Gaveston,
And all in vain ; for, when I speak him fair,
He turns away, and smiles upon his minion.

Y. Mor. Cease to lament, and tell us where's the king?

Queen. What would you with the king ? is't him you
seek ?   30

Lan. No, madam, but that cursèd Gaveston.
Far be it from the thought of Lancaster
To offer violence to his sovereign.
We would but rid the realm of Gaveston :
Tell us where he remains, and he shall die.

Queen. He's gone by water unto Scarborough ;
Pursue him quickly, and he cannot scape ;
The king hath left him, and his train is small.

War. Foreslow [1] no time, sweet Lancaster, let's march.

Y. Mor. How comes it that the king and he is
parted ?   40

---

[1] Delay.   The word occurs in 3 *Henry VI.* ii. 3, l. 56 ; *Arden of
Feversham, &c.*

Queen. That thus[1] your army, going several ways,
Might be of lesser force : and with the power
That he intendeth presently to raise,
Be easily suppressed ; therefore[2] be gone.
  Y. Mor. Here in the river rides a Flemish hoy ;
Let's all aboard, and follow him amain.
  Lan. The wind that bears him hence will fill our sails :
Come, come aboard, 'tis but an hour's sailing.
  Y. Mor. Madam, stay you within this castle here.
  Queen. No, Mortimer, I'll to my lord the king.   50
  Y. Mor. Nay, rather sail with us to Scarborough.
  Queen. You know the king is so suspicious,
As if he hear I have but talked with you,
Mine honour will be called in question :
And therefore, gentle Mortimer, be gone.
  Y. Mor. Madam, I cannot stay to answer you,
But think of Mortimer as he deserves. [*Exeunt* Barons.
  Queen. So well hast thou deserved, sweet Mortimer,
As Isabel could live with thee for ever.
In vain I look for love at Edward's hand,   60
Whose eyes are fixed on none but Gaveston
Yet once more I'll importune him with prayer,
If he be strange and not regard my words,
My son and I will over into France,
And to the king my brother there complain,
How Gaveston hath robbed me of his love :
But yet I hope my sorrows will have end,
  d Gaveston this blessèd day be slain.   [*Exit.*

---

1 Old eds. "this."
2 So ed. 1622.—Eds. 1598, 1612, "*and* therefore."

SCENE V.

Enter [1] GAVESTON, *pursued.*

Gav. Yet, lusty lords, I have escaped your hands,
Your threats, your larums, and your hot pursuits ;
And though divorcèd from King Edward's eyes,
Yet liveth Pierce of Gaveston unsurprised,
Breathing, in hope (malgrado [2] all your beards,
That muster rebels thus against your king),
To see [3] his royal sovereign once again.

Enter the Nobles.

War. Upon him, soldiers, take away his weapons.
Y. Mor. Thou proud disturber of thy country's peace,
Corrupter of thy king ; cause of these broils,   10
Base flatterer, yield ! and were it not for shame,
Shame and dishonour to a soldier's name,
Upon my weapons point here should'st thou fall,
And welter in thy gore.
Lan. Monster of men !
That, like the Greekish strumpet, trained to arms
And bloody wars so many valiant knights ,
Look for no other fortune, wretch, than death !
King Edward is not here to buckler thee.
War. Lancaster, why talk'st thou to the slave ?

---

1 "There is such uncertainty about the location of this scene that I can only mark it—an open country. *—Dyce.*
2 The Italian form of " maugre."
3 So ed. 1612.—Ed. 1598 " these."

Go, soldiers, take him hence, for by my sword 20
His head shall off: Gaveston, short warning
Shall serve thy turn.   It is our country's cause,
That here severely we will execute
Upon thy person : hang him at a bough.
 Gav. My lords !—
 War. Soldiers, have him away;
But for thou wert the favourite of a king,
Thou shalt have so much honour at our hands [1]—
 Gav. I thank you all, my lords: then I perceive,
That heading is one, and hanging is the other,
And death is all.
Enter Earl of ARUNDEL.

 Lan. How now, my lord of Arundel? 30
 Arun. My lords, King Edward greets you all by me.
 War. Arundel, say your message.
 Arun. His majesty,
Hearing that you had taken Gaveston,
Intreateth you by me, but that he may
See him before he dies; for why, he says,
And sends you word, he knows that die he shall;
And if you gratify his grace so far,
He will be mindful of the courtesy.
 War. How now?
 Gav. Renowmèd Edward, how thy name
Revives poor Gaveston !
 War. No, it needeth not; 40

---

[1] A line, as Dyce remarks, in which Warwick says that Gaveston shall
b *beheaded*, has dropped out.

Arundel, we will gratify the king
In other matters ; he must pardon us in this.
Soldiers, away with him !

Gav. Why, my lord of Warwick,
Will not these delays beget my hopes ? [1]
I know it, lords, it is this life you aim at,
Yet grant King Edward this.

Y. Mor. Shalt thou appoint
What we shall grant?   Soldiers, away with him :
Thus we'll gratify the king,
We'll send his head by thee ; let him bestow
His tears on that, for that is all he gets   50
Of Gaveston, or else his senseless trunk.

Lan. Not so, my lords, lest he bestow more cost
In burying him than he hath ever earned.

Arun. My lords, it is his Majesty's request,
And in the honour of a king he swears,
He will but talk with him, and send him back.

War. When ? can you tell ? [2]   Arundel, no ; we wot,
He that the care of his [3] realm remits,
And drives his nobles to these exigents
For Gaveston, will, if he seize [4] him once,   60
Violate any promise to possess him.

---

[1] The passage is corrupt : I have followed the reading of the old
eds. Dyce gives—
        " Will *now* these *short* delays beget my hopes ? "

[2] " When ? can you tell ? "—a sort of proverbial expression. See
Dyce's *Shakespeare Glossary.*

[3] So Dyce.—Ed. 1598 omits " his." Eds. 1612, 1622, read :—" He
that *hath* the care of Realme-remits." (" Care " must be pronounced as
a dissyllable.)

[4] Cunningham reads " sees."

Arun. Then if you will not trust his grace in keep,
My lords, I will be pledge for his return.

Y. Mor. 'Tis[1] honourable in thee to offer this :
But for we know thou art a noble gentleman,
We will not wrong thee so, to make away
A true man for a thief.

Gav. How mean'st thou, Mortimer? that is over-base.

Y. Mor. Away, base groom, robber of king's renown,
Question with thy companions and mates.　　　70

Pem. My Lord Mortimer, and you, my lords, each one,
To gratify the king's request therein.
Touching the sending of this Gaveston,
Because his majesty so earnestly
Desires to see the man before his death,
I will upon mine honour undertake
To carry him, and bring him back again ;
Provided this, that you my lord of Arundel
Will join with me.

War. Pembroke, what wilt thou do?
Cause yet more bloodshed? is it not enough　　80
That we have taken him, but must we now
Leave him on "had I wist,"[2] and let him go?

Pem. My lords, I will not over-woo your honours,
But if you dare trust Pembroke with the prisoner,
Upon mine oath, I will return him back.

Arun. My lord of Lancaster, what say you in this?

Lan. Why, I say, let him go on Pembroke's word.

---

[1] Old eds. " It is."
[2] " The exclamation of those who repent what they have rashly
done."—*Dyce.*

Pem. And you, Lord Mortimer?

Y. Mor. How say you, my lord of Warwick?

War. Nay, do your pleasures, I know how 'twill prove.

Pem. Then give him me.

Gav. Sweet sovereign, yet I come   90
To see thee ere I die.

War. Yet not perhaps,
If Warwick's wit and policy prevail.   [*Aside.*

Y. Mor. My lord of Pembroke, we deliver him you :
Return him on your honour.   Sound, away!
> [*Exeunt all but* PEMBROKE, ARUNDEL,[1]
> GAVESTON, *and* PEMBROKE'S men.

Pem. My lord [of Arundel], you shall go with me.
My house is not far hence; out of the way
A little, but our men shall go along.
We that have pretty wenches to our wives,
Sir, must not come so near to baulk their lips.

Arun. 'Tis very kindly spoke, my lord of Pembroke; 100
Your honour hath an adamant of power
To draw a prince.

Pem. So, my lord.   Come hither, James
I do commit this Gaveston to thee,
Be thou this night his keeper, in the morning
We will discharge thee of thy charge : be gone.

Gav. Unhappy Gaveston, whither goest thou now?
> [*Exit with* JAMES *and* PEMBROKE'S men.

Horse-boy. My lord, we'll quickly be at Cobham.
> [*Exeunt.*

---

[1] Here and throughout iii. 11, the 4tos give "Mat" and "Matreuis" for "Arundel." The mistake arose, as Dyce pointed out, by the parts of Arundel and Matrevis having been taken by the same actor.

ACT THE THIRD.

SCENE I.

Enter [1] GAVESTON *mourning,* JAMES, *and the* EARL of PEMBROKE'S men.

Gav. O treacherous Warwick! thus to wrong thy
    friend.

James. I see it is your life these arms pursue.

Gav. Weaponless must I fall, and die in bands?
O! must this day be period of my life?
Centre of all my bliss! An ye be men,
Speed to the king.

          Enter WARWICK *and his company.*

War. My lord of Pembroke's men,
Strive you no longer—I will have that Gaveston.

James. Your lordship does dishonour to yourself,
And wrong our lord, your honourable friend.

War. No, James, it is my country's cause I follow. 10
Go, take the villain; soldiers, come away.
We'll make quick work. Commend me to your master,

---

[1] Scene · the open country (near Warwick?).

My friend, and tell him that I watched it well.
Come, let thy shadow[1] parley with King Edward.

Gav. Treacherous earl, shall I not see the king?

War. The king of Heaven perhaps, no other king.
Away! [*Exeunt* WARWICK *and his* Men *with* GAVESTON

James. Come, fellows, it booted not for us to strive,
We will in haste go certify our lord. [*Exeunt.*

SCENE II.

Enter[2] KING EDWARD *and* YOUNG SPENCER, BALDOCK,
and Nobles *of the king's side, with drums and fifes.*

Edw. I long to hear an answer from the barons
Touching my friend, my dearest Gaveston.
Ah! Spencer, not the riches of my realm
Can ransom him: ah, he is marked to die!
I know the malice of the younger Mortimer,
Warwick I know is rough, and Lancaster
Inexorable, and I shall never see
My lovely Pierce of Gaveston again
The barons overbear me with their pride.

Y. Spen. Were I King Edward, England's sovereign, 10
Son to the lovely Eleanor of Spain,
Great Edward Longshanks' issue, would I bear
These braves,[3] this rage, and suffer uncontrolled
These barons thus to beard me in my land,

---

[1] The meaning is surely "ghost, spirit," not, as Mr. Fleay interprets,
"representative, plenipotentiary."

[2] Scene : neighbourhood of Borrowbridge.

[3] Braggard challenges.

In mine own realm?   My lord, pardon my speech,
Did you retain your father's magnanimity,
Did you regard the honour of your name,
You would not suffer thus your majesty
Be counterbuft of your nobility.
Strike off their heads, and let them preach on poles !   20
No doubt, such lessons they will teach the rest,
As by their preachments they will profit much,
And learn obedience to their lawful king.

Edw. Yea, gentle Spencer, we have been too mild,
Too kind to them ; but now have drawn our sword,
And if they send me not my Gaveston,
We'll steel it on their crest, and poll their tops.

Bald. This haught[1] resolve becomes your majesty
Not to be tied to their affection,
As though your highness were a schoolboy still,   30
And must be awed and governed like a child.

Enter HUGH SPENCER, *father to the* YOUNG SPENCER,
with his truncheon and Soldiers.

O. Spen. Long live my sovereign, the noble Edward—
In peace triumphant, fortunate in wars !

Edw. Welcome, old man, com'st thou in Edward's aid ?
Then tell thy[2] prince of whence, and what thou art.

O. Spen. Lo, with a band of bowmen and of pikes,
Brown bills and targeteers, four hundred strong,
Sworn to defend King Edward's royal right,
I come in person to your majesty,

---

[1] Fr. haut.   Old eds. "the."

Spencer, the father of Hugh Spencer there,　　　40
Bound to your highness everlastingly,
For favour done, in him, unto us all.

　Edw. Thy father, Spencer?

　Y. Spen. True, an it like your grace,
That pours, in lieu of all your goodness shown,
His life, my lord, before your princely feet.

　Edw. Welcome ten thousand times, old man, again.
Spencer, this love, this kindness to thy king,
Argues thy noble mind and disposition.
Spencer, I here create thee Earl of Wiltshire,
And daily will enrich thee with our favour,　　　50
That, as the sunshine, shall reflect o'er thee.
Beside, the more to manifest our love,
Because we hear Lord Bruce doth sell his land,
And that the Mortimers are in hand withal,
Thou shalt have crowns of us t'outbid the barons ·
And, Spencer, spare them not, lay it on.
Soldiers, a largess, and thrice welcome all!

　Y. Spen. My lord, here comes [1] the queen.

Enter the QUEEN *and her* Son, *and* LEVUNE, *a Frenchman.*

　Edw. Madam, what news?

　Queen. News of dishonour, lord, and discontent.
Our friend Levune, faithful and full of trust,　　　60
Informeth us, by letters and by words,
That Lord Valois our brother, King of France,
Because your highness hath been slack in homage,

---

[1] So ed. 1612.—Ed. 1598 "come."

Hath seizèd Normandy into his hands.
These be the letters, this the messenger.

Edw. Welcome, Levune. Tush, Sib, if this be all,
Valois and I will soon be friends again.—
But to my Gaveston : shall I never see,
Never behold thee now?[1]—Madam, in this matter,
We will employ you and your little son :   70
You shall go parley with the King of France.
Boy, see you bear you bravely to the king,
And do your message with a majesty.

Prince. Commit not to my youth things of more weight
Than fits a prince so young as I to bear,
And fear not, lord and father, heaven's great beams
On Atlas' shoulder shall not lie more safe,
Than shall your charge committed to my trust.

Queen. Ah, boy ! this towardness makes thy mother fear
Thou art not marked to many days on earth.   80

Edw. Madam, we will that you with speed be shipped,
And this our son : Levune shall follow you
With all the haste we can despatch him hence.
Chuse of our lords to bear you company ;
And go in peace, leave us in wars at home.

Queen. Unnatural wars, where subjects brave their king ;
God end them once ! My lord, I take my leave,
To make my preparation for France.

[*Exit with* Prince.

Enter ARUNDEL.

Edw. What, Lord Arundel, dost thou come alone ?

---

[1] Cunningham and Mr Fleay silently print " more."

Arun. Yea, my good lord, for Gaveston is dead.   90
Edw. Ah, traitors! have they put my friend to death?
Tell me, Arundel, died he ere thou cam'st,
Or didst thou see my friend to take his death?
Arun. Neither, my lord; for as he was surprised,
Begirt with weapons and with enemies round,
I did your highness' message to them all;
Demanding him of them, entreating rather,
And said, upon the honour of my name,
That I would undertake to carry him
Unto your highness, and to bring him back.   100
Edw. And tell me, would the rebels deny me that?
Y. Spen. Proud recreants!
Edw. Yea, Spencer, traitors all.
Arun. I found them at the first inexorable;
The Earl of Warwick would not bide the hearing,
Mortimer hardly, Pembroke and Lancaster
Spake least: and when they flatly had denied,
Refusing to receive my pledge for him,
The Earl of Pembroke mildly thus bespake:
"My lord, because our sovereign sends for him,
And promiseth he shall be safe returned,   110
I will this undertake, to have him hence,
And see him re-delivered to your hands."
Edw. Well, and how fortunes [it] that he came not?
Y. Spen. Some treason, or some villany, was the cause.
Arun. The Earl of Warwick seized him on his way;
For being delivered unto Pembroke's men,
Their lord rode home thinking his prisoner safe·
But ere he came, Warwick in ambush lay,

And bare him to his death ; and in a trench
Strake off his head, and marched unto the camp.   120
   Y. Spen. A bloody part, flatly 'gainst law of arms.
   Edw. O shall I speak, or shall I sigh and die !
   Y. Spen. My lord, refer your vengeance to the sword
Upon these barons ; hearten up your men ;
Let them not unrevenged murder your friends !
Advance your standard, Edward, in the field,
And march to fire them from their starting holes.
                         [EDWARD *kneels*
   Edw. By earth, the common mother of us all,
By heaven, and all the moving orbs thereof,
By this right hand, and by my father's sword,   130
And all the honours 'longing to my crown,
I will have heads, and lives for him, as many
As I have manors, castles, towns, and towers !   [*Rises.*
Treacherous Warwick ! traitorous Mortimer '
If I be England's king, in lakes of gore
Your headless trunks, your bodies will I trail,
That you may drink your fill, and quaff in blood,
And stain my royal standard with the same,
That so my bloody colours may suggest
Remembrance of revenge immortally   140
On your accursèd traitorous progeny,
You villains, that have slain my Gaveston !
And in his place of honour and of trust,
Spencer, sweet Spencer, I adopt thee here :
And merely of our love we do create thee
Earl of Gloucester, and Lord Chamberlain,
Despite of times, despite of enemies.

Y. Spen. My Lord, here is[1] a messenger from the
   barons
Desires access unto your majesty.
 Edw. Admit him near.   150

Enter the Herald *from the* Barons, *with his coat of
arms.*

 Her. Long live King Edward, England's lawful lord !
 Edw. So wish not they, I wis, that sent thee hither.
Thou com'st from Mortimer and his complices,
A ranker rout[2] of rebels never was.
Well, say thy message.
 Her. The barons up in arms, by me salute
Your highness with long life and happiness :
And bid me say, as plainer to your grace,
That if without effusion of blood
You will this grief have ease and remedy,   160
That from your princely person you remove
This Spencer, as a putrefying branch,
That deads the royal vine, whose golden leaves[3]
Empale your princely head, your diadem,
Whose brightness such pernicious upstarts dim,
Say they ; and lovingly advise your grace,
To cherish virtue and nobility,
And have old servitors in high esteem,
And shake off smooth dissembling flatterers :

---

[1] Ed. 1598 "heres is."— Ed. 1612, 1622, "heres.
[2] So ed. 1622.—Eds. 1598, 1612, "roote."
[3] So ed. 1612.—Ed. 1598 "leave."

This granted, they, their honours, and their lives,   170
Are to your highness vowed and consecrate.

    Y. Spen. Ah, traitors! will they still display their
           pride?

    Edw. Away, tarry no answer, but be gone!
Rebels, will they appoint their sovereign
His sports, his pleasures, and his company?
Yet, ere thou go, see how I do divorce

                         [*Embraces* SPENCER.

Spencer from me.—-Now get thee to thy lords,
And tell them I will come to chastise them
For murdering Gaveston : hie thee, get thee gone
Edward with fire and sword follows at thy heels.   180
My lord[s], perceive you how these rebels swell?
Soldiers, good hearts, defend your sovereign's right,
For now, even now, we march to make them stoop.
Away!   [*Exeunt. Alarums, excursions, a great fight,*
                       and a retreat.

SCENE III.

Enter the KING, OLD SPENCER, YOUNG SPENCER, *and*
the Noblemen *of the* KING'S *side.*

    Edw. Why do we sound retreat? upon them, lords!
This day I shall pour vengeance with my sword
On those proud rebels that are up in arms,
And do confront and countermand their king.

    Y. Spen. I doubt it not, my lord, right will prevail.

    O. Spen. 'Tis not amiss, my liege, for either part
To breathe awhile; our men, with sweat and dust

All choked well near, begin to faint for heat ;
And this retire refresheth horse and man.

   Y. Spen. Here come the rebels.   10

     Enter YOUNG MORTIMER, LANCASTER, WARWICK,
            PEMBROKE, *&c.*

   E. Mor. Look, Lancaster, yonder is Edward
Among his flatterers.

   Lan. And there let him be
Till he pay dearly for their company.

   War. And shall, or Warwick's sword shall smite in
       vain,

   Edw. What, rebels, do you shrink and sound retreat ?

   Y. Mor. No, Edward, no, thy flatterers faint and fly.

   Lan. They'd best betimes forsake thee, and their
       trains,[1]
For they'll betray thee, traitors as they are.

   Y. Spen. Traitor on thy face, rebellious Lancaster !

   Pem. Away, base upstart, bravest thou nobles thus ? 20

   O. Spen. A noble attempt, and honourable deed,
Is[2] it not, trow ye, to assemble aid,
And levy arms against your lawful king !

   Edw. For which ere long their heads shall satisfy,
To appease the wrath of their offended king.

   Y. Mor. Then, Edward, thou wilt fight it to the last,
And rather bathe thy sword in subjects' blood,
Than banish that pernicious company ?

   Edw. I, traitors all, rather than thus be braved,

---

[1] Schemes.   [2] So ed. 1612.—Ed. 1589 " It is."

Make England's civil towns huge heaps of stones,   30
And ploughs to go about our palace-gates.

 War. A desperate and unnatural resolution!
Alarum!—to the fight!
St. George for England, and the barons' right.

  Edw. St. George for England, and King Edward's
   right.   [*Alarums. Exeunt.*

 Re-enter EDWARD *and his followers, with the* Barons
   and KENT, *captives.*

 Edw. Now, lusty lords, now, not by chance of war,
But justice of the quarrel and the cause,
Vailed is your pride; methinks you hang the heads,
But we'll advance them, traitors; now 'tis time
To be avenged on you for all your braves,   40
And for the murder of my dearest friend,
To whom right well you knew our soul was knit,
Good Pierce of Gaveston, my sweet favourite:
Ah, rebels! recreants' you made him away.

 Kent. Brother, in regard of thee, and of thy land,
Did they remove that flatterer from thy throne.

  Edw. So, sir, you have spoke; away, avoid our
   presence.   [*Exit* KENT.
Accursèd wretches, was't in regard of us,
When we had sent our messenger to request
He might be spared to come to speak with us,   50
And Pembroke undertook for his return,
That thou, proud Warwick, watched the prisoner,
Poor Pierce, and headed him 'gainst law of arms;

For which thy head shall overlook the rest,
As much as thou in rage outwent'st the rest.

War. Tyrant, I scorn thy threats and menaces,
It is but temporal that thou canst inflict.

Lan. The worst is death, and better die to live
Than live in infamy under such a king.

Edw. Away with them, my lord of Winchester !   60
These lusty leaders, Warwick and Lancaster,
I charge you roundly---off with both their heads '
Away !

War. Farewell, vain world '

Lan. Sweet Mortimer, farewell.

Y. Mor. England, unkind to thy nobility,
Groan for this grief, behold how thou art maimed !

Edw. Go, take that haughty Mortimer to the Tower,
There see him safe bestowed ; and for the rest,
Do speedy execution on them all.
Begone !   70

Y. Mor. What, Mortimer ! can ragged stony walls
Immure thy virtue that aspires to heaven ?
No, Edward, England's scourge, it may not be,
Mortimer's hope surmounts his fortune far.

                         [The captive Barons *are led off.*

Edw. Sound drums and trumpets ! March with me,
       my friends,
Edward this day hath crowned him king anew.

                  [Exeunt all e ept YOUNG
                      SPENCER, LEVUNE, *and*
                      BALDOCK.

Y. Spen. Levune, the trust that we repose in thee,

Begets the quiet of King Edward's land.
Therefore begone in haste, and with advice
Bestow that pleasure on the lords of France,   80
That, therewith all enchanted, like the guard
That suffered Jove to pass in showers of gold
To Danae, all aid may be denied
To Isabel, the queen, that now in France
Makes friends, to cross the seas with her young son,
And step into his father's regiment.[1]

Levune. That's it these barons and the subtle queen
Long levelled [2] at.

Bal. Yea, but, Levune, thou seest
These barons lay their heads on blocks together;
What they intend, the hangman frustrates clean.   90

Levune. Have you no doubt, my lords, I'll clap [3] so
            close
Among the lords of France with England's gold,
That Isabel shall make her plaints in vain,
And France shall be obdurate with her tears.

Y. Spen. Then make for France, amain—Levune,
            away :
Proclaim King Edward's wars and victories.

                            [*Exeunt omnes.*

---

[1] Rule.   [2] Old eds. "leuied."   [3] Old eds. "claps close."

ACT THE FOURTH.

SCENE I.

Enter [1] KENT.

Kent. Fair blows the wind for France; blow gentle
      gale,
Till Edmund be arrived for England's good :
Nature, yield to my country's cause in this.
A brother? no, a butcher of thy friends!
Proud Edward, dost thou banish me thy presence?
But I'll to France, and cheer the wrongèd queen,
And certify what Edward's looseness is.
Unnatural king! to slaughter noblemen
And cherish flatterers!   Mortimer, I stay
Thy sweet escape; stand gracious, gloomy night,   10
To his device.

Enter YOUNG MORTIMER, *disguised.*

Y. Mor. Holla : who walketh there?
Is't you, my lord?
   Kent. Mortimer, 'tis I;
But hath thy portion wrought so happily?

---

[1] Scene : London, near the Tower.

Y. Mor. It hath, my lord : the warders all asleep,
I thank them, gave me leave to pass in peace.
But hath your grace got shipping unto France?

Kent. Fear it not.   [*Exeunt.*

SCENE II.

Enter[1] *the* QUEEN *and her* Son.

Queen. Ah, boy ! our friends do fail us all in France :
The lords are cruel, and the king unkind :
What shall we do?[2]

Prince. Madam, return to England,
And please my father well, and then a fig
For all my uncle's friendship here in France.
I warrant you, I'll win his highness quickly ;
He loves me better than a thousand Spencers.

Queen. Ah, boy, thou art deceived, at least in this,
To think that we can yet be tuned together ;
No, no, we jar too far.   Unkind Valois !   10
Unhappy Isabel ! when France rejects,
Whither, oh ! whither dost thou bend thy steps ?

Enter SIR JOHN *of* Hainault.

Sir J. Madam, what cheer?

Queen. Ah ! good Sir John of Hainault,
Never so cheerless, nor so far distrest.

Sir J. I hear, sweet lady, of the king's unkindness ;
But droop not, madam : noble minds contemn

---

1 Scene : Paris.
2 So eds. 1598, 1622.—Ed. 1612 "goe."

Despair : will your grace with me to Hainault,
And there stay time's advantage with your son?
How say you, my lord, will you go with your friends,
And shake off all our fortunes equally ?   20
   Prince. So pleaseth [1] the queen, my mother, me it
       likes :
The king of England, nor the court of France,
Shall have me from my gracious mother's side,
Till I be strong enough to break a staff :
And then have at the proudest Spencer's head.
   Sir J. Well said, my lord.
   Queen. O, my sweet heart, how do I moan thy
       wrongs,
Yet triumph in the hope of thee, my joy !
Ah, sweet Sir John ! even to the utmost verge
Of Europe, or [2] the shore of Tanais,   30
We will with thee to Hainault—so we will :—
The marquis is a noble gentleman ;
His grace, I dare presume, will welcome me.
But who are these ?

     Enter KENT *and* YOUNG MORTIMER.

   Kent. Madam, long may you live,
Much happier than your friends in England do !
   Queen. Lord Edmund and Lord Mortimer alive !
Welcome to France ! the news was here, my lord,
That you were dead, or very near your death.

---

[1] Mr. Fleay reads "please," supposing that the letters *th* are repeated
from the next word.
   [2] Dyce's correction "on" seems to be quite unnecessary.

Y. Mor. Lady, the last was truest of the twain :
But Mortimer, reserved for better hap,   40
Hath shaken off the thraldom of the Tower,
And lives t' advance your standard, good my lord.

    Prince. How mean you ? and the king, my father, lives !
No, my Lord Mortimer, not I, I trow.

    Queen. Not, son ; why not ? I would it were no
         worse.
But, gentle lords, friendless we are in France.

    Y. Mor. Monsieur le Grand, a noble friend of yours,
Told us, at our arrival, all the news :
How hard the nobles, how unkind the king
Hath showed himself ; but, madam, right makes room 50
Where weapons want ; and, though so many friends
Are made away, as Warwick, Lancaster,
And others of our party [1] and faction ;
Yet have we friends, assure your grace, in England
Would cast up caps, and clap their hands for joy,
To see us there, appointed [2] for our foes.

    Kent. Would all were well, and Edward well reclaimed,
For England's honour, peace, and quietness.

    Y. Mor. But by the sword, my lord, 't must be de-
         served ; [3]
The king will ne'er forsake his flatterers.   60

    Sir J. My lords of England, sith th' ungentle king
Of France refuseth to give aid of arms

---

[1] Dyce needlessly reads " part.
    Equipped to meet our foes.
[2] Earned.

To this distressèd queen his sister here,
Go you with her to Hainault ; doubt ye not,
We will find comfort, money, men and friends
Ere long, to bid the English king a base.[1]
How say, young prince ? what think you of the match ?
   Prince. I think King Edward will outrun us all.
   Queen. Nay, son, not so : and you must not dis-
      courage
Your friends, that are so forward in your aid.   70
   Kent. Sir John of Hainault, pardon us, I pray ;
These comforts that you give our woful queen
Bind us in kindness all at your command.
   Queen. Yea, gentle brother ; and the God of heaven
Prosper your happy motion, good Sir John.
   Y. Mor. This noble gentleman, forward in arms,
Was born, I see, to be our anchor-hold.
Sir John of Hainault, be it thy renown,
That England's queen, and nobles in distress,
Have been by thee restored and comforted.   80
   Sir. J. Madam, along, and you my lord[s], with me,
That England's peers may Hainault's welcome see.
                              [*Exeunt.*

---

[1] An allusion to the game of *Prisoner's Base.* To " bid a base " is
for a player to run into the centre and challenge one of the opposite
party to pursue.

SCENE III.

Enter [1] *the* KING, ARUNDEL,[2] *the two* SPENCERS, *with others.*

Edw. Thus after many threats of wrathful war,
Triumpheth England's Edward with his friends ;
And triumph, Edward, with his friends uncontrolled !
My lord of Gloucester, do you hear the news ?

Y. Spen. What news, my lord ?

Edw. Why, man, they say there is great execution
Done through the realm ; my lord of Arundel,
You have the note, have you not ?

Arun.[3] From the lieutenant of the Tower, my lord.

Edw. I pray let us see it.　What have we there ?　10
Read it, Spencer.　　　　　　　[SPENCER *reads their names.*
Why so : they barked apace a month [4] ago :
Now, on my life, they'll neither bark nor bite.
Now, sirs, the news from France ? Gloucester, I trow,
The lords of France love England's gold so well,
As Isabella [5] gets no aid from thence.
What now remains ; have you proclaimed, my lord,
Reward for them can bring in Mortimer ?

---

[1] Scene : the royal palace, London.
[2] Old eds. "*Matr.*" and "*Matreuis.*"—The elder Spencer is a *muta persona.* Mr. Fleay, who ousts him altogether from this scene, observes "There is no hint of Old Spencer being on the stage after the third act,"—strangely forgetting that he is introduced in the fifth scene of the present act.
[3] Old eds. "*Matr.*"
[4] So ed. 1598.—Eds. 1612, 1622, 'not long ago."
[5] Old eds. "Isabell."

Y. Spen. My lord, we have ; and if he be in England,
'A will be had ere long, I doubt it not.   20

Edw. If, dost thou say?   Spencer, as true as death,
He is in England's ground ; our portmasters
Are not so careless of their king's command.

Enter a Messenger.

How now, what news with thee? from whence come
        these?

Mes. Letters, my lord, and tidings forth of France,
To you, my lord of Gloucester, from Levune.

Edw. Read.

[SPENCER *reads the letter.*]

"*My duty to your honour premised, &c., I have, according to
instructions in that behalf, dealt with the King of France his lords,
and effected, that the queen, all discontented and discomforted, is gone.
Whither, if you ask, with Sir John of Hainault, brother to the marquis, into Flanders: with them are gone Lord Edmund, and the
Lord Mortimer, having in their company divers of your nation, and
others ; and, as constant report goeth, they intend to give King Edward battle in England, sooner than he can look for them: this is
all the news of import.*

                Your honour's in all service, LEVUNE."   36

Edw. Ah, villains ! hath that Mortimer escaped?
With him is Edmund gone associate?
And will Sir John of Hainault lead the round?
Welcome, a God's name, madam, and your son :   40
England shall welcome you and all your rout.
Gallop apace [1] bright Phœbus, through the sky,

---

[1] Cf. *Romeo and Juliet,* iii. 2 :—"Gallop apace you fiery-footed
steeds," &c.

And dusky night, in rusty iron car,
Between you both shorten the time, I pray,
That I may see that most desirèd day,
When we may meet those traitors in the field.
Ah, nothing grieves me, but my little boy
Is thus misled to countenance their ills.
Come, friends, to Bristow, there to make us strong ;
And, winds, as equal be to bring them in,   50
As you injurious were to bear them forth !   [*Exeunt.*

SCENE IV.

Enter [1] *the* QUEEN, *her* SON, KENT, MORTIMER, *and* SIR
JOHN HAINAULT.

Queen. Now, lords, our loving friends and country-
        men,
Welcome to England all, with prosperous winds ;
Our kindest friends in Belgia have we left,
To cope with friends at home : a heavy case
When force to force is knit, and sword and glaive
In civil broils make kin and countrymen
Slaughter themselves in others, and their sides
With their own weapons gored !   But what's the help?
Misgoverned kings are cause of all this wreck ;
And, Edward, thou art one among them all,   10
Whose looseness hath betrayed thy land to spoil,
Who made the channel [2] overflow with blood

---

[1] Scene: the neighbourhood of Harwich.
[2] Kennel.

Of thine own people ; patron shouldst thou be,
But thou——

Y. Mor. Nay, madam, if you be a warrior,
You must not grow so passionate in speeches.
Lords,
Sith that we are by sufferance of heaven
Arrived, and armèd in this prince's right,
Here for our country's cause swear we to him   20
All homage, fealty, and forwardness ;
And for the open wrongs and injuries
Edward hath done to us, his queen and land,
We come in arms to wreak it with the sword ;
That England's queen in peace may repossess
Her dignities and honours : and withal
We may remove these flatterers from the king,
That havoc England's wealth and treasury.

Sir. J. Sound trumpets, my lord, and forward let us
          march.
Edward will think we come to flatter him.   30

Kent. I would he never had been flattered more !

                              [*Exeunt.*

SCENE V.

Enter[1] the KING, BALDOCK, *and* YOUNG SPENCER, *flying
about the stage.*

Y. Spen. Fly, fly, my lord ! the queen is over-strong ;
Her friends do multiply, and yours do fail.
Shape we our course to Ireland, there to breathe.

---

[1] Scene : the neighbourhood of Bristol.

Edw. What! was I born to fly and run away,
And leave the Mortimers conquerors behind?
Give me my horse, and let's re'nforce our troops:
And in this bed of honour die with fame.

Bald. O no, my lord, this princely resolution
Fits not the time; away, we are pursued.   [*Exeunt.*

Enter KENT *alone, with his sword and target.*

Kent. This way he fled, but I am come too late.   10
Edward, alas! my heart relents for thee.
Proud traitor, Mortimer, why dost thou chase
Thy lawful king, thy sovereign, with thy sword?
Vild wretch! and why hast thou, of all unkind,
Borne arms against thy brother and thy king?
Rain showers of vengeance on my cursèd head,
Thou God, to whom in justice it belongs
To punish this unnatural revolt!
Edward, this Mortimer aims at thy life!
O fly him, then! but, Edmund, calm this rage,   20
Dissemble, or thou diest; for Mortimer
And Isabel do kiss, while they conspire:
And yet she bears a face of love forsooth.
Fie on that love that hatcheth death and hate!
Edmund, away; Bristow to Longshanks' blood
Is false: be not found single for suspect:
Proud Mortimer pries near unto thy walks.

Enter the QUEEN, MORTIMER, *the* Young Prince, *and*
SIR JOHN OF HAINAULT.

Queen. Successful[1] battle gives the God of kings

---

[1] So ed. 1622.—Eds. 1598, 1612, "successfulls."

To them that fight in right, and fear his wrath.
Since then successfully we have prevailed,   30
Thankèd be heaven's great architect, and you.
Ere farther we proceed, my noble lords,
We here create our well-belovèd son,
Of love and care unto his royal person,
Lord Warden of the realm, and sith the fates
Have made his father so infortunate,
Deal you, my lords, in this, my loving lords,
As to your wisdoms fittest seems in all.
    Kent. Madam, without offence, if I may ask,
How will you deal with Edward in his fall?   40
        Prince. Tell me, good uncle, what Edward do you
            mean?
    Kent. Nephew, your father: I dare not call him king.
    Mor. My lord of Kent, what needs these questions?
'Tis not in her controlment, nor in ours,
But as the realm and parliament shall please,
So shall your brother be disposèd of.—
I like not this relenting mood in Edmund.
Madam, 'tis good to look to him betimes.
                        [*Aside to the* QUEEN.
    Queen. My lord, the Mayor of Bristow knows our mind.
    Y. Mor. Yea, madam, and they scape not easily   50
That fled the field.
    Queen. Baldock is with the king.
A goodly chancellor, is he not, my lord?
    Sir J. So are the Spencers, the father and the son.
    Kent.[1] This Edward is the ruin of the realm.

---

[1] As in l. 21 Kent determined to "dissemble," I have not changed

Enter RICE AP HOWELL, *and the* MAYOR OF BRISTOW, *with*
OLD SPENCER *prisoner.*

Rice. God save queen Isabel, and her princely son!
Madam, the mayor and citizens of Bristow,
In sign of love and duty to this presence,
Present by me this traitor to the state,
Spencer, the father to that wanton Spencer,
That, like the lawless Catiline of Rome,   60
Revelled in England's wealth and treasury.

Queen. We thank you all.

Y. Mor. Your loving care in this
Deserveth princely favours and rewards.
But where's the king and the other Spencer fled?

Rice. Spencer the son, created Earl of Gloucester,
Is with that smooth-tongued scholar Baldock gone,
And shipped but late for Ireland with the king.

Y. Mor. Some whirlwind fetch them back or sink them
         all!   [*Aside.*
They shall be started thence, I doubt it not.

Prince. Shall I not see the king my father yet?   70

Kent. Unhappy 's Edward, chased from England's
         bounds.   [*Aside.*

Sir. J. Madam, what resteth, why stand you in a muse?

Queen. I rue my lord's ill-fortune; but alas!
Care of my country called me to this war.

---

the prefix of the old eds.   Dyce gives the words to *Y. Mor.*   Mr. Fleay
prints—

    "*Kent.* This, Edward, is the ruin, &c.

                              [*To the Prince.*"

Y. Mor. Madam, have done with care and sad com-
   plaint ;
Your King hath wronged your country and himself,
And we must seek to right it as we may.
Meanwhile, have hence this rebel to the block.

 O. Spen. Rebel is he that fights against the prince ;
So fought not they that fought in Edward's right.   80

 Y. Mor. Take him away, he prates ; you, Rice ap
   Howell,
Shall do good service to her majesty,
Being of countenance in your country here,
To follow these rebellious runagates.
We in meanwhile, madam, must take advice,
How Baldock, Spencer, and their complices,
May in their fall be followed to their end.

          [Exeunt Omnes.

SCENE VI.

Enter[1] *the* Abbot, Monks, EDWARD, YOUNG SPENCER,
and BALDOCK.

 Abbot. Have you no doubt, my lord ; have you no fear ;
As silent and as careful we will be,
To keep your royal person safe with us,
Free from suspect, and fell invasion
Of such as have your majesty in chase,
Yourself, and those your chosen company,
As danger of this stormy time requires.

 Edw. Father, thy face should harbour no deceit.
O ! hadst thou ever been a king, thy heart,

---

[1] Scene : the Abbey of Neath, Glamorganshire.

Pierced deeply with [a] sense of my distress,   10
Could not but take compassion of my state.
Stately and proud, in riches and in train,
Whilom I was, powerful, and full of pomp:
But what is he whom rule and empery
Have not in life or death made miserable?
Come, Spencer; come, Baldock, come, sit down by me;
Make trial now of that[1] philosophy,
That in our famous nurseries of arts
Thou suck'dst from Plato and from Aristotle.
Father, this life contemplative is heaven.   20
O that I might this life in quiet lead!
But we, alas! are chased: and you, my friends,
Your lives and my dishonour they pursue.
Yet, gentle monks, for treasure, gold nor fee,
Do you betray us and our company.

Monk. Your grace may sit secure, if none but we
Do wot of your abode.

Y. Spen. Not one alive, but shrewdly I suspect
A gloomy fellow in a mead below.
'A gave a long look after us, my lord,   30
And all the land I know is up in arms,
Arms that pursue our lives with deadly hate.

Bald. We were embarked for Ireland, wretched we!
With awkward winds and sore[2] tempests driven
To fall on shore, and here to pine in fear
Of Mortimer and his confederates.

Edw. Mortimer! who talks of Mortimer?

---

[1] So ed. 1598.—Omitted in ed. 1612. (Ed. 1622 "thy.")
[2] So eds. 1598, 1612.—Ed. 1622 "*with* sore" (and so Dyce.)

Who wounds me with the name of Mortimer,
That bloody man? Good father, on thy lap
Lay I this head, laden with mickle care.   40
O might I never ope[1] these eyes again!
Never again lift up this drooping head!
O never more lift up this dying heart!
   Y. Spen. Look up, my lord.—Baldock, this drowisness
Betides no good; here even we are betrayed.

Enter, with Welsh hooks, RICE AP HOWELL, *a* Mower, *and
the* EARL OF LEICESTER.

   Mow. Upon my life, these be the men ye seek,
   Rice. Fellow, enough.—My lord, I pray be short,
A fair commission warrants what we do.
   Leices. The queen's commission, urged by Mortimer;
What cannot gallant Mortimer with the queen?   50
Alas! see where he sits, and hopes unseen
To escape their hands that seek to reave his life.
Too true it is, *Quem*[2] *dies vidit veniens superbum,
Hunc dies vidit fugiens jacentem.*
But, Leicester, leave to grow so passionate.
Spencer and Baldock, by no other names.
I [do] arrest you of high treason here.
Stand not on titles, but obey th' arrest;
'Tis in the name of Isabel the queen.
My lord, why droop you thus?   60
   Edw. O day the last of all my bliss on earth!

---

[1] So eds. 1612, 1622.—Ed. 1598 "open."
[2] Seneca *Thyestes*, 613.

Centre of all misfortune! O my stars,
Why do you lour unkindly on a king?
Come[s] Leicester, then in Isabella's name
To take my life, my company from me?
Here, man, rip up this panting breast of mine,
And take my heart in rescue of my friends!

Rice. Away with them!

Y. Spen. It may become thee yet
To let us take our farewell of his grace.

Abbot. My heart with pity earns[1] to see this sight,   70
A king to bear these words and proud commands.

Edw. Spencer, ah, sweet Spencer, thus then must we
    part?

Y. Spen. We must, my lord, so will the angry heavens.

Edw. Nay, so will hell and cruel Mortimer;
The gentle heavens have not to do in this.

Bald. My lord, it is in vain to grieve or storm.
Here humbly of your grace we take our leaves;
Our lots are cast; I fear me, so is thine.

Edw. In heaven we may, in earth ne'er shall we meet:
And, Leicester, say, what shall become of us?   80

Leices. Your majesty must go to Killingworth.

Edw. Must! it is somewhat hard, when kings must go.

Leices. Here is a litter ready for your grace,
That waits your pleasure, and the day grows old.

Rice. As good be gone, as stay and be benighted.

Edw. A litter hast thou? lay me in a hearse,
And to the gates of hell convey me hence;

---

[1] Old form of "yearns."

Let Pluto's bells ring out my fatal knell,
And hags howl for my death at Charon's shore,
For friend hath Edward none, but these and these :[1]   90
And these must die under a tyrant's sword.

Rice. My lord, be going ; care not for these,
For we shall see them shorter by the heads.

Edw. Well, that shall be, shall be : part we must !
Sweet Spencer, gentle Baldock, part we must !
Hence feignèd weeds ! unfeignèd are my woes ;

> [*Casts off his disguise.*

Father, farewell ! Leicester, thou stay'st for me,
And go I must.   Life, farewell, with my friends.

> [*Exeunt* EDWARD *and* LEICESTER.

Y. Spen. O ! is he gone ? is noble Edward gone ?
Parted from hence ? never to see us more ?   100
Rent, sphere of heaven ! and, fire, forsake thy orb !
Earth, melt to air ! gone is my sovereign,
Gone, gone, alas ! never to make return.

Bald. Spencer, I see our souls are fleeting hence ;
We are deprived the sunshine of our life :
Make for a new life, man ; throw up thy eyes,
And heart and hands to heaven's immortal throne ;
Pay nature's debt with cheerful countenance ;
Reduce we all our lessons unto this,

---

[1] So old eds. The repetition of "and these" in the next line is
certainly suspicious.   Dyce proposed
> " For friends hath *hapless* Edward none but these,
>   And these must die," &c.

Mr. Fleay's suggestion that "these and these" are "the 'hags' and
'Spencer and Baldock,'" seems very questionable.

To die, sweet Spencer, therefore live we all ; 110
Spencer, all live to die, and rise to fall.

Rice.[1] Come, come, keep these preachments till you
come to the place appointed.   You, and such as you are,
have made wise work in England ; will your lordships
away?

Mow. Your Lordship, I trust, will remember me?

Rice. Remember thee?   Fellow, what else?   Follow
me to the town.   [*Exeunt.*

---

[1] Mr. Fleay prints this speech as verse :
   " Come, come, keep these preachments till you come
      To th' place appointed.   You, and such as you are,
      Have made wise work in England ; will you away."
The lines hobble badly.

ACT THE FIFTH.

SCENE I.

Enter[1] *the* KING, LEICESTER, *the* BISHOP OF WIN-
CHESTER, *and* TRUSSEL.

Leices. Be patient, good my lord, cease to lament,
Imagine Killingworth Castle were your court,
And that you lay for pleasure here a space,
Not of compulsion or necessity.

Edw. Leicester, if gentle words might comfort me,
Thy speeches long ago had eased my sorrows;
For kind and loving hast thou always been.
The griefs of private men are soon allayed,
But not of kings. The forest deer, being struck,
Runs to an herb[2] that closeth up the wounds;   10

---

[1] Scene: Kenilworth Castle.
[2] Dittany. Cf. Virgil *Aen.* xii. 411-15 :—

> " Hic Venus, indigno nati concussa dolore,
> *Dictamnum* genitrix Cretaea carpit ab Ida,
> Puberibus caulem foliis et flore comantum
> Purpureo : *non illa feris incognita capris*
> *Gramina cum tergo volucres hausere sagittæ.*"

Elizabethan poets are fond of alluding to the virtues of this herb. Cf.
(one of many instances) Peele's *Arraignment of Paris*, iii. 1 :—

> " And whither wends yon thriveless swain? like to the stricken deer,
> Seeks he *dictamnum* for his wound within our forest here."

But, when the imperial lion's flesh is gored,
He rends and tears it with his wrathful paw,
[And] highly scorning that the lowly earth
Should drink his blood, mounts up to the air.
And so it fares with me, whose dauntless mind
The ambitious Mortimer would seek to curb,
And that unnatural queen, false Isabel,
That thus hath pent and mewed me in a prison;
For such outrageous passions cloy my soul,
As with the wings of rancour and disdain,   20
Full oft[en] am I soaring up to heaven,
To plain me to the gods against them both.
But when I call to mind I am a king,
Methinks I should revenge me of my wrongs,
That Mortimer and Isabel have done.
But what are kings, when regiment [1] is gone,
But perfect shadows in a sunshine day?
My nobles rule, I bear the name of king;
I wear the crown, but am controlled by them,
By Mortimer, and my unconstant queen,   30
Who spots my nuptial bed with infamy;
Whilst I am lodged within this cave of care,
Where sorrow at my elbow still attends,
To company my heart with sad laments,
That bleeds within me for this strange exchange.
But tell me, must I now resign my crown,
To make usurping Mortimer a king?

   Winch. Your grace mistakes, it is for England's good,
And princely Edward's right we crave the crown.

---

[1] Rule.

Edw. No, 'tis for Mortimer, not Edward's head; 40
For he's a lamb, encompassèd by wolves,
Which in a moment will abridge his life.
But if proud Mortimer do wear this crown,
Heaven turn it to a blaze of quenchless fire ![1]
Or like the snaky wreath of Tisiphon,
Engirt the temples of his hateful head;
So shall not England's vine[2] be perished,
But Edward's name survives,[3] though Edward dies.

Leices. My lord, why waste you thus the time away?
They stay your answer; will you yield your crown? 50

Edw. Ah, Leicester, weigh how hardly I can brook
To lose my crown and kingdom without cause;
To give ambitious Mortimer my right,
That like a mountain overwhelms my bliss,
In which extreme my mind here murdered is.
But what the heavens appoint, I must obey!
Here, take my crown; the life of Edward too;

                        [*Taking off the crown.*
Two kings in England cannot reign at once.
But stay awhile, let me be[4] king till night,
That I may gaze upon this glittering crown; 60
So shall my eyes receive their last content,
My head, the latest honour due to it,
And jointly both yield up their wishèd right.

---

1 An allusion (as Steevens observed) to Creusa's crown in Euripides'
Medea.
2 Old eds. "vines."
3 Ed. 1622 "survive" (and so Dyce).
4 So eds. 1612, 1622.—Omitted in ed. 1598.

Continue ever thou celestial sun ;
Let never silent night possess this clime :
Stand still you watches of the element ;
All times and seasons, rest you at a stay,
That Edward may be still fair England's king !
But day's bright beam doth vanish fast away,
And needs I must resign my wishèd crown.   70
Inhuman creatures ! nursed with tiger's milk !
Why gape you for your sovereign's overthrow !
My diadem I mean, and guiltless life.
See, monsters, see, I'll wear my crown again !

                              [*He puts on the crown.*

What, fear you not the fury of your king ?
But, hapless Edward, thou art fondly led,
They pass not for thy frowns as late they did,
But seek to make a new-elected king !
Which fills my mind with strange despairing thoughts,
Which thoughts are martyrèd with endless torments, 80
And in this torment comfort find I none,
But that I feel the crown upon my head,
And therefore let me wear it yet awhile.

    Trus. My lord, the parliament must have present
        news,
And therefore say will you resign or no ?

                              [*The* KING *rageth.*

    Edw. I'll not resign, but whilst I live [1] [be king].
Traitors, be gone ! and join you with Mortimer !
Elect, conspire, install, do what you will :—
Their blood and yours shall seal these treacheries !

---

[1] Ed. 1612 "*not* whilst I live."

Winch. This answer we'll return, and so farewell. 90

Leices. Call them again, my lord, and speak them fair;

For if they go, the prince shall lose his right.

Edw. Call thou them back, I have no power to speak.

Leices. My lord, the king is willing to resign.

Winch. If he be not, let him choose.

Edw. O would I might! but heavens and earth conspire

To make me miserable!   Here receive my crown:

Receive it? no, these innocent hands of mine

Shall not be guilty of so foul a crime.

He of you all that most desires my blood, 100

And will be called the murderer of a king,

Take it.   What, are you moved? pity you me?

Then send for unrelenting Mortimer,

And Isabel, whose eyes, being turned to steel,

Will sooner sparkle fire than shed a tear.

Yet stay, for rather than I'll look on them,

Here, here! *[He gives them the crown.*

Now, sweet God of heaven,

Make me despise this transitory pomp,

And sit for aye enthronizèd in heaven!

Come, death, and with thy fingers close my eyes, 110

Or if I live, let me forget myself.[1]

Winch. My lord.

Edw. Call me not lord: away—out of my sight:

Ah, pardon me: grief makes me lunatic!

---

[1] In old eds. after this line the entrance of Berkeley is marked. I
have followed Dyce in giving the words "My lord" to Winchester,
and in placing Berkeley's entrance after line 127.

Let not that Mortimer protect my son;
More safety there is in a tiger's jaws,
Than his embracements—bear this to the queen,
Wet with my tears, and dried again with sighs;

> [*Gives a handkerchief.*

If with the sight thereof she be not moved,
Return it back and dip it in my blood.   120
Commend me to my son, and bid him rule
Better than I.   Yet how have I transgressed,
Unless it be with too much clemency?

   Trus. And thus most humbly do we take our leave.

> [*Exeunt* BISHOP *and* TRUSSEL.

   Edw. Farewell; I know the next news that they bring
Will be my death; and welcome shall it be;
To wretched men, death is felicity.

Enter BERKELEY, *who gives a paper to* LEICESTER.

   Leices. Another post! what news brings he?

   Edw. Such news as I expect—come, Berkeley, come,
And tell thy message to my naked breast.   130

   Berk. My lord, think not a thought so villainous
Can harbour in a man of noble birth.
To do your highness service and devoir,
And save you from your foes, Berkeley would die.

   Leices. My lord, the council of [1] the queen commands
That I resign my charge.

   Edw. And who must keep me now?   Must you, my
      lord?

---

[1] Eds. 1612, 1622, "and."

Berk. I, my most gracious lord—so 'tis decreed.

Edw. [*taking the paper.*] By Mortimer, whose name is
    written here !

Well may I rent his name that rends my heart !   140

                             [*Tears it.*

This poor revenge has something eased my mind.

So may his limbs be torn, as is this paper !

Hear me, immortal Jove, and grant it too !

Berk. Your grace must hence with me to Berkeley
    straight.

Edw. Whither you will, all places are alike,

And every earth is fit for burial.

Leices. Favour him, my lord, as much as lieth in you.

Berk. Even so betide my soul as I use him.

Edw. Mine enemy hath pitied my estate,

And that's the cause that I am now removed.   150

Berk. And thinks your grace that Berkeley will be
    cruel ?

Edw. I know not ; but of this am I assured,

That death ends all, and I can die but once.

Leicester, farewell !

Leices. Not yet, my lord : I'll bear you on your way.

                          [*Exeunt omnes.*

SCENE II.

Enter[1] MORTIMER *and* QUEEN ISABEL.

Y. Mor. Fair Isabel, now have we our desire,

The proud corrupters of the light-brained king

---

[1] Scene: the royal palace, London.

Have done their homage to the lofty gallows,
And he himself lies in captivity.
Be ruled by me, and we will rule the realm.
In any case take heed of childish fear,
For now we hold an old wolf[1] by the ears,
That, if he slip, will seize upon us both,
And gripe the sorer, being grip'd himself.
Think therefore, madam, that [it] imports us[2] much   10
To erect your son with all the speed we may,
And that I be protector over him ;
For our behoof, 'twill[3] bear the greater sway
Whenas a king's name shall be under writ.

   Queen. Sweet Mortimer, the life of Isabel,
Be thou persuaded that I love thee well,
And therefore, so the prince my son be safe,
Whom I esteem as dear as these mine eyes,
Conclude against his father what thou wilt,
And I myself will willingly subscribe.   20

   Y. Mor. First would I hear news he were deposed,
And then let me alone to handle him.

Enter Messenger.

Letters ! from whence ?
   Mess. From Killingworth, my lord,
   Queen. How fares my lord the king ?
   Mess. In health, madam, but full of pensiveness.
   Queen. Alas, poor soul, would I could ease his grief !

---

[1] An allusion to the Greek proverb, τὸν λύκον τῶν ὤτων ἔχω.
[2] So eds. 1612, 1622.—Ed. 1598 "as."
[3] So eds. 1612, 1622.—Ed. 1598 "will."

Enter WINCHESTER [1] *with the Crown.*

Thanks, gentle Winchester. [*To the Messenger.*] Sirrah,
      be gone. [*Exit Messenger.*
  Winch. The king hath willingly resigned his crown.
  Queen. O happy news! send for the prince, my son.
  Winch. Further, or this letter [2] was sealed, Lord
      Berkeley came, 30
So that he now is gone from Killingworth;
And we have heard that Edmund laid a plot
To set his brother free; no more but so.
The Lord of Berkeley is so [as?] pitiful
As Leicester that had charge of him before.
  Queen. Then let some other be his guardian.
  Y. Mor. Let me alone, here is the privy seal.
                [*Exit* WINCHESTER.
Who's there?—call hither Gurney and Matrevis.
To dash the heavy-headed Edmund's drift,
Berkeley shall be discharged, the king removed, 40
And none but we shall know where he lieth.
  Queen. But, Mortimer, as long as he survives,
What safety rests for us, or for my son?
  Y. Mor. Speak, shall he presently be despatched and
      die?
  Queen. I would he were, so 'twere not by my means.

---

1 The entrance and exit of Winchester are not marked in the old
eds. I have followed Dyce.
  2 Dyce proposed to omit the word "letter."
  3 Mr. Fleay reads:—
      "And where he lieth none but we shall know."

Enter MATREVIS *and* GURNEY.

Y. Mor. Enough.—
Matrevis, write a letter presently
Unto the Lord of Berkeley from ourself
That he resign the king to thee and Gurney :
And when 'tis done, we will subscribe our name.   50
  Mat. It shall be done, my lord.
  Y. Mor. Gurney.
  Gur. My lord.
  Y. Mor. As thou intend'st to rise by Mortimer,
Who now makes Fortune's wheel turn as he please,
Seek all the means thou canst to make him droop,
And neither give him kind word nor good look.
  Gur. I warrant you, my lord.
  Y. Mor. And this above the rest : because we hear
That Edmund casts to work his liberty,
Remove him still from place to place by night,
Till at the last he come to Killingworth,   60
And then from thence to Berkeley back again ?
And by the way, to make him fret the more,
Speak curstly to him ; and in any case
Let no man comfort him if he chance to weep,
But amplify his grief with bitter words.
  Mat. Fear not, my lord, we'll do as you command.
  Y. Mor. So now away ; post thitherwards amain.
  Queen. Whither goes this letter? to my lord the king?
Commend me humbly to his majesty,
And tell him that I labour all in vain   70
To ease his grief, and work his liberty ;

And bear him this as witness of my love. [*Gives a ring.*
 Mat. I will, madam.
   [*Exeunt* MATREVIS *and* GURNEY ; *manent* ISABEL
    and MORTIMER.

Enter the Young Prince, *and the* EARL OF KENT *talking
   with him.*

 Y. Mor. Finely dissembled ? Do so still, sweet queen.
Here comes the young prince with the Earl of Kent.
 Queen. Something he whispers in his childish ears.
 Y. Mor. If he have such access unto the prince,
Our plots and stratagems will soon be dashed.
 Queen. Use Edmund friendly as if all were well.
 Y. Mor. How fares my honourable lord of Kent ? 80
 Kent. In health, sweet Mortimer : how fares your
  grace ?
 Queen. Well, if my lord your brother were enlarged.
 Kent. I hear of late he hath deposed himself.
 Queen. The more my grief.
 Y. Mor. And mine.
 Kent. Ah, they do dissemble ?   [*Aside.*
 Queen. Sweet son, come hither, I must talk with
  thee.
 Y. Mor. You being his uncle, and the next of blood,
Do look to be protector o'er the prince.
 Kent. Not I, my lord ; who should protect the son, 90
But she that gave him life ? I mean the queen.
 Prince. Mother, persuade me not to wear the crown :
Let him be king—I am too young to reign.

Queen. But be content, seeing 'tis [1] his highness'
    pleasure.

Prince. Let me but see him first, and then I will.

Kent. I, do, sweet nephew.

Queen. Brother, you know it is impossible.

Prince. Why, is he dead?

Queen. No, God forbid.

Kent. I would those words proceeded from your
    heart.   100

Y. Mor. Inconstant Edmund, dost thou favour him,
That wast a cause of his imprisonment?

Kent. The more cause have I now to make amends.

Y. Mor. I tell thee, 'tis not meet that one so false
Should come about the person of a prince.
My lord, he hath betrayed the king his brother,
And therefore trust him not.

Prince. But he repents, and sorrows for it now,

Queen. Come, son, and go with this gentle lord and me.

Prince. With you I will, but not with Mortimer.   110

Y. Mor. Why, youngling, 'sdain'st thou so of
    Mortimer?
Then I will carry thee by force away.

Prince. Help, uncle Kent, Mortimer will wrong me.

Queen. Brother Edmund, strive not; we are his
    friends;
Isabel is nearer than the Earl of Kent.

Kent. Sister, Edward is my charge, redeem him.

Queen. Edward is my son, and I will keep him.

---

[1] Ed. 1598 "it."—Eds. 1612, 1622, "it is."

Kent. Mortimer shall know that he hath wrongèd me!—
Hence will I haste to Killingworth Castle,
And rescue aged Edward from his foes,   120
To be revenged on Mortimer and thee.

                                        [*Aside.   Exeunt omnes.*

SCENE III.

Enter[1] MATREVIS *and* GURNEY *with the* KING.

Mat. My lord, be not pensive, we are your friends :
Men are ordained to live in misery,
Therefore come,—dalliance dangereth our lives.

Edw. Friends, whither must unhappy Edward go ?
Will hateful Mortimer appoint no rest ?
Must I be vexèd like the nightly bird,
Whose sight is loathsome to all wingèd fowls ?
When will the fury of his mind assuage ?
When will his heart be satisfied with blood ?
If mine will serve, unbowel straight this breast,   10
And give my heart to Isabel and him ;
It is the chiefest mark they level at.

Gur. Not so, my liege, the queen hath given this charge
To keep your grace in safety ;
Your passions make your dolours to increase.

Edw. This usage makes my misery to increase.
But can my air[2] of life continue long
When all my senses are annoyed with stench ?
Within a dungeon England's king is kept,
Where I am starved for want of sustenance.   20

---

[1] Scene : precincts of Kenilworth Castle.   [2] Aura vitæ.

My daily diet is heart-breaking sobs,
That almost rent the closet of my heart;
Thus lives old [1] Edward not relieved by any,
And so must die, though pitièd by many.
O, water, gentle friends, to cool my thirst,
And clear my body from foul excrements!

   Mat. Here's channel water, as your charge is
          given;
Sit down, for we'll be barbers to your grace.

   Edw. Traitors, away! what, will you murder me,
Or choke your sovereign with puddle water?   30

   Gur. No;
But wash your face, and shave away your beard,
Lest you be known and so be rescued.

   Mat. Why strive you thus? your labour is in vain?

   Edw. The wren may strive against the lion's strength,
But all in vain: so vainly do I strive
To seek for mercy at a tyrant's hand.

      [*They wash him with puddle water, and shave his
        beard away.*

Immortal powers! that knows the painful cares
That waits upon my poor distressèd soul!

---

   1 Edward II. was only forty-three when he was murdered. Stow often speaks of Edward II. as the "old king." Malone on *Richard II.* i. 1 ("Old John of Gaunt, time-honoured Lancaster"), remarks:—"Our ancestors, in their estimate of old age, appear to have reckoned somewhat differently from us, and to have considered men as old whom we should esteem middle-aged. With them every man that had passed fifty seems to have been accounted an old man. . . . I believe this is made to arise from its being customary to enter into life in former times at an earlier period than we do now. Those who were married at fifteen had at fifty been masters of a house and family for thirty-five years."

O level all your looks upon these daring men,   40
That wrongs their liege and sovereign, England's king.
O Gaveston, 'tis for thee that I am wronged,
For me, both thou and both the Spencers died !
And for your sakes a thousand wrongs I'll take.
The Spencers' ghosts, wherever they remain,
Wish well to mine ; then tush, for them I'll die.
  Mat. 'Twixt theirs and yours shall be no enmity.
Come, come away ; now put the torches out,
We'll enter in by darkness to Killingworth.

Enter KENT.

  Gur. How now, who comes there ?   50
  Mat. Guard the king sure : it is the Earl of Kent.

Enter Soldiers.

  Edw. O gentle brother, help to rescue me !
  Mat. Keep them asunder ; thrust in the king.
  Kent. Soldiers, let me but talk to him one word.
  Gur. Lay hands upon the earl for his assault.
  Kent. Lay down your weapons, traitors, yield the king.
  Mat. Edmund, yield thou thyself, or thou shalt die.
  Kent. Base villains, wherefore do you gripe me thus !
  Gur. Bind him and so convey him to the court.
  Kent. Where is the court but here ? here is the king; 60
And I will visit him : why stay you me ?
  Mat. The court is where Lord Mortimer remains ;
Thither shall your honour go ; and so farewell.

[*Exeunt* MATREVIS *and* GURNEY, *with the* KING.
KENT *and the* Soldiers *remain.*

Kent. O miserable is that commonweal,
Where lords keep courts, and kings are locked in prison?
    Sol. Wherefore stay we? on, sirs, to the court.
    Kent. I, lead me whither you will, even to my death,
Seeing that my brother cannot be released.

                                        [Exeunt.

SCENE IV.

Enter [1] YOUNG MORTIMER.

    Y. Mor. The king must die, or Mortimer goes down.
The commons now begin to pity him.
Yet he that is the cause of Edward's death,
Is sure to pay for it when his son's of age;
And therefore will **I** do it cunningly.
This letter, written by a friend of ours,
Contains his death, yet bids them save his life.   *[Reads.*
Edwardum occidere nolite timere bonum est
Fear not to kill the king 'tis good he die.
But read it thus, and that's another sense: 10
Edwardum occidere nolite timere bonum est
Kill not the king 'tis good to fear the worst.
Unpointed as it is, thus shall it go,
That, being dead, if it chance to be found,
Matrevis and the rest may bear the blame,
And we be quit that caused it to be done.
Within this room is locked the messenger,

---

        [1] Scene: the Royal Palace, London.

That shall convey it, and perform the rest :
And by a secret token that he bears,
Shall he be murdered when the deed is done.—   20
Lightborn, come forth !

Enter LIGHTBORN.

    Art thou so resolute as thou wast ?
 Light. What else, my lord ? and far more resolute.
 Y. Mor. And hast thou cast how to accomplish it ?
 Light. I, I, and none shall know which way he died.
 Y. Mor. But at his looks, Lightborn, thou wilt relent.
 Light. Relent ! ha, ha ! I use much to relent.
 Y. Mor. Well, do it bravely, and be secret.
 Light. You shall not need to give instructions :
'Tis not the first time I have killed a man.   30
I learned in Naples how to poison flowers ;
To strangle with a lawn thrust through [1] the throat ;
To pierce the windpipe with the needle's point ;
Or whilst one is asleep, to take a quill
And blow a little powder in his ears :
Or open his mouth and pour quicksilver down.
And yet I have a braver way than these.
 Y. Mor. What's that ?
 Light. Nay, you shall pardon me ; none shall know
   my tricks.
 Y. Mor. I care not how it is, so it be not spied.   40
Deliver this to Gurney and Matrevis.
At every ten mile end thou hast a horse.
Take this, away, and never see me more.

---

[1] So ed. 1598.—Eds. 1612, 1622, "down."

Light. No!

Y. Mor. No;

Unless thou bring me news of Edward's death.

Light. That will I quickly do; farewell, my lord.

[*Exit.*

Y. Mor. The prince I rule, the queen do I command,
And with a lowly congé to the ground,
The proudest lords salute me as I pass :
I seal, I cancel, I do what I will :
Feared am I more than loved—let me be feared ;
And when I frown, make all the court look pale.
I view the prince with Aristarchus' eyes,
Whose looks were as a breeching to a boy.
They thrust upon me the protectorship,
And sue to me for that that I desire.
While at the council-table, grave enough,
And not unlike a bashful puritan,
First I complain of imbecility,   60
Saying it is *onus quam gravissimum ;*
TIll being interrupted by my friends,
Suscepi that *provinciam* as they term it;
And to conclude, I am Protector now.
Now is all sure, the queen and Mortimer
Shall rule the realm, the king; and none rules us.
Mine enemies will I plague, my friends advance ;
And what I list command who dare control?
Major sum quam cui possit fortuna nocere.[1]
And that this be the coronation-day,   70

---

[1] Ovid *Metam.* vi. 195.

It pleaseth me, and Isabel the queen.

[*Trumpets within.*

The trumpets sound, I must go take my place.

Enter[1] *the* YOUNG KING, ARCHBISHOP,[2] CHAMPION,
Nobles, QUEEN.

Archbishop. Long live King Edward, by the grace of
God,
King of England, and Lord of Ireland !
Cham. If any Christian, Heathen, Turk, or Jew,
Dare but affirm that Edward's not true king,
And will avouch his saying with the sword,
I am the champion that will combat with him.
Y. Mor. None comes, sound trumpets.
King. Champion, here's to thee.   [*Gives a purse.*
Queen. Lord Mortimer, now take him to your charge. 80

Enter Soldiers, *with the* EARL OF KENT *prisoner.*

Y. Mor. What traitor have we there with blades and
bills ?
Sol. Edmund, the Earl of Kent.
King. What hath he done?
Sol. 'A would have taken the king away perforce,
As we were bringing him to Killingworth.
Y. Mor. Did you attempt his rescue, Edmund? speak.
Kent. Mortimer, I did; he is our king,
And thou compell'st this prince to wear the crown.

---

1 The scene shifts to Westminster.
2 Old eds. " Bishop."

Y. Mor. Strike off his head, he shall have martial
    law.

Kent. Strike off my head ! base traitor, I defy thee.

King. My lord, he is my uncle, and shall live.   90

Y. Mor. My lord, he is your enemy, and shall die.

Kent. Stay, villains !

King. Sweet mother, if I cannot pardon him,

Entreat my Lord Protector for his life.

Queen. Son, be content ; I dare not speak a word.

King. Nor I, and yet methinks I should command :

But, seeing I cannot, I'll entreat for him,—

My lord, if you will let my uncle live,

I will requite it when I come to age.

Y. Mor. 'Tis for your highness' good, and for the
    realm's.—   100

How often shall I bid you bear him hence ?

Kent. Art thou king ? must I die at thy command ?

Y. Mor. At our command ! once more away with
    him.

Kent. Let me but stay and speak : I will not go.

Either my brother or my son is king,

And none of both them thirst for Edmund's blood.

And therefore, soldiers, whither will you hale me ?

    [*They hale* KENT *away, and carry him to be beheaded.*

King. What safety may I look for at his hands,

If that my uncle shall be murdered thus ?

Queen. Fear not, sweet boy, I'll guard thee from thy
    foes ;   110

Had Edmund lived, he would have sought thy death.

Come, son, we'll ride a hunting in the park.

King. And shall my uncle Edmund ride with us?
Queen. He is a traitor; think not on him: come.

                             [Exeunt omnes.

SCENE V.

Enter [1] MATREVIS *and* GURNEY.

Mat. Gurney, I wonder the king dies not,
Being in a vault up to the knees in water,
To which the channels of the castle run,
From whence a damp continually ariseth,
That were enough to poison any man,
Much more a king brought up so tenderly.
  Gur. And so do I, Matrevis: yesternight
I opened but the door to throw him meat,
And I was almost stifled with the savour.
  Mat. He hath a body able to endure   10
More than we can inflict: and therefore now
Let us assail his mind another while.
  Gur. Send for him out thence, and I will anger him.
  Mat. But stay, who's this?

Enter LIGHTBORN.

  Light. My Lord Protector greets you.
  Gur. What's here? I know not how to construe it.
  Mat. Gurney, it was left unpointed for the nonce:
Edwardum occidere nolite timere,
That's his meaning.
  Light. Know ye this token? I must have the king.
  Mat. I, stay awhile, thou shalt have answer straight. 20

---

          [1] Scene: Berkeley Castle.

This villain's sent to make away the king.   [*Aside.*

     Gur. I thought as much.   [*Aside.*

     Mat. And when the murder's done,

See how he must be handled for his labour.

Pereat iste!   Let him have the king.   [*Aside.*

What else? here is the keys, this is the lake,[1]

Do as you are commanded by my lord.

     Light. I know what I must do ; get you away.

Yet be not far off, I shall need your help ;

See that in the next room I have a fire,

And get me a spit, and let it be red-hot.   30

     Mat. Very well.

     Gur. Need you anything besides?

     Light. What else?   A table and a feather-bed.

     Gur. That's all?

     Light. I, I : so, when I call you, bring

It in.

     Mat. Fear not thou that.

     Gur. Here's a light,

To go into the dungeon.

                   [*Gives light, and exit with* MATREVIS.

     Light. So [2] now

Must I about this gear ;[3] ne'er was there any

So finely handled as this king shall be.

Foh, here's a place indeed, with all my heart !

     Edw. Who's there? what light is that? wherefore

           com'st thou?

---

[1] *I.e.*, the dungeon full of mire and puddle.   But perhaps we should read "lock."

[2] A curtain is drawn and the king is discovered in the dungeon.

[3] Business.

Light. **To** comfort you, and bring you joyful news. 40
Edw. Small comfort finds poor Edward in thy looks.
Villain, I know thou com'st to murder me.
Light. To murder you, my most gracious lord !
Far is it from my heart to do you harm.
The queen sent me to see how you were used,
For she relents at this your misery :
And what eyes can refrain from shedding tears,
To see a king in this most piteous state ?
Edw. Weep'st thou already ? list awhile to me.
And then thy heart, were it as Gurney's is,   50
Or as Matrevis', hewn from the Caucasus,
Yet will it melt, ere I have done my tale.
This dungeon where they keep me is the sink
Wherein the filth of all the castle falls.
Light. O villains !
Edw. And there in mire and puddle have I stood
This ten days' space ; and, lest that I should sleep,
One plays continually upon a drum.
They give me bread and water, being a king ;
So that, for want of sleep and sustenance,   60
My mind's distempered, and my body's numbed,
And whether I have limbs or no I know not.
O, would my blood dropped out from every vein,
As doth this water from my tattered [1] robes.
Tell Isabel, the queen, I looked not thus,
When for her sake I ran at tilt in France,
And there unhorsed the Duke of Cleremont.

---

[1] So eds. 1598, 1612.—Ed. 1622 "tottered."

Light. O speak no more, my lord! this breaks my
　　　heart.
Lie on this bed,[1] and rest yourself awhile,
　Edw. These looks of thine can harbour nought but
　　　death :　　　　　　　　　　　　　　　　　70
I see my tragedy written in thy brows.
Yet stay; awhile forbear thy bloody hand,
And let me see the stroke before it comes,
That [2] even then when I shall lose my life,
My mind may be more steadfast on my God.
　Light. What means your highness to mistrust me thus?
　Edw. What mean'st thou to dissemble with me
　　　thus?
　Light. These hands were never stained with innocent
　　　blood,
Nor shall they now be tainted with a king's.　　79
　Edw. Forgive my thought [3] for having such a thought.
One jewel have I left, receive thou this.　　[*Giving jewel.*
Still fear I, and I know not what's the cause,
But every joint shakes as I give it thee.
O, if thou harbour'st murder in thy heart,
Let this gift change thy mind, and save thy soul!
Know that I am a king : O! at that name
I feel a hell of grief; where is my crown?
Gone, gone; and do I remain alive? [4]

---

　1 The feather-bed mentioned in l. 32.　"It was no doubt thrust upon
the stage from the wing after the exit of Gurney and Matrevis."—*Dyce.*
　2 Old eds. "That *and* even."
　3 Mr. Fleay would read "fau't" (*i.e.* fault), comparing *Richard III.*
ii. 1, 104 :—"His *fault* was thought."
　4 So ed. 1598.—Omitted in eds. 1612, 1622.

Light. You're overwatched, my lord : lie down and
      rest.
Edw. But that grief keeps me waking, I should sleep, 90
For not these ten days have these eyes' lids [1] closed.
Now as I speak they fall, and yet with fear
Open again.   O wherefore sitt'st thou here?
Light. If you mistrust me, I'll begone, my lord.
Edw. No, no, for if thou mean'st to murder me,
Thou wilt return again, and therefore stay.   [*Sleeps.*
Light. He sleeps.
Edw. [*awakes*]. O let me not die yet ; [2] stay, O stay a
      while !
Light. How now, my lord?
Edw. Something still buzzeth in mine ears, 100
And tells me if I sleep I never wake ;
This fear is that which makes me tremble thus.
And therefore tell me, wherefore art thou come.
Light. To rid thee of thy life ; Matrevis, come.

     Enter MATREVIS *and* GURNEY.

Edw. I am too weak and feeble to resist :
Assist me, sweet God, and receive my soul.
Light. Run for the table.
Edw. O spare me, or despatch me in a trice.

---

1 So eds. 1598, 1612, ("eies-lids ").—Ed. 1622 "eye lids."
2 Eds. 1598, 1612, "O let me not die, yet stay, O stay a while."   Ed.
1622 "O let me not die yet! O stay a while" (and so Dyce).   Mr.
Fleay prints :—
     "Oh !
     Let me not die yet ; stay, oh stay a while."

Light. So, lay the table down, and stamp on it,
But not too hard, lest that you bruise his body.   110
                    [KING EDWARD *is murdered.*

Mat. I fear me that this cry will raise the town,
And therefore, let us take horse and away.

Light. Tell me, sirs, was it not bravely done?

Gur. Excellent well: take this for thy reward.
                    [GURNEY *stabs* LIGHTBORN.
Come, let us cast the body in the moat,
And bear the king's to Mortimer our lord:
Away!   [*Exeunt with the bodies.*

SCENE VI.

Enter[1] MORTIMER *and* MATREVIS.

Y. Mor. Is't done, Matrevis, and the murderer dead?

Mat. I, my good lord; I would it were undone.

Y. Mor. Matrevis, if thou now[2] growest penitent
I'll be thy ghostly father; therefore chuse,
Whether thou wilt be secret in this,
Or else die by the hand of Mortimer.

Mat. Gurney, my lord, is fled, and will, I fear,
Betray us both, therefore let me fly.

Y. Mor. Fly to the savages.

Mat. I humbly thank your honour.   10

Y. Mor. As for myself, I stand as Jove's huge tree;
And others are but shrubs compared to me.

---

[1] Scene: the royal palace, London.
[2] So ed. 1598.—Omitted in eds. 1612, 1622.

All tremble at my name, and I fear none ;
Let's see who dare impeach me for his death.

Enter the QUEEN.

Queen. Ah, Mortimer, the king my son hath news
His father's dead, and we have murdered him.

   Y. Mor. What if he have ? the king is yet a child.

   Queen. I,[1] but he tears his hair, and wrings his hands,
And vows to be revenged upon us both.
Into the council-chamber he is gone,   20
To crave the aid and succour of his peers.
Aye me ! see where he comes, and they with him ;
Now, Mortimer, begins our tragedy.

Enter the KING, *with the* Lords.

   First[2] *Lord.* Fear not, my lord, know that you are a
          king.

   King. Villain !

   Y. Mor. Ho,[3] now, my lord !

   King. Think not that I am frighted with thy words !
My father's murdered through thy treachery ;
And thou shalt die, and on his mournful hearse
Thy hateful and accursèd head shall lie,
To witness to the world, that by thy means   30
His kingly body was too soon interred.

   Queen. Weep not, sweet son !

   King. Forbid me not to weep, he was my father ;

---

[1] The old eds. repeat "I."

[2] The prefix in the old eds. is "*Lords.*"

[3] So ed. 1598.—Eds. 1612, 1622, "*How now*, my Lord?" (which is
perhaps the right reading).

And, had you loved him half so well as I,
You could not bear his death thus patiently.
But you, I fear, conspired with Mortimer.

First[1] *Lord.* Why speak you not unto my lord the king?

Y. Mor. Because I think scorn to be accused.
Who is the man dares say I murdered him?

King. Traitor! in me my loving father speaks,   40
And plainly saith, 'twas thou that murder'dst him.

Y. Mor. But has your grace no other proof than this?

King. Yes, if this be the hand of Mortimer.

Y. Mor. False Gurney hath betrayed me and himself.
                                        [*Aside.*

Queen. I feared as much; murder cannot be hid.
                                        [*Aside.*

Y. Mor. It is my hand: what gather you by this?

King. That thither thou didst send a murderer.

Y. Mor. What murderer? Bring forth the man I sent.

King, I, Mortimer, thou knowest that he is slain:
And so shalt thou be too.   Why stays he here?   50
Bring him unto a hurdle, drag him forth,
Hang him, I say, and set his quarters up,
But bring his head back presently to me.

Queen. For my sake, sweet son, pity Mortimer.

Y. Mor. Madam, entreat not, I will rather die,
Than sue for life unto a paltry boy.

King. Hence with the traitor! with the murderer!

Y. Mor. Base Fortune, now I see, that in thy wheel
There is a point, to which when men aspire,

---

[1] Old eds. "*Lords.*"

They tumble headlong down : that point I touched, 60
And, seeing there was no place to mount up higher,
Why should I grieve at my declining fall?
Farewell, fair queen ; weep not for Mortimer,
That scorns the world, and, as a traveller,
Goes to discover countries yet unknown.
 King. What ! suffer you the traitor to delay?
       [MORTIMER *is taken away.*
 Queen. As thou receivedst thy life from me,
Spill not the blood of gentle Mortimer.
 King. This argues that you spilt my father's blood,
Else would you not entreat for Mortimer. 70
 Queen. I spill his blood? no.[1]
 King. I, madam, you ; for so the rumour runs.
 Queen. That rumour is untrue ; for loving thee,
Is this report raised on poor Isabel.
 King. I do not think her so unnatural.
 Second[2] *Lord.* My lord, I fear me it will prove too true.
 King. Mother, you are suspected for his death,
And therefore we commit you to the Tower
Till farther trial may be made thereof ;
If you be guilty, though I be your son, 80
Think not to find me slack or pitiful.
 Queen. Nay, to my death, for too long have I lived,
Whenas my son thinks to abridge my days.
 King. Away with her, her words enforce these tears,
And I shall pity her if she speak again.

---

1 Omitted in eds. 1612, 1622.
2 Old eds. "*Lords.*"

Queen. Shall I not mourn for my beloved lord,
And with the rest accompany him to his [1] grave ?
Second [2] *Lord.* Thus, madam, 'tis the king's will you shall
      hence.
Queen. He hath forgotten me ; stay, I am his mother.
Second [2] *Lord.* That boots not; therefore, gentle
      madam, go.
Queen. Then come, sweet death, and rid me of this
      grief.   [*Exit.*   90

Re-enter a Lord, *with the head of* MORTIMER.

Lord. My lord, here is the head of Mortimer.
King. Go fetch my father's hearse, where it shall lie ;
And bring my funeral robes.   Accursèd head,
Could I have ruled thee then, as I do now,
Thou had'st not hatched this monstrous treachery.
Here comes the hearse ; help me to mourn, my lords.
Sweet father, here unto thy murdered ghost
I offer up this wicked traitor's head :
And let these tears, distilling from mine eyes,
Be witness of my grief and innocency.   [*Exeunt.*   100

---

[1] So ed. 1598.—Eds. 1612, 1622, "the."
[2] Old eds. "*Lords.*"

THE MASSACRE AT PARIS.

OF *The Massacre at Paris* there is only one early edition, an undated 8vo. (printed *circ.* 1596?) The title is :—

The Massacre at Paris : With the death of the Duke of Guise. As it was plaide by the right honourable the Lord high Admirall his Seruants. Written by Christopher Marlowe. At London Printed by E. A. for Edward White, dwelling neere the little North doore of S. Paules Church at the signe of the Gun.

PERSONS REPRESENTED.

CHARLES THE NINTH, *king of France.*
DUKE OF ANJOU, *his Brother, afterwards* KING HENRY THE THIRD.
KING OF NAVARRE.
PRINCE OF CONDÉ, *his Cousin.*
DUKE OF GUISE,
CARDINAL OF LORRAINE, } *Brothers.*
DUKE DUMAINE,
Son to the DUKE OF GUISE, *a Boy.*
THE LORD HIGH ADMIRAL.
DUKE JOYEUX.
EPERNOUN.
PLESHÈ.
BARTUS.
TWO LORDS OF POLAND.
GONZAGO.
RETES.
MOUNTSORRELL.
MUGEROUN.
LOREINE, *a Preacher.*
SEROUNE.
RAMUS.
TALÆUS.
Friar.
Surgeon.
English Agent.
Apothecary.
Cutpurse.
Captain of the Guard, Protestants, Schoolmasters, Soldiers, Murderers, Attendants, &c.

CATHERINE, the Queen-Mother of France.
MARGARET, *her Daughter, wife to the* KING OF NAVARRE.
THE OLD QUEEN OF NAVARRE.
DUCHESS OF GUISE.
Wife to SEROUNE.
Maid to the DUCHESS OF GUISE.

THE MASSACRE AT PARIS.

—o—

SCENE I.

Enter CHARLES,[1] *the French king;* CATHERINE, *the Queen-*
Mother; the KING OF NAVARRE ; MARGARET, *Queen*
of Navarre; the PRINCE OF CONDÉ ; *the* LORD HIGH
ADMIRAL ; *the* OLD QUEEN OF NAVARRE ; *with*
others.

Char. Prince of Navarre, my honourable brother,
Prince Condé, and my good Lord Admiral,
I wish this union and religious league,
Knit in these hands, thus joined in nuptial rites,
May not dissolve till death dissolve our lives ;
And that the native sparks of princely love,
That kindled first this motion in our hearts,
May still be fuelled in our progeny.

Nav. The many favours which your grace hath shown,
From time to time, but specially in this,   10
Shall bind me ever to your highness' will,
In what Queen-Mother or your grace commands.

---

1 In the old copy there is no division into scenes.   Scene : an apartment in the Louvre.

Cath. Thanks, son Navarre. You see we love you
  well,
That link you in marriage with our daughter here;
And, as you know, our difference in religion
Might be a means to cross you in your love,—
 Char. Well, madam, let that rest.—
And now, my lords, the marriage rites performed,
We think it good to go and cònsummate
The rest with hearing of a holy mass.—   20
Sister, I think yourself will bear us company.
 Mar. I will, my good lord.
 Char. The rest that will not go, my lords, may stay.—
Come, mother,
Let us go to honour this solemnity.
 Cath. Which I'll dissolve with blood and cruelty.
             [Aside.
  [Exeunt all except the KING OF NAVARRE,
    CONDÉ, *and the* ADMIRAL.
 Nav. Prince Condé, and my good Lord Admiral,
Now Guise may storm, but do us little hurt,
Having the king, Queen-Mother on our sides,
To stop the malice of his envious heart,   30
That seeks to murder all the Protestants.
Have you not heard of late how he decreed
(If that the king had given consent thereto)
That all the Protestants that are in Paris
Should have been murderèd the other night?
 Adm. My lord, I marvel that th' aspiring Guise
Dares once adventure, without the king's consent,
To meddle or attempt such dangerous things.

Con. My lord, you need not marvel at the Guise,
For what he doth, the Pope will ratify,   40
In murder, mischief, or in tyranny.

Nav. But he that sits and rules above the clouds
Doth hear and see the prayers of the just,
And will revenge the blood of innocents,
That Guise hath slain by treason of his heart,
And brought by murder to their timeless[1] ends.

Adm. My lord, but did you mark the Cardinal,
The Guise's brother, and the Duke Dumaine,
How they did storm at these your nuptial rites,
Because the house of Bourbon now comes in,   50
And joins your lineage to the crown of France?

Nav. And that's the cause that Guise so frowns at us,
And beats his brains to catch us in his trap,
Which he hath pitched within his deadly toil.
Come, my lords, let's go to the church, and pray
That God may still defend the right of France,
And make his Gospel flourish in this land.   [*Exeunt.*

SCENE II.

Enter GUISE.[2]

Guise. If ever Hymen lour'd at marriage rites,
And had his altars decked with dusky lights :
If ever sun stained heaven with bloody clouds,
And made it look with terror on the world ;

---

[1] Untimely.
[2] Scene: an apartment in a house near the Louvre.

If ever day were turned to ugly night,
And night made semblance of the hue of hell;
This day, this hour, this fatal night,
Shall fully show the fury of them all.—
Apothecary!

Enter Apothecary.

 Apoth. My lord?   10
 Guise. Now shall I prove, and guerdon to the full,
The love thou bear'st unto the house of Guise.
Where are those perfumed gloves which [late] I sent
To be poisoned? hast thou done them? speak;
Will every savour breed a pang of death?
 Apoth. See where they be, my good lord; and he that
     smells
But to them, dies.
 Guise. Then thou remainest resolute?
 Apoth. I am, my lord, in what your grace commands,
Till death.
 Guise. Thanks, my good friend: I will requite thy love.
Go, then, present them to the Queen Navarre;   20
For she is that huge blemish in our eye,
That makes these upstart heresies in France:
Be gone, my friend, present them to her straight.
        [*Exit* Apothecary.
Soldier!

Enter a Soldier.

 Sold. My lord?
 Guise. Now come thou forth and play thy tragic part:

Stand in some window,[1] opening near the street,
And when thou see'st the Admiral ride by,
Discharge thy musket, and perform his death:
And then I'll guerdon thee with store of crowns.   30
  Sold. I will, my lord.   [*Exit.*
  Guise. Now, Guise, begin those deep-engendered
          thoughts
To burst abroad those never-dying flames
Which cannot be extinguished but by blood.
Oft have I levelled, and at last have learn'd
That peril is the cheapest way to happiness,
And resolution honour's fairest aim.
What glory is there in a common good,
That hangs for every peasant to achieve?
That like I best that flies beyond my reach.   40
Set me to scale the high Pyramides,
And thereon set the diadem of France;
I'll either rend it with my nails to naught,
Or mount the top with my aspiring wings,
Although my downfall be the deepest hell.
For this I wake, when others think I sleep;

---

1 "About noone, when he [the Admiral] was in returning home from
the Counsell, with a greate companie of noblemen and gentlemen, be-
holde a harquebuzier out of a window of a house neere adjoyning shot
the Admiral with two bullets of lead through both the arms. . . . The name
of him that shot was very diligently kept secret. Some, saye it was
Manrevet, which in the third Civill War traitorously slew his Captaine,
Monsieur de Mony, a most valiant and noble gentleman, and straightway
fled into the enemie's campe. Some say it was Bondot, one of the
archers of the king's guard."—*The Three Partes of Commentaries containing the whole and perfect discourse of the Civill Wars of France*, &c.
1574 (Book x.).

For this I wait, that scorn attendance else;
For this, my quenchless thirst, whereon I build,
Hath often pleaded kindred to the king;
For this, this head, this heart, this hand, and sword,   50
Contrives, imagines, and fully executes,
Matters of import aimèd at by many,
Yet understood by none;
For this, hath heaven engendered me of earth;
For this, this earth sustains my body's weight,
And with this weight I'll counterpoise a crown,
Or with seditions weary all the world;
For this, from Spain the stately Catholics
Send Indian gold to coin me French ecues;[1]
For this, have I a largess from the Pope,   60
A pension, and a dispensation too;
And by that privilege to work upon,
My policy hath fram'd religion.
Religion! *O Diabole!*
Fie, I am asham'd, however that I seem,
To think a word of such a simple sound,
Of so great matter should be made the ground!
The gentle king, whose pleasure uncontroll'd
Weakeneth his body, and will waste his realm,
If I repair not what he ruinates,[2]—   70
Him, as a child, I daily win with words,
So that for proof he barely bears the name;
I execute, and he sustains the blame.

---

[1] Crowns.

[2] This word occurs in 3 *Henry VI.*, v. 1, and *Titus Andronicus*, v. 3; also in Shakespeare's *Sonnets* and *Rape of Lucrece.*

The Mother-Queen works wonders for my sake,
And in my love entombs the hope of France,
Rifling the bowels of her treasury,
To supply my wants and necessity.
Paris hath full five hundred colleges,
As monasteries, priories, abbeys, and halls,
Wherein are thirty thousand able men, 80
Besides a thousand sturdy student Catholics :
And more,—of my knowledge, in one cloister keep [1]
Five hundred fat Franciscan friars and priests :
All this, and more, if more may be comprised,
To bring the will of our desires to end.
Then, Guise,
Since thou hast all the cards within thy hands,
To shuffle or cut, take this as surest thing,
That, right or wrong, thou deal thyself a king.—
I, but, Navarre,[2]—'tis but a nook of France, 90
Sufficient yet for such a petty king,
That, with a rabblement of his heretics,
Blinds Europe's eyes, and troubleth our estate.
Him will we—[*Pointing to his sword*] but first let's follow
     those in France
That hinder our possession to the crown.
As Cæsar to his soldiers, so say I,—
Those that hate me will I learn to loathe.
Give me a look, that, when I bend the brows,
Pale death may walk in furrows of my face :
A hand, that with a grasp may gripe the world ; 100

---

[1] Dwell. (In this sense the word " keep " is still used at Cambridge.)
[2] Old ed. " Nauarre, Nauarre."

An ear to hear what my detractors say;
A royal seat, a sceptre, and a crown;
That those which do behold, they [1] may become
As men that stand and gaze against the sun.
The plot is laid, and things shall come to pass
Where resolution strives for victory.   [*Exit.*

SCENE III.

Enter the KING OF NAVARRE,[2] QUEEN MARGARET, *the*
OLD QUEEN OF NAVARRE, *the* PRINCE OF CONDÉ,
and the ADMIRAL; *they are met by the* Apothecary
with the gloves, which he gives to the OLD QUEEN.

Apoth. Madam,
I beseech your grace to accept this simple gift.
     Old Q. of Nav. Thanks, my good friend.   Hold, take
          thou this reward.   [*Gives a purse.*
     Apoth. I humbly thank your majesty.   [*Exit.*
     Old Q. of Nav. Methinks the gloves have a very strong
          perfume,
The scent whereof doth make my head to ache.
     Nav. Doth not your grace know the man that gave
          them you?
     Old Q. of Nav. Not well; but do remember such a
          man.
     Adm. Your grace was ill-advised to take them, then,
Considering of these dangerous times.   10

---

[1] So old ed.—Dyce reads, "That those which do behold them."
[2] Scene: a street.

Old Q. of Nav. Help, son Navarre! I am poisoned!

Mar. The heavens forbid your highness such mishap!

Nav. The late suspicion of the Duke of Guise
Might well have moved your highness to beware
How you did meddle with such dangerous gifts.

Mar. Too late it is, my lord, if that be true,
To blame her highness; but I hope it be
Only some natural passion makes her sick.

Old Q. of Nav. O no, sweet Margaret! the fatal poison
Works within my head; my brain-pan breaks;   20
My heart doth faint; I die!   [*Dies.*

Nav. My mother poisoned here before my face!
O gracious God, what times are these!
O grant, sweet God, my days may end with hers,
That I with her may die and live again!

Mar. Let not this heavy chance, my dearest lord
(For whose effects my soul is massacrèd),
Infect thy gracious breast with fresh supply
To aggravate our sudden misery.

Adm. Come, my lords, let us bear her body hence, 30
And see it honoured with just solemnity.

> [*As they are going out, the* Soldier *dischargeth his
> musket at the* ADMIRAL.

Con. What, are you hurt, my Lord High Admiral?

Adm. I, my good lord, shot through the arm.

Nav. We[1] are betrayed! Come, my lords,
And let us go tell the king of this.

---

[1] Cunningham arranges ll. 34-5 thus:
   " We are betrayèd! come, my lords, and let us
   Go tell the king of this."

Adm. These are
The cursèd Guisians, that do seek our death.
O fatal was this marriage to us all!

     [*Exeunt, bearing out the body of the*
      OLD QUEEN OF NAVARRE.

SCENE IV.

Enter[1] KING CHARLES, CATHERINE *the Queen-Mother*,
  GUISE, ANJOU, *and* DUMAINE.

 Cath. My noble son, and princely Duke of Guise,
Now have we got the fatal, straggling deer
Within the compass of a deadly toil,
And, as we late decreed, we may perform.
 Char. Madam, it will be noted through the world
An action bloody and tyrannical;
Chiefly, since under safety of our word
They justly challenge their protection:
Besides, my heart relents that noblemen,
Only corrupted in religion,   10
Ladies of honour, knights, and gentlemen,
Should, for their conscience, taste such ruthless ends.
 Anj. Though gentle minds should pity others' pain,
Yet will the wisest note their proper griefs,
And rather seek to scourge their enemies
Than be themselves base subjects to the whip.
 Guise. Methinks my Lord Anjou hath well advised

---

[1] Scene: an apartment in the Louvre.

Your highness to consider of the thing,
And rather choose to seek your country's good
Than pity or relieve these upstart heretics.   20

Cath. I hope these reasons may serve my princely son
To have some care for fear of enemies.

Char. Well, madam, I refer it to your majesty,
And to my nephew here, the Duke of Guise :
What you determine, I will ratify.

Cath. Thanks to my princely son.—Then tell me,
          Guise,
What order will you set down for the massacre?

Guise. Thus, madam.   They
That shall be actors in this massacre,
Shall wear white crosses on their burgonets,   30
And tie white linen scarfs about their arms :
He that wants these, and is suspect [1] of heresy,
Shall die, be he king or emperor.   Then I'll have
A peal of ordnance shot from the tower, at which
They all shall issue out, and set [2] the streets ;
And then,
The watch-word being given, a bell shall ring,
Which when they hear, they shall begin to kill,
And never cease until that bell shall cease ;
Then breathe a while.   40

Enter the ADMIRAL'S Serving-Man.

Char. How now, fellow ! what news?

---

[1] So Dyce.—Old ed. "suspected."
[2] Beset.

Serv.-M. An it please your grace, the Lord High
          Admiral,
Riding the streets, was traitorously shot :
And most humbly [1] entreats your majesty
To visit him, sick in his bed.
     Char. Messenger, tell him I will see him straight.
                                   [*Exit* Serv.-M.

What shall we do now with the Admiral?
     Cath. Your majesty were best go visit him,
And make a show as if all were well.
     Char. Content ; I will go visit the Admiral.   50
     Guise. And I will go take order for his death.
                                   [*Exeunt.*[2]

SCENE V.

The [3] ADMIRAL *discovered in bed.* *Enter* KING CHARLES.

     Char. How fares it with my Lord High Admiral?
Hath he been hurt with villains in the street?
I vow and swear, as I am king of France,
To find and to repay the man with death,
With death delayed and torments never us'd,
That durst presume, for hope of any gain,
To hurt the nobleman their [4] sovereign loves.

---

[1] Old ed. "humble."

[2] Not marked in old ed.

[3] Old ed. "Enter the Admirall in his bed," a stage-direction meaning
that a bed containing the Admiral should be thrust upon the stage.
Cf. a stage-direction in Heywood's *Golden Age* :—"*Enter the foure old
Beldams, drawing out Danae's bed, she in it.*"

[4] Dyce reads "his."

Adm. Ah, my good lord, these are the Guisians,
That seek to massacre our guiltless lives !

    Char. Assure yourself, my good Lord Admiral,   10
I deeply sorrow for your treacherous wrong;
And that I am not more secure myself
Than I am careful you should be preserv'd.—
Cousin, take twenty of our strongest guard,
And, under your direction, see they keep
All treacherous violence from our noble friend ;
Repaying all attempts with present death
Upon the cursèd breakers of our peace.—
And so be patient, good Lord Admiral,
And every hour I will visit you.   20

    Adm. I humbly thank your royal majesty.
                    [*Exit* CHARLES.   *The bed is drawn in.*

SCENE VI.

Enter[1] GUISE, ANJOU, DUMAINE, GONZAGO, RETES,
    MOUNTSORRELL, *and* Soldiers, *to the massacre.*

    Guise. Anjou, Dumaine, Gonzago, Retes, swear,
By the argent crosses in your burgonets,
To kill all that you suspect of heresy.

    Dum. I swear by this, to be unmerciful.

    Anj. I am disguis'd, and none knows who I am,
And therefore mean to murder all I meet.

    Gon. And so will I.

---

[1] Scene : a street.

Retes. And I.

Guise. Away, then ! break into the Admiral's house.

Retes. I, let the Admiral be first despatch'd.

Guise. The Admiral,   10
Chief standard-bearer to the Lutherans,
Shall in the entrance [1] of this massacre
Be murder'd in his bed.
Gonzago, conduct them thither ; and then
Beset his house, that not a man may live.

   Anj. That charge is mine.—Switzers, keep you the
         streets :
And at each corner shall the king's guard stand.

   Gon. Come, sirs, follow me.

                         [*Exit* GONZAGO *with others.*

   Anj. Cousin, the captain of the Admiral's guard,
Plac'd by my brother, will betray his lord.   20
Now, Guise, shall Catholics flourish once again :
The head being off, the members cannot stand.

   Retes. But look, my lord, there's some in the Admiral's
         house.

GONZAGO *and others enter the* ADMIRAL'S *house ; the*
ADMIRAL *discovered in bed.*

   Anj. In lucky time : come, let us keep this lane,
And slay his servants that shall issue out,

   Gon. Where is the Admiral?

   Adm. O let me pray before I die !

---

[1] Commencement.   Dyce quotes from Heywood's *Four Prentises of London* :—

      " Take them to guard: this *entrance* to our warres
        Is full of spirit, and begets much hope."

Gon. Then pray unto our Lady; kiss this cross.

> [*Stabs him.*

Adm. O God, forgive my sins!   [*Dies.*

Guise. Gonzago, what, is he dead?

Gon. I, my lord.   30

Guise. Then throw him down.[1]

> [*The body of the* ADMIRAL *is thrown down.*

Anj. Now, cousin, view him well:
It maybe 'tis some other, and he escap'd.

Guise. Cousin, 'tis he; I know him by his look:
See where my soldier shot him through the arm;
He miss'd him near, but we have struck him now.—
Ah, base Chatillon and degenerate,
Chief Standard-bearer to the Lutherans,
Thus, in despite of thy religion,
The Duke of Guise stamps on thy lifeless bulk!

Anj. Away with him! cut off his head and
                hands,   40
And send them for a present to the Pope;[2]
And, when this just revenge is finishèd,
Unto Mount Falcon[3] will we drag his corse;

---

1 From the upper stage.

2 " Then a certain Italian of Gonzague's band cut off the Admiral's head, and sent it, preserved with spices, to Rome to the Pope and the Cardinal of Lorraine. Others cut off his hands."—*Three Parts of Commentaries*, &c., Book x. p. 14.

3 " So the old ed. ; and so indeed our early authors usually wrote the name :
      ' O, may they once as high as Haman mount,
         And from *Mount Faulcon* give a sad account,' &c.
Sylvester's *Du Bartas's.*"—*Dyce.*

And he, that living hated so the Cross,
Shall, being dead, be hanged thereon in chains.

Guise. Anjou, Gonzago, Retes, if that you three
Will be as resolute as I and Dumaine,
There shall not a Huguenot breathe in France.

Anj. I swear by this cross, we'll not be partial,
But slay as many as we can come near. 50

Guise. Mountsorrell, go shoot the ordnance off,
That they, which have already set the street,
May know their watchword; then toll the bell,
And so let's forward to the massacre.

Mount. I will, my lord. [*Exit.*

Guise. And now, my lords, let's closely to our business.

Anj. Anjou will follow thee.

Dum. And so will Dumaine.

[*The ordnance being shot off, the bell tolls.*

Guise. Come, then, let's away. [*Exeunt.*

SCENE VII.

Enter [1] GUISE *and the rest with their swords drawn,
chasing the Protestants.*

Guise. Tuez, tuez, tuez!
Let none escape! murder the Huguenots!

Anj. Kill them! kill them! [*Exeunt.*

Enter LOREINE *running;* GUISE *and the rest pursuing him.*

Guise. Loreine, Loreine! follow Loreine!—Sirrah,
Are you a preacher of these heresies?

---

[1] Scene : a street.

Lor. I am a preacher of the word of God;
And thou a traitor to thy soul and him.

    Guise. "Dearly belovèd brother,"—thus 'tis written.

                  [*Stabs* LOREINE, *who dies.*

    Anj. Stay, my lord, let me begin the psalm.

    Guise. Come, drag him away, and throw him in a
        ditch.   [*Exeunt with the body.* 10

SCENE VIII.

Enter [1] MOUNTSORRELL, *and knocks at* SEROUNE'S *door.*

    Seroune's Wife [*within*]. Who is that which knocks
        there?

    Mount. Mountsorrell, from the Duke of Guise.

    Seroune's Wife [*within*]. Husband, come down : here's
        one would speak with you
From the Duke of Guise.

        Enter SEROUNE *from the house.*

    Ser. To speak with me, from such a man as he?

    Mount. I, I, for this, Seroune ; and thou shalt ha't.

                  [*Showing his dagger.*

    Ser. O, let me pray, before I take my death !

    Mount. Despatch, then, quickly.

    Ser. O Christ, my Saviour !

    Mount. Christ, villain !
Why, darest thou presume to call on Christ,   10

---

[1] Scene : the entrance to Seroune's house.

Without the intercession of some saint ?
Sanctus[1] *Jacobus*, he's[2] my saint ; pray to him.
　Ser. O let me pray unto my God !
　Mount. Then take this with you.
　　　　　[*Stabs* SEROUNE, *who dies ; and then exit.*

SCENE IX.

Enter RAMUS, *in his study.*

Ramus. What fearful cries come from the river Seine,[3]
That fright poor Ramus sitting at his book !
I fear the Guisians have pass'd the bridge,
And mean once more to menace me.

Enter TALÆUS.

　Tal. Fly, Ramus, fly, if thou wilt save thy life !
　Ramus. Tell me, Talæus, wherefore should I fly ?
　Tal. The Guisians are
Hard at thy door, and mean to murder us :
Hark, hark, they come ! I'll leap out at the window.
　Ramus. Sweet Talæus, stay.　　　　　　　10

Enter GONZAGO *and* RETES.

　Gon. Who goes there ?
　Retes. 'Tis Talæus, Ramus' bedfellow.
　Gon. What art thou ?
　Tal. I am, as Ramus is, a Christian.
　Retes. O, let him go ; he is a Catholic. [*Exit* TALÆUS.

---

　　　[1] Old ed. "Sancta."　　　　　[2] Old ed. " he was."
　　　[3] Old ed. "Rene."

Gon. Come, Ramus, more gold, or thou shalt have
    the stab.

Ramus. Alas, I am a scholar ! how should I have gold ?
All that I have is but my stipend from the king,
Which is no sooner receiv'd but it is spent.

Enter GUISE, ANJOU, DUMAINE, MOUNTSORRELL, *and*
        Soldiers.

Anj. Who have you there ?
Retes. 'Tis Ramus, the king's Professor of Logic.   20
Guise. Stab him.
Ramus. O, good my lord,
Wherein hath Ramus been so offensious ?
Guise. Marry, sir, in having a smack in all,
And yet didst never sound anything to the depth.
Was it not thou that scoff'dst [1] the *Organon,*
And said it was a heap of vanities ?
He that will be a flat dichotomist,
And seen in nothing but epitomes,
Is in your judgment thought a learnèd man ;
And he, forsooth, must go and preach in Germany,   30
Excepting against doctors' axioms, [2]
And *ipse dixi* with this quiddity,
Argumentum testimonii est inartificiale. [3]
To contradict which, I say, Ramus shall die :
How answer you that ? your *nego argumentum*
Cannot serve, sirrah.—Kill him.

---

1 Old ed. "scoftes."   2 Old ed. "actions."
  3 I have adopted Mitford's emendation. The reading of the old ed.
is "Argumentum testimonis est in arte fetialis."

Ramus. O, good my lord, let me but speak a word !

Anj. Well, say on.

Ramus. Not for my life do I desire this pause ;

But in my latter hour to purge myself,   40
In that I know the things that I have wrote,
Which, as I hear, one Scheckius [1] takes it ill,
Because my places,[2] being but three, contain all his.
I knew the *Organon* to be confus'd,
And I reduc'd it into better form :
And this for Aristotle will I say,
That he that despiseth him can ne'er
Be good in logic or philosophy :
And that's because the blockish Sorbonnists [3]
Attribute as much unto their [own] works   50
As to the service of the eternal God.

Guise. Why suffer you that peasant to declaim ?
Stab [4] him, I say, and send him to his friends in hell.

Anj. Ne'er was there collier's [5] son so full of pride.

[*Stabs* RAMUS, *who dies.*

---

[1] Old ed. "Shekins."

[2] Grounds of proof,—in the scholastic sense of τόποι, or loci. "Itaque licet definire, *locum esse argumenti sedem.*"—Cicero, *Top.* ii. 3.

[3] Old ed. "thorbonest."

[4] ". . . tandemque P. Ramum diu quaesitum vicariorum coryphaeus unus offendit, eique veniam frustra deprecanti vulnus in brachio infligit, et plurimis aliis ictibus postea confoditur. . . . E fenestra spiritum trahens praecipitatur in aream, pedibusque fune devinctis per urbis sordes devolvitur et capite a chirurgo quodam truncato cadaver in . . . Sequanam flumen misere projicitur."—Theophilus Banosius' *Vita Rami*, prefixed to *Commentarii de Religione Christiana* (Francofurti, 1577).

[5] "'Carbonarius pater probri loco illi [sc. Ramo] objectus est.' *Rami Vita per Freigium.*"—*Dyce.*

Guise. My Lord of Anjou, there are a hundred Pro-
    testants
Which we have chased into the river Seine,[1]
That swim about, and so preserve their lives :
How may we do ? I fear me they will live.
    Dum. Go place some men upon the bridge,
With bows and darts, to shoot at them they see,   60
And sink them in the river as they swim.
    Guise. 'Tis well advis'd, Dumaine ; go see it straight
        be done.   [*Exit* DUMAINE.
And in the meantime, my lord, could we devise
To get those pedants from the King Navarre,
That are tutors to him and the Prince of Condé—
    Anj. For that, let me alone : cousin, stay you here,
And when you see me in, then follow hard.[2]

ANJOU *knocketh at the door: and enter the* KING OF
    NAVARRE *and the* PRINCE OF CONDÉ,[3] *with their*
    two Schoolmasters.

How now, my lords ! how fare you ?
    Nav. My lord, they say
That all the Protestants are massacred.
    Anj. I, so they are : but yet, what remedy ?   70
I have done what I could to stay this broil.
    Nav. But yet, my lord, the report doth run
That you were one that made this massacre.

---

1 Old ed. "Rene."
2 The scene shifts to the King of Navarre's quarters in the Louvre.
3 The young Prince of Condé, cousin to the King of Navarre.

Anj. Who, I ? you are deceiv'd ; I rose but now.
> [GUISE *and the others come forward*[1] *from
> the back of the stage.*

Guise. Murder the Huguenots ! take those pedants
  hence !

Nav. Thou traitor, Guise, lay off thy bloody hands !

Con. Come, let us go tell the king.
> [*Exit with the* KING OF NAVARRE.

Guise. Come, sirs,
I'll whip you to death with my poniard's point.
> [*Stabs the* Schoolmasters, *who die.*

Anj. Away with them both !
> [*Exeunt* ANJOU *and* Soldiers *with the bodies.*

Guise. And now, sirs, for this night let our fury stay.
Yet will we not that the massacre shall end :   81
Gonzago, post you to Orleans,
Retes to Dieppe, Mountsorrell unto Rouen,
And spare not one that you suspect of heresy.
And now stay
That bell, that to the devil's matins rings.
Now every man put off his burgonet,
And so convey him closely to his bed.   [*Exeunt.*

SCENE X.

Enter [2] ANJOU, *with two* Lords of Poland.

Anj. My lords of Poland, I must needs confess,
The offer of your Prince Elector's far

---

[1] The stage-direction in old ed. is " Enter Guise."
[2] Scene : a room in the Louvre.

Beyond the reach of my deserts ;
For Poland is, as I have been inform'd,
A martial people, worthy such a king
As hath sufficient counsel in himself
To lighten doubts, and frustrate subtle foes ;
And such a king, whom practice long hath taught
To please himself with manage of the wars,
The greatest wars within our Christian bounds,— 10
I mean our wars against the Muscovites,
And, on the other side, against the Turk,
Rich princes both, and mighty emperors.
Yet, by my brother Charles, our King of France,
And by his grace's council, it is thought
That, if I undertake to wear the crown
Of Poland, it may prejudice their hope
Of my inheritance to the crown of France ;
For, if th' Almighty take my brother hence,
By due descent the regal seat is mine. 20
With Poland, therefore, must I covenant thus,—
That if, by death of Charles, the diadem
Of France be cast on me, then, with your leaves,
I may retire me to my native home.
If your commission serve to warrant this,
I thankfully shall undertake the charge
Of you and yours, and carefully maintain
The wealth and safety of your kingdom's right.
 First Lord. All this, and more, your highness shall
   command,
For Poland's crown and kingly diadem. 30
 Anj. Then, come, my lords, let's go. [*Exeunt.*

SCENE XI.

Enter [1] *two* Men, *with the* ADMIRAL'S *body.*

First Man. Now, sirrah, what shall we do with the Admiral?

Sec. Man. Why, let us burn him for an heretic.

First Man. O no! his body will infect the fire, and the fire the air, and so we shall be poisoned with him.

Sec. Man. What shall we do, then?

First Man. Let's throw him into the river.

Sec. Man. O, 'twill corrupt the water, and the water the fish, and the [2] fish ourselves when we eat them!

First Man. Then throw him into a ditch.   10

Sec. Man. No, no.   To decide all doubts, be ruled by me: let's hang him here upon this tree.

First Man. Agreed.

    [*They hang up the body on a tree, and then exeunt.*

Enter GUISE, CATHERINE *the Queen-Mother, and the* CARDINAL OF LORRAINE, *with* Attendants.

Guise. Now, madam, how like you our lusty Admiral?

Cath. Believe me, Guise, he becomes the place so well As I could long ere this have wish'd him there.
But come,
Let's walk aside; the air's not very sweet.

Guise. No, by my faith, madam.—

---

[1] Scene; near Paris.   [2] Old ed. "*by* the."

Sirs, take him away, and throw him in some ditch.   20
      [*The* Attendants *bear off the* ADMIRAL'S *body.*
And now, madam, as I understand,
There are a hundred Huguenots and more,
Which in the woods do hold their synagogue,
And daily meet about this time of day ;
And thither will I, to put them to the sword.
    Cath. Do so, sweet Guise ; let us delay no time ;
For, if these stragglers gather head again,
And disperse themselves throught the realm of France,
It will be hard for us to work their deaths.
Be gone ; delay no time, sweet Guise.
    Guise. Madam,   30
I go as whirlwinds rage before a storm.   [*Exit.*
    Cath. My Lord of Lorraine, have you marked of late,
How Charles our son begins for to lament
For the late night's work which my Lord of Guise
Did make in Paris among the Huguenots?
    Card. Madam, I have heard him solemnly vow,
With the rebellious King of Navarre,
To revenge their deaths upon us all.   ·
    Cath. I, but, my lord, let me alone for that ;
For Catherine must have her will in France.   40
As I do live, so surely shall he die,
And Henry then shall wear the diadem ;
And, if he grudge or cross his mother's will,
I'll disinherit him and all the rest ;
For I'll rule France, but they shall wear the crown,
And, if they storm, I then may pull them down.
Come, my lord, let us go.   [*Exeunt.*

SCENE XII.

Enter[1] *five or six* Protestants, *with books, and kneel
together.   Then enter* GUISE *and others.*

Guise. Down with the Huguenots! murder them!
First Pro. O Monsieur de Guise, hear me but speak!
Guise. No, villain; that tongue of thine,
That hath blasphem'd the holy Church of Rome,
Shall drive no plaints into the Guise's ears,
To make the justice of my heart relent.—
Tuez, tuez, tuez! let none escape.

> [*They kill the* Protestants.

So drag them away.   [*Exeunt with the bodies.*

SCENE XIII.

Enter[2] KING CHARLES, *supported by the* KING OF NA-
VARRE *and* EPERNOUN; CATHERINE *the Queen-
Mother, the* CARDINAL OF LORRAINE, PLESHÉ,[3] *and*
Attendants.

Char. O, let me stay, and rest me here awhile!
A griping pain hath seiz'd upon my heart;
A sudden pang, the messenger of death.
Cath. O, say not so! thou kill'st thy mother's heart.

---

[1] Scene: a wood near Paris.
[2] Scene: a room in the Castle of Vincennes.
[3] Du-Plessis Mornay.

Char. I must say so ; pain forceth me complain.

Nav. Comfort yourself, my lord, and have no doubt
But God will sure restore you to your health.

Cha.. O no, my loving brother of Navarre !
I have deserved a scourge, I must confess ;
Yet is their[1] patience of another sort   10
Than to misdo the welfare of their king :
God grant my nearest friends may prove no worse !
O, hold me up, my sight begins to fail,
My sinews shrink, my brains turn upside down ;
My heart doth break : I faint and die.   *[Dies.*

Cath. Art thou dead, sweet son ? speak to thy mother !
O no, his soul is fled from out his breast,
And he nor hears nor sees us what we do !
My lords, what resteth there now to be done,
But that we presently despatch ambassadors   20
To Poland, to call Henry back again,
To wear his brother's crown and dignity ?
Epernoun, go see it presently be done,
And bid him come without delay to us.

Eper. Madam, I will.   *[Exit.*

Cath. And now,

---

[1] Old ed. "there," which Dyce silently retains. The correction was
made by Cunningham, who explains the passage thus :—"There are per-
sons (you yourself and my Protestant subjects, for instance) from whom
I have deserved a scourge, but their feelings would never lead them to
poison their king ; God grant that my dearest relations may prove to have
been no worse than those who ought to be my enemies," &c.—"Scourge"
must surely be the scourge of God. Navarre had said, "God will sure
restore you :" to which the king answers, "I have deserved a scourge"
from God. Before l. 10 a line or more referring to the massacre of the
Protestants must have dropped out.

My lords, after these funerals be done,
We will, with all the speed we can, provide
For Henry's coronation from Polony.
Come, let us take his body hence.   30

> [*The body of* KING CHARLES *is borne out; and
> exeunt all except the* KING OF NAVARRE *and*
> PLESHÉ.

   Nav. And now, Pleshé,[1] whilst that these broils do
     last,
My opportunity may serve it fit
To steal from France, and hie me to my home,
For there's no safety in this realm for me:
And now that Henry is call'd from Poland,
It is my due, by just succession;
And therefore, as speedily as I can perform,
I'll muster up an army secretly,
For fear that Guise, join'd with the king of Spain,
Might seek[2] to cross me in mine enterprise.   40
But God, that always doth defend the right,
Will show his mercy, and preserve us still.

   Pleshé. The virtues of our true religion
Cannot but march, with many graces more,
Whose army shall discomfort all your foes,
And, at the length, in Pampelonia[3] crown
(In spite of Spain, and all the popish power,
That holds it from your highness wrongfully)
Your majesty her rightful lord and sovereign.

---

[1] Old ed. " Nauarre."   [2] Old ed. "seeme."
[3] Pampeluna.

Nav. Truth, Pleshé; and God so prosper me in all, 50
As I intend to labour for the truth,
And true profession of his holy word !
Come, Pleshé, let's away whilst time doth serve.

[*Exeunt.*

SCENE XIV.

*Trumpets sound within, and a cry of " Vive le Roi"
two or three times. Enter* [1] ANJOU *crowned as King
Henry the Third;* CATHERINE *the Queen Mother,
the* CARDINAL OF LORRAINE, GUISE, EPERNOUN,
MUGEROUN, *the* Cutpurse, *and others.*

All. Vive le Roi, Vive le Roi ! [*A flourish of trumpets.*
Cath. Welcome from Poland, Henry, once again !
Welcome to France, thy father's royal seat !
Here hast thou a country void of fears,
A warlike people to maintain thy right,
A watchful senate for ordaining laws,
A loving mother to preserve thy state,
And all things that a king may wish besides ;
All this, and more, hath Henry with his crown.
    Card. And long may Henry enjoy all this, and more ! 10
All. Vive le Roi, Vive le Roi ! [*A flourish of trumpets.*
Henry. Thanks to you all.   The guider of all crowns
Grant that our deeds may well deserve your loves !
And so they shall if fortune speed my will,
And yield your thoughts to height of my deserts.

---

[1] Scene : a ball in the Louvre.

What say our minions? think they Henry's heart
Will not both harbour love and majesty?
Put off that fear, they are already join'd:
No person, place, or time, or circumstance,
Shall slack my love's affection from his bent: 20
As now you are, so shall you still persist,
Removeless from the favours of your king.

  Mug. We know that noble minds change not their
     thoughts
For wearing of a crown, in that your grace
Hath worn the Poland diadem before
You were invested in the crown of France.

  Henry. I tell thee, Mugeroun, we will be friends,
And fellows too, whatever storms arise.

  Mug. Then[1] may it please your majesty to give me
     leave
To punish those that do profane this holy feast.   30

  Henry. How mean'st thou that?

    [MUGEROUN *cuts off the* Cutpurse's *ear, for cutting
     the gold buttons off his cloak.*

  Cutp. O Lord, mine ear!

  Mug. Come, sir, give me my buttons, and here's your
     ear.

  Guise. Sirrah, take him away.

  Henry. Hands off, good fellow; I will be his bail
For this offence.—Go, sirrah, work no more

---

[1] I should prefer to read :—
  " Then may it please
   Your majesty to give me leave to punish
   Those that do [dare] profane this holy feast."

Till this our coronation day be past.—
And now,
Our solemn rites of coronation done,[1]
What now remains but for a while to feast,   40
And spend some days in barriers, tourney, tilt,
And like disports, such as do fit the court?
Let's go, my lords; our dinner stays for us.

> [*Exeunt all except* CATHERINE *the Queen Mother
> and the* CARDINAL OF LORRAINE.

Cath. My Lord Cardinal of Lorraine, tell me,
How likes your grace my son's pleasantness?
His mind, you see, runs on his minions,
And all his heaven is to delight himself;
And, whilst he sleeps securely thus in ease,
Thy brother Guise and we may now provide
To plant ourselves with such authority   50
As not a man may live without our leaves.
Then shall the Catholic faith of Rome
Flourish in France, and none deny the same.

Card. Madam, as in secrecy I was told,
My brother Guise hath gather'd a power of men,
Which are,[1] he saith, to kill the Puritans;
But 'tis the house of Bourbon that he means.
Now, madam, must you insinuate with the king,
And tell him that 'tis for his country's good,
And common profit of religion.   60

Cath. Tush, man, let me alone with him,
To work the way to bring this thing to pass;

---

[1] Old ed. "as."

And, if he do deny what I do say,
I'll despatch him with his brother presently,
And then shall Monsieur wear the diadem.
Tush, all shall die unless I have my will;
For, while she lives, Catherine will be queen.
Come, my lord,[1] let us go seek the Guise,
And then determine of this enterprise.   [*Exeunt.*

SCENE XV.

Enter [2] *the* DUCHESS OF GUISE *and her* Maid.

Duch. of G. Go fetch me pen and ink,—
Maid. I will, madam.
Duch. That I may write unto my dearest lord.
                                        [*Exit* Maid.

Sweet Mugeroun,[3] 'tis he that hath my heart,
And Guise usurps it 'cause I am his wife.
Fain would I find some means to speak with him,
But cannot, and therefore am enforced to write,
That he may come and meet me in some place,
Where we may one enjoy the other's sight.

        Re-enter the Maid, *with pen, ink, and paper.*
So, set it down, and leave me to myself.
                        [*Exit* Maid.   *The* DUCHESS *writes.*

---

[1] Old ed. "lords."
[2] Scene: a room in the Duke of Guise's house.
[3] "The gallant of the Duchess was not Mugeroun (Maugiron), but Saint-Mégrin, another of the King's 'Mignons.' See Anquetil.—*Hist. de France,* t. v. 345, ed. 1817."—*Dyce.*

O, would to God, this quill that here doth write   10
Had late been pluck'd from out fair Cupid's wing,
That it might print these lines within his heart!

Enter GUISE.

Guise. What, all alone, my love? and writing too?
I prithee, say to whom thou writ'st.
Duch. To such
A one, my Lord, as, when she reads my lines,
Will laugh, I fear me, at their good array.
Guise. I pray thee, let me see.
Duch. O no, my lord; a woman only must
Partake the secrets of my heart.
Guise. But, madam, I must see.   20

[*Seizes the paper.*

Are these your secrets that no man must know!
Duch. O, pardon me, my lord!
Guise. Thou trothless and unjust! what lines are
        these?
Am I grown old, or is thy lust grown young?
Or hath my love been so obscured in thee,
That others need to comment on my text?
Is all my love forgot, which held thee dear,
I, dearer than the apple of mine eye?
Is Guise's glory but a cloudy mist,
In sight and judgment of thy lustful eye?   30
Mort Dieu! were[1] not the fruit within thy womb,
Of whose increase I set some longing hope,

---

1 Old ed. "wert."

This wrathful hand should strike thee to the heart.
Hence, strumpet! hide thy head for shame ;
And fly my presence if thou look to live !

[*Exit* DUCHESS.

O wicked sex, perjùrèd and unjust !
Now do I see that from the very first
Her eyes and looks sow'd seeds of perjury.
But villain, he, to whom these lines should go,
Shall buy her love even with his dearest blood. [*Exit.* 40

SCENE XVI.

Enter [1] *the* KING OF NAVARRE, PLESHÉ, BARTUS, *and
train, with drums and trumpets.*

Nav. My lords, sith in a quarrel just and right
We undertake to manage these our wars
Against the proud disturbers of the faith
(I mean the Guise, the Pope, and king of Spain,
Who set themselves to tread us under foot,
And rent our true religion from this land :
But for you know our quarrel is no more
But to defend [2] their strange inventions,
Which they will put us to with sword and fire),
We must with resolute minds resolve to fight,   10
In honour of our God, and country's good.

---

[1] " I must leave the location of this scene to the reader. I should
have marked it—La Rochelle, but that the Messenger presently informs
the King that ' a mighty army comes *from France.*' "—*Dyce.*
[2] Hinder.

Spain is the council-chamber of the Pope,
Spain is the place where he makes peace and war;
And Guise for Spain hath now incensed the king
To send his power to meet us in the field.

Bar. Then in this bloody brunt they may behold
The sole endeavour of your princely care,
To plant the true succession of the faith,
In spite of Spain and all his heresies.

Nav. The power of vengeance now encamps itself 20
Upon the haughty mountains of my breast;
Plays with her gory colours of revenge,
Whom I respect as leaves of boasting green,
That change their colour when the winter comes,
When I shall vaunt as victor in revenge.

Enter a Messenger.

How now, sirrah! what news?

Mes. My lord, as by our scouts we understand,
A mighty army comes from France with speed;
Which are already mustered in the land,
And mean to meet your highness in the field. 30

Nav. In God's name, let them come!
This is the Guise that hath incensed the king
To levy arms, and make these civil broils.
But canst thou tell who is their general?

Mes. Not yet, my lord, for thereon do they stay;
But, as report doth go, the Duke of Joyeux
Hath made great suit unto the king therefore.

Nav. It will not countervail his pains, I hope.
I would the Guise in his stead might have come!

But he doth lurk within his drowsy couch,　　　　　40
And makes his footstool on security :
So he be safe, he cares not what becomes
Of king or country ; no, not for them both.
But come, my lords, let us away with speed,
And place ourselves in order for the fight.　　*[Exeunt.*

SCENE XVII.

Enter [1] KING HENRY, GUISE, EPERNOUN, *and* JOYEUX.

Henry. My sweet Joyeux, I make thee general
Of all my army, now in readiness
To march 'gainst the rebellious King Navarre ;
At thy request I am content thou go,
Although my love to thee can hardly suffer['t],
Regarding still the danger of thy life.

　　Joyeux. Thanks to your majesty : and so, I take my
　　　　　leave.—
Farewell to my Lord of Guise, and Epernoun.

　　Guise. Health and hearty farewell to my Lord Joyeux.
　　　　　　　　　　　　　　[Exit JOYEUX.

　　Henry. So kindly, cousin of Guise, you and your wife
Do both salute our lovely minions.　　　　　　11
Remember you the letter, gentle sir,
Which your wife writ
To my dear minion, and her chosen friend ?
　　　　　　　　　　　　[Makes horns at GUISE.

---

[1] Scene : an apartment in the Louvre.

Guise. How now, my Lord ! faith, this is more than
      need.
Am I thus to be jested at and scorn'd?
'Tis more than kingly or emperious :
And, sure, if all the proudest kings
In Christendom should bear me such derision,
They should know how I scorn'd them and their mocks. 20
I love your minions ! dote on them yourself;
I know none else but holds them in disgrace ;
And here, by all the saints in heaven, I swear,
That villain for whom I bear this deep disgrace,
Even for your words that have incens'd me so,
Shall buy that strumpet's favour with his blood '
Whether he have dishonour'd me or no,
Par la mort de Dieu [1] *il mourra !*   [*Exit.*
    Henry. Believe me, this jest bites sore.
    Eper. My lord, 'twere good to make them friends,   30
For his oaths are seldom spent in vain.

           Enter MUGEROUN.

    Henry. How now, Mugeroun ! mett'st thou not the
      Guise at the door ?
    Mug. Not I, my lord : what if I had?
    Henry. Marry, if thou hadst, thou mightst have had
      the stab,
For he hath solemnly sworn thy death.
    Mug. I may be stabb'd, and live till he be dead :
But wherefore bears he me such deadly hate?
    Henry. Because his wife bears thee such kindly love.

---

[1] Old ed. "mor du."

Mug. If that be all, the next time that I meet
      her,
I'll make her shake off love with her heels.   40
But which way is he gone? I'll go take [1] a walk
On purpose from the court to meet with him.   [*Exit.*
   Henry. I like not this. Come, Epernoun,
Let us go seek the duke, and make them friends.
                              [*Exeunt.*

SCENE XVIII.

Alarums within, and a cry—" The DUKE JOYEUX *is slain."*
   Enter [2] *the* KING OF NAVARRE, BARTUS, *and train.*

   Nav. The duke is slain, and all his power dispers'd,
And we are graced with wreaths of victory.
Thus God, we see, doth ever guide the right,
To make his glory great upon the earth.
   Bar. The terror of this happy victory,
I hope, will make the king surcease his hate,
And either never manage army more,
Or else employ them in some better cause.
   Nav. How many noblemen have lost their lives
In prosecution of these cruel arms,   10
Is ruth, and almost death, to call to mind.
But God we know will always put them down
That lift themselves against the perfect truth :
Which I'll maintain so long as life doth last,

---

     [1] Old ed. "make."   [2] Scene : near Coutras.

And with the Queen of England join my force
To beat the papal monarch from our lands,
And keep those relics from our countries' coasts.
Come, my lords ; now that this storm is over-past,
Let us away with triumph to our tents.   [*Exeunt.*

SCENE XIX.

Enter [1] *a* Soldier.

Sold. Sir, to you, sir, that dares make the duke a

---

[1] Scene : outside the Louvre.—In his *Hist. of Eng. Dram. Poetry*, iii. 134 (old ed.), Collier printed a portion (given below) of this scene from a fragment of a MS. copy. It will be seen that the printed text was much mutilated.

" Enter a Souldier with a muskett.

Souldier. Now, sir, to you that dares make a duke a cuckolde, and use a counterfeyt key to his privye chamber : though you take out none but your owne treasure, yett you put in that displeases him, and fill up his rome that he shold occupye.   Herein, sir, you forestalle the markett, and sett up your standinge where you shold not.   But you will saye you leave him rome enoghe besides : that's no answere ; he's to have the choyce of his owne freeland ; yf it be not too free, there's the questione.   Nowe, for where he is your landlorde, you take upon you to be his, and will needs enter by defaulte : what though you were once in possession, yett comminge upon you once unawares, he frayde you out againe ; therefore your entrye is mere intrusione : this is against the law, sir : and though I come not to keepe possessione (as I wolde I might !), yet I come to keepe you out, sir.

Enter MINION.

You are wellcome, sir : have at you !   [*He kills him.*
   Minion. Trayterouse Guise, ah, thou hast morthered me !

Enter GUISE.

Guise. Hold the[e], tall soldier ! take the[e] this, and flye.
                    [*Exit* [*Soldier*].
        Thus fall, imperfett exhalatione,
        Which our great sonn of France cold not effecte ;

cuckold, and use a counterfeit key to his privy-chamber-
door; and although you take out nothing but your own,
yet you put in that which displeaseth him, and so forestall
his market, and set up your standing where you should
not ; and whereas he is your landlord, you will take upon
you to be his, and till the ground that he himself should
occupy, which is his own free land; if it be not too free
—there's the question; and though I come not to take
possession (as I would I might !), yet I mean to keep you
out; which I will, if this gear hold.   11

Enter MUGEROUN.

What, are ye come so soon? have at ye, sir !
                    [*Shoots at* MUGEROUN *and kills him.*[1]

A fyery meteor in the fermament :
Lye there, the kinge's delyght and Guise's scorne !
Revenge it, Henry, yf thou list or darst :
I did it onely in dispight of thee.
Fondlie hast thou incenste the Guise's sowle,
That of it selfe was hote enough to worke
Thy just degestione with extreamest shame.
The armye I have gatherd now shall ayme,
More at thie end then exterpatione ;
And when thou thinkst I have forgotten this,
And that thou most reposest in my faythe,
Than will I wake thee from thy folishe dreame,
And lett thee see thie selfe my prysoner.   [*Exeunt.*"

[1] "Mugeroun (Maugiron) fell in a duel: Anquetil, *Hist. de France*,
t. v. 344, ed. 1817 : but Saint-Mégrin, the gallant of the Duchess of
Guise, *was* assassinated. 'Ils dressèrentu ne embuscade à la porte du
Louvre. Comme Saint-Mégrin, en sortoit la nuit, des assassins apostés
se jetèrent sur lui, et l'étendirent sur le pavé, percé de trente-cinq coups.
Il vécut cependant jusqu'au lendemain.' Anquetil, *Ibid.* p. 347."—*Dyce.*

Enter GUISE *and* Attendants.

Guise [*Giving a purse*]. Hold thee, tall soldier, take
      thee this, and fly.   [*Exit* Soldier.
Lie there, the king's delight, and Guise's scorn !
Revenge it, Henry, as thou list or dare ;
I did it only in despite of thee.
          [Attendants *bear off* MUGEROUN's *body.*

Enter KING HENRY *and* EPERNOUN.

Henry. My Lord of Guise, we understand
That you have gatherèd a power of men :
What your intent is yet we cannot learn,
But we presume it is not for our good.   20
  Guise. Why, I am no traitor to the crown of France ;
What I have done, 'tis for the Gospel's sake.
  Eper. Nay, for the Pope's sake, and thine own benefit.
What peer in France but thou, aspiring Guise,
Durst be in arms without the king's consent?
I challenge thee for treason in the cause.
  Guise. Ah, base Epernoun ! were not his highness here,
Thou shouldst perceive the Duke of Guise is mov'd.
  Henry. Be patient, Guise, and threat not Epernoun,
Lest thou perceive the king of France be mov'd.   30
  Guise. Why, I'm a prince of the Valois line,
Therefore an enemy to the Bourbonites ;
I am a juror in the holy league,
And therefore hated of the Protestants :
What should I do but stand upon my guard ?
And, being able, I'll keep an host in pay.

Eper. Thou able to maintain an host in pay,
That liv'st by foreign exhibition ![1]
The Pope and King of Spain are thy good friends :
Else all France knows how poor a duke thou art.   40

   Henry. I, those are they that feed him with their
        gold,
To countermand our will, and check our friends.

   Guise. My lord, to speak more plainly, thus it is.
Being animated by religious zeal,
I mean to muster all the power I can,
To overthrow those factious[2] Puritans :
And know, my lord, the Pope will sell his triple
        crown,
I, and the Catholic Philip, king of Spain,
Ere I shall want, will cause his Indians
To rip the golden bowels of America.   50
Navarre, that cloaks them underneath his wings,
Shall feel the house of Lorraine is his foe.
Your highness needs not fear mine army's force :
'Tis for your safety, and your enemies' wreck.

   Henry. Guise, wear our crown, and be thou king of
        France,
And, as dictator, make or war or peace,
Whilst I cry *placet*, like a senator !
I cannot brook thy haughty insolence :
Dismiss thy camp, or else by our edict
Be thou proclaim'd a traitor throughout France.   60

---

[1] Pension, maintenance.
[2] Collier's correction for the old copy's "sexious."

Guise. The choice is hard ; I must dissemble.—

                                     [*Aside.*

My lord, in token of my true humility,
And simple meaning to your majesty,
I kiss your grace's hand, and take my leave,
Intending to dislodge my camp with speed.

    Henry. Then farewell, Guise ; the king and thou are
            friends.   [*Exit* GUISE.

    Eper. But trust him not, my lord ; for, had your high-
            ness

Seen with what a pomp he enter'd Paris,
And how the citizens with gifts and shows
Did entertain him,   70
And promisèd to be at his command—
Nay, they fear'd not to speak it in the streets,
That the Guise durst stand in arms against the king,
For not effecting of his holiness' will.

    Henry. Did they of Paris entertain him so ?
Then means he present treason to our state.
Well, let me alone.—Who's within there?

Enter an Attendant, *with pen and ink.*

Make a discharge of all my council straight,
And I'll subscribe my name, and seal it straight.—

                            [Attendant *writes.*

My head shall be my council ; they are false ;   80
And, Epernoun, I will be rul'd by thee.

    Eper. My lord,
I think, for safety of your royal person,

It would be good the Guise were made away,
And so to quite [1] your grace of all suspect.

   Henry. First let us set our hand and seal to this,
And then I'll tell thee what I mean to do.—   [*Writes.*
So ; convey this to the council presently.

                          [*Exit* Attendant.

And, Epernoun, though I seem mild and calm,
Think not but I am tragical within.   90
I'll secretly convey me unto Blois ;
For, now that Paris takes the Guise's part,
Here is no staying for the king of France,
Unless he mean to be betray'd and die :
But, as I live, so sure the Guise shall die.   [*Exeunt.*

SCENE XX.

Enter [2] *the* KING OF NAVARRE, *reading a letter, and*
BARTUS.

   Nav. My lord, I am advertisèd from France
That the Guise hath taken arms against the king,
And that Paris is revolted from his grace.

   Bar. Then hath your grace fit opportunity
To show your love unto the king of France,
Offering him aid against his enemies,
Which cannot but be thankfully receiv'd.

   Nav. Bartus, it shall be so : post, then, to France,

---

   [1] Quit, free.
   [2] It cannot be determined where this scene takes place.

And there salute his highness in our name ;
Assure him all the aid we can provide   10
Against the Guisians and their complices.
Bartus, be gone : commend me to his grace,
And tell him, ere it be long, I'll visit him.

   Bar. I will, my lord.   [*Exit.*
   Nav. Pleshè !

Enter PLESHÈ.

   Pleshè. My lord?
   Nav. Pleshè, go muster up our men with speed,
And let them march away to France amain,
For we must aid the king against the Guise.
Begone, I say : 'tis time that we were there.   20

   Pleshè. I go, my lord.   [*Exit.*
   Nav. That wicked Guise, I fear me much, will be
The ruin of that famous realm of France ;
For his aspiring thoughts aim at the crown,
And[1] takes his vantage on religion,
To plant the Pope and Popelings in the realm,
And bind it wholly to the see of Rome.
But, if that God do prosper mine attempts,
And send us safely to arrive in France,
We'll beat him back, and drive him to his death,   30
That basely seeks the ruin of his realm.   [*Exit.*

---

[1] Dyce reads "'A takes" (*i.e.* "He takes") ; but the omission of a
personal pronoun, where the sense is plain, occurs not unfrequently.

SCENE XXI.

Enter[1] *the* Captain of the Guard, *and three* Murderers.

Cap. Come on, sirs.   What, are you resolutely bent,
Hating the life and honour of the Guise?
What, will you not fear, when you see him come?

First Murd. Fear him, said you? tush, were he here,
we would kill him presently.

Sec. Murd. O that his heart were leaping in my hand!

Third Murd. But when will he come, that we may
            murder him?

Cap. Well, then, I see you are resolute.

First Murd. Let us alone; I warrant you.

Cap. Then, sirs, take your standings within this
            chamber;   10
For anon the Guise will come.

All three Murderers. You will give us our money?

Cap. I, I, fear not: stand close: so; be resolute.
                                    [*Exeunt* Murderers.
Now falls the star whose influence governs France,
Whose light was deadly to the Protestants:
Now must he fall, and perish in his height.

Enter KING HENRY *and* EPERNOUN.

Henry. Now, captain of my guard, are these murderers
            ready?

Cap. They be, my good lord.

---

[1] Scene: a room in the royal palace at Blois.

Henry. But are they resolute, and armed to kill,
Hating the life and honour of the Guise?   20
    Cap. I warrant ye, my lord.   [*Exit.*
    Henry. Then come, proud Guise, and here disgorge
             thy breast,
Surcharged with surfeit of ambitious thoughts ;
Breathe out that life wherein my death was hid,
And end thy endless treasons with thy death.
                        [*Knocking within.*
    Guise [*within*]. *Holà, varlet, hé !*—Epernoun, where is
        the king ?
    Eper. Mounted [1] his royal cabinet.
    Guise [*within*]. I prithee, tell him that the Guise is here.
    Eper. An please your grace, the Duke of Guise doth
        crave
Access unto your highness.
    Henry. Let him come in.—   30
Come, Guise, and see thy traitorous guile outreach'd,
And perish in the pit thou mad'st for me.

Enter GUISE.

    Guise. Good morrow to your majesty.
    Henry. Good morrow to my loving cousin of Guise :
How fares it this morning with your excellence?
    Guise. I heard your majesty was scarcely pleased,
That in the court I bear so great a train.
    Henry. They were to blame that said I was displeased ;

---

[1] Cf. 2 *Tamburlaine* iv. 3 :—" Mounted his shining chariot " (for
" mounted *in* ").

And you, good cousin, to imagine it.
'Twere hard with me, if I should doubt my kin,   40
Or be suspicious of my dearest friends,
Cousin, assure you I am resolute,
Whatsoever any whisper in mine ears,
Not to suspect disloyalty in thee :
And so, sweet coz, farewell.   [*Exit with* EPERNOUN.
     Guise. So ;
Now sues the king for favour to the Guise,
And all his minions stoop when I command :
Why, this 'tis to have an army in the field.
Now, by the holy sacrament, I swear,   50
As ancient Romans o'er their captive lords.
So will I triumph o'er this wanton king ;
And he shall follow my proud chariot's wheels.
Now do I but begin to look about,
And all my former time was spent in vain.
Hold, sword,
For in thee is the Duke of Guise's hope.

Re-enter Third Murderer.

Villain, why dost thou look so ghastly ? speak.
     Third Murd. O, pardon me, my Lord of Guise !
     Guise. Pardon thee ! why, what hast thou done?   60
     Third Murd. O my lord, I am one of them that is set
to murder you !
     Guise. To murder me, villain !
     Third Murd. I, my lord : the rest have ta'en their
standings in the next room ; therefore, good my lord, go
not forth.

Guise. Yet Cæsar shall go forth.
Let mean conceits and baser men fear death :
Tut, they are peasants ; I am Duke of Guise ;
And princes with their looks engender fear.　　　70
　　First Murd. [*within*] Stand close ; he is coming ; I
　　　　know him by his voice.
　　Guise. As pale as ashes !¹ nay, then, it is time
To look about.

　　　　Enter First *and* Second Murderers.

　　First and Sec. Murderers. Down with him, down with
　　　　him !　　　　　　　　　　[*They stab* GUISE.
　　Guise. O, I have my death's wound ! give me leave to
　　　　speak.
　　Sec. Murd. Then pray to God, and ask forgiveness of
the king.
　　Guise. Trouble me not ; I ne'er offended him,
Nor will I ask forgiveness of the king.
O, that I have not power to stay my life,
Nor immortality to be revenged :　　　　　　80
To die by peasants, what a grief is this !
Ah, Sixtus, be reveng'd upon the king !
Philip and Parma, I am slain for you !
Pope, excommunicate, Philip, depose
The wicked branch of curs'd Valois his line !
Vive la messe! perish Huguenots !
Thus Cæsar did go forth, and thus he died.　　　[*Dies.*

---

¹ Dyce conjectures that Guise must have seen himself in a mirror as
he uttered these words.

Enter the Captain of the Guard.

Cap. What, have you done?
Then stay a while, and I'll go call the king.
But see, where he comes.   90

Enter KING HENRY, EPERNOUN, *and* Attendants.

My lord, see, where the Guise is slain.
   Henry. Ah, this sweet sight is physic to my soul!
Go fetch his son for to behold his death.—
                              [*Exit an* Attendant.
Surcharg'd with guilt of thousand massacres,
Monsieur of Lorraine, sink away to hell!
And, in remembrance of those bloody broils,
To which thou didst allure me, being alive,
And here, in presence of you all, I swear,
I ne'er was king of France until this hour.
This is the traitor that hath spent my gold   100
In making foreign wars and civil broils.
Did he not draw a sort[1] of English priests
From Douay to the seminary at Rheims,
To hatch forth treason 'gainst their natural queen?
Did he not cause the king of Spain's huge fleet
To threaten England, and to menace me?
Did he not injure Monsieur that's deceas'd?
Hath he not made me, in the Pope's defence,
To spend the treasure, that should strength my land,
In civil broils between Navarre and me?   110

---

[1] Set.

Tush, to be short, he meant to make me monk,
Or else to murder me, and so be king.
Let Christian princes, that shall hear of this
(As all the world shall know our Guise is dead),
Rest satisfied with this, that here I swear,
Ne'er was there king of France so yoked as I.

    Eper. My lord, here is his son.

Enter GUISE'S Son.

    Henry. Boy, look where your father lies.
    G.'s Son. My father slain! who hath done this deed?
    Henry. Sirrah, 'twas I that slew him; and will slay 120
Thee too, an thou prove such a traitor.
    G.'s Son. Art thou king, and hast done this bloody
        deed?
I'll be reveng'd.   [*Offers to throw his dagger.*
    Henry. Away to prison with him! I'll clip his wings
Or e'er he pass my hands.   Away with him!
        [*Some of the* Attendants *bear off* GUISE'S Son.
But what availeth that this traitor's dead,
When Duke Dumaine, his brother, is alive,
And that young cardinal that is grown so proud?
Go to the governor of Orleans,
And will[1] him, in my name, to kill the duke.   130
        [*To the* Captain of the Guard.
Get you away, and strangle the cardinal.
           [*To the* Murderers.
      [*Exeunt* Captain of the Guard *and* Murderers.

---

[1] Order.

These two will make one entire Duke of Guise,
Especially with our old mother's help.

   Eper. My lord, see, where she comes, as if she droop'd
To hear these news.

   Henry. And let her droop; my heart is light enough.

Enter CATHERINE *the Queen Mother.*

Mother, how like you this device of mine?
I slew the Guise, because I would be king.

   Cath. King! why, so thou wert before:
Pray God thou be a king now this is done!   140

   Henry. Nay, he was king, and countermanded me:
But now I will be king, and rule myself,
And make the Guisians stoop that are alive.

   Cath. I cannot speak for grief.—When thou wast born,
I would that I had murdered thee, my son:
My son? thou art a changeling, not my son:
I curse thee, and exclaim thee miscreant,
Traitor to God and to the realm of France!

   Henry. Cry out, exclaim, howl till thy throat be hoarse!
The Guise is slain, and I rejoice therefore: 150
And now will I to arms.—Come, Epernoun,
And let her grieve her heart out, if she will.

             [Exit with EPERNOUN.

   Cath. Away! leave me alone to meditate.

             [Exeunt Attendants.

Sweet Guise, would he had died, so thou wert here!
To whom shall I bewray my secrets now,
Or who will help to build religion?
The Protestants will glory and insult;

Wicked Navarre will get the crown of France;
The Popedom cannot stand; all goes to wreck;
And all for thee, my Guise! What may I do?   160
But sorrow seize upon my toiling soul!
For, since the Guise is dead, I will not live.   [*Exit.*

SCENE XXII.

Enter [1] *two* Murderers, *dragging in the* CARDINAL.

Card. Murder me not; I am a cardinal.

First Murd. Wert thou the Pope thou might'st not
    scape from us.

Card. What, will you file your hands with churchmen's
    blood?

Sec. Murd. Shed your blood! O Lord, no! for we
intend to strangle you.

Card. Then there is no remedy, but I must die?

First Murd. No remedy; therefore prepare yourself.

Card. Yet lives my brother Duke Dumaine, and many
    mo,
To revenge our deaths upon that cursèd king:
Upon whose heart may all the Furies gripe,   10
And with their paws drench his black soul in hell!

First Murd. Yours, my Lord Cardinal, you should
    have said.—   [*They strangle him.*
So, pluck amain:
He is hard-hearted; therefore pull with violence.
Come, take him away.   *Exeunt with the body.*

---

[1] Scene: the interior of a prison at Blois.

SCENE XXIII.

Enter [1] DUMAINE, *reading a letter ; with others.*

Dum. My noble brother murder'd by the king [1]
O, what may I do for to revenge thy death?
The king's alone, it cannot satisfy.
Sweet Duke of Guise, our prop to lean upon,
Now thou art dead, here is no stay for us.
I am thy brother, and I'll revenge thy death,
And root Valois his line from forth of France ;
And beat proud Bourbon to his native home,
That basely seeks to join with such a king,
Whose murderous thoughts will be his overthrow.   10
He will'd the governor of Orleans, in his name,
That I with speed should have been put to death :
But that's prevented, for to end his life,
And [2] all those traitors to the Church of Rome
That durst attempt to murder noble Guise.

Enter Friar.

Fri. My lord, I come to bring you news that your
brother the Cardinal of Lorraine, by the king's consent,
is lately strangled unto death.

Dum. My brother Cardinal slain, and I alive !
O words of power to kill a thousand men !—   20
Come, let us away, and levy men ;
'Tis war that must assuage this tyrant's pride.

---

[1] Scene : a room in Dumaine's house, at Paris.
[2] Old ed. " *His life* and all," &c.

Fri. My lord, hear me but speak.
I am a friar of the order of the Jacobins,
That for my conscience' sake will kill the king.

Dum. But what doth move thee, above the rest, to do
the deed?

Fri. O my lord, I have been a great sinner in my
days! and the deed is meritorious.

Dum. But how wilt thou get opportunity?   30

Fri. Tush, my lord, let me alone for that.

Dum. Friar, come with me;
We will go talk more of this within.   [*Exeunt.*

SCENE XXIV.

Drums and Trumpets. Enter[1] KING HENRY, *the* KING
OF NAVARRE, EPERNOUN, BARTUS, PLESHÈ, Soldiers,
and Attendants.

Henry. Brother of Navarre, I sorrow much
That ever I was prov'd your enemy,
And that the sweet and princely mind you bare
Was ever troubled with injurious wars.
I vow, as I am lawful king of France,
To recompense your reconcilèd love,
With all the honours and affections
That ever I vouchsaf'd my dearest friends.

Nav. It is enough if that Navarre may be
Esteemèd faithful to the king of France,   10
Whose service he may still command till death.

---

[1] Scene : Saint-Cloud.

Henry. Thanks to my kingly brother of Navarre.
Then here we'll lie before Lutetia-walls,[1]
Girting this strumpet city with our siege,
Till, surfeiting with our afflicting arms,
She cast her hateful stomach to the earth.

Enter a Messenger.

Mes. An it please your majesty, here is a friar of the
order of the Jacobins, sent from the President of Paris,
that craves access unto your grace.
Henry. Let him come in.   [*Exit* Mess.   20

Enter Friar, *with a letter.*

Eper. I like not this friar's look :
'Twere not amiss, my lord, if he were search'd.
Henry. Sweet Epernoun, our friars are holy men,
And will not offer violence to their king
For all the wealth and treasure of the world.—
Friar, thou dost acknowledge me thy king?
Fri. I, my good lord, and will die therein.
Henry. Then come thou near, and tell what news
          thou bring'st.
Fri. My lord,
The President of Paris greets your grace,   30
And sends his duty by these speedy lines,
Humbly craving your gracious reply.   [*Gives letter.*

---

1 Old ed. "Lucrecia walles."

Henry. I'll read them, friar, and then I'll answer
 thee.

Fri. Sancte Jacobe,[1] now have mercy upon me!

 [*Stabs the king with a knife, as he reads the
  letter; and then the king gets the knife, and
  kills him.*

Eper. O my lord, let him live a while!

Henry. No, let the villain die, and feel in hell
Just torments for his treachery.

Nav. What, is your highness hurt?

Henry. Yes, Navarre; but not to death, I hope.

Nav. God shield your grace from such a sudden
 death :—   40
Go call a surgeon hither straight. [*Exit an* Attendant.

Henry. What irreligious pagans' parts be these,
Of such as hold them of the holy church '
Take hence that damnèd villain from my sight.

    [Attendants *carry out the* Friar's *body.*

Eper. Ah, had your highness let him live,
We might have punish'd him to his deserts!

Henry. Sweet Epernoun, all rebels under heaven
Shall take example by his[2] punishment,
How they bear arms against their sovereign.—
Go call the English agent hither straight: 50

      [*Exit an* Attendant.
I'll send my sister England news of this,
And give her warning of her treacherous foes.

---

[1] Old ed. "Jacobus."   [2] Old ed. "their."

Enter a Surgeon.

Nav. Pleaseth your grace to let the surgeon search
    your wound?
Henry. The wound, I warrant ye, is deep, my lord.—
Search, surgeon, and resolve me what thou see'st.

              [*The* Surgeon *searches the wound.*

Enter the English Agent.

Agent for England, send thy mistress word
What this detested Jacobin hath done.
Tell her, for all this, that I hope to live;
Which if I do, the papal monarch goes
To wreck, and antichristian kingdom falls: 60
These bloody hands shall tear his triple crown,
And fire accursèd Rome about his ears;
I'll fire his crazèd buildings, and enforce
The papal towers to kiss the lowly [1] earth.
Navarre, give me thy hand: I here do swear
To ruinate that wicked Church of Rome,
That hatcheth up such bloody practices;
And here protest eternal love to thee,
And to the Queen of England specially,
Whom God hath bless'd for hating papistry.   70
   Nav. These words revive my thoughts, and comfort me,
To see your highness in this virtuous mind.

---

[1] Dyce's correction for "*incense* . . . to kiss the *holy* earth." He
compares *Edward II.* (I. 4, ll. 100, 101):—
      "I'll fire thy crazed buildings, and *enforce*
      The papal towers to kiss the *lowly* ground."

Henry. Tell me, surgeon, shall I live?

Surg. Alas, my lord, the wound is dangerous,
For you are stricken with a poison'd knife!

 Henry. A poison'd knife! what, shall the French king
    die,
Wounded and poison'd both at once?

 Eper. O, that
That damnèd villain were alive again,   79
That we might torture him with some new-found death!

 Bar. He died a death too good:
The devil of hell torture his wicked soul!

 Henry. Ah, curse him not, sith he is dead!—
O, the fatal poison works within my breast!—
Tell me, surgeon, and flatter not—may I live?

 Surg. Alas, my lord, your highness cannot live!

 Nav. Surgeon, why say'st thou so? the king may live.

 Henry. O no, Navarre! thou must be king of France.

 Nav. Long may you live, and still be king of France!

 Eper. Or else, die Epernoun!   90

 Henry. Sweet Epernoun, thy king must die.—My lords,
Fight in the quarrel of this valiant prince,
For he's your lawful king, and my next heir;
Valois's line ends in my tragedy.
Now let the house of Bourbon wear the crown;
And may it ne'er end in blood as mine hath done!—
Weep not, sweet Navarre, but revenge my death.—
Ah, Epernoun, is this thy love to me?
Henry, thy king, wipes off these childish tears,
And bids thee whet thy sword on Sixtus' bones, 100
That it may keenly slice the Catholics.

He loves me not [the most [1]] that sheds most tears,
But he that makes most lavish of his blood.
Fire Paris, where these treacherous rebels lurk.—
I die, Navarre: come bear me to my sepulchre.
Salute the Queen of England in my name,
And tell her Henry dies her faithful friend.   [*Dies.*

  Nav. Come, lords, take up the body of the king,
That we may see it honourably interr'd:
And then I vow so [2] to revenge his death,   110
As Rome, and all these popish prelates there,
Shall curse the time that e'er Navarre was king,
And ruled in France by Henry's fatal death.

> [*They march out, with the body of* KING HENRY
>   *lying on four men's shoulders, with a dead
>   march, drawing weapons on the ground.*

---

[1] The bracketed words were inserted by Dyce.
[2] Dyce's correction for the old copy's "for."

THE TRAGEDY

OF

DIDO, QUEEN OF CARTHAGE.

Dido was published in 1594, with the following title :—

The Tragedie of Dido Queene of Carthage: Played by the Children of her Maiesties Chappell. Written by Christopher Marlowe, and Thomas Nash, Gent.

Actors.

Jupiter.	*Ascanius.*
Ganimed.	*Dido.*
Venus.	*Anna.*
Cupid.	*Achates.*
Juno.	*Ilioneus.*
Mercurie, or	*Iarbas.*
Hermes.	*Cloanthes.*
Æneas.	*Sergestus.*

At London, Printed, by the Widdowe Orwin, for Thomas Wood-cocke, and are to be sold at his shop, in Paules Churchyeard, at the signe of the blacke Beare. 1594. 4to.

A copy of this edition is in the Bodleian Library; and I am indebted to my friend Mr. C. H. Firth for kindly comparing Dyce's text with the text of the Bodleian copy.

PERSONS REPRESENTED.

JUPITER.
GANYMEDE.
HERMES.
CUPID.

JUNO.
VENUS.

ÆNEAS.
ASCANIUS, his son.
ACHATES.
ILIONEUS.
CLOANTHUS.
SERGESTUS.
Other Trojans.
IARBAS.
Carthaginian Lords.

DIDO.
ANNA, her sister.
Nurse

THE TRAGEDY OF

DIDO, QUEEN OF CARTHAGE.

—o—

ACT I.

SCENE I.

Here the curtains draw: there is discovered JUPITER
dandling GANYMEDE *upon his knee, and* HERMES
lying asleep.

Jup. Come, gentle Ganymede, and play with me :
I love thee well, say Juno what she will.

Gan. I am much better for your worthless love,
That will not shield me from her shrewish blows !
To-day, whenas I filled into your cups,
And held the cloth of pleasance whiles you drank,
She reached me such a rap for that I spilled,
As made the blood run down about mine ears.

Jup. What? dares she strike the darling of my thoughts?
By Saturn's soul, and this earth-threatening hair,[1]   10
That, shaken thrice, makes nature's buildings quake,
I vow, if she but once frown on thee more,

---

[1] Old ed. "aire."

To hang her, meteor-like, 'twixt heaven and earth,
And bind her, hand and foot, with golden cords,
As once I did for harming Hercules!

Gan. Might I but see that pretty sport a-foot,
O, how would I with Helen's brother laugh,
And bring the gods to wonder at the game!
Sweet Jupiter, if e'er I pleased thine eye,
Or seemèd fair, wall'd-in with eagle's wings,[1]   20
Grace my immortal beauty with this boon,
And I will spend my time in thy bright arms.

Jup. What is't, sweet wag, I should deny thy youth?
Whose face reflects such pleasure to mine eyes,
As I, exhaled with thy fire-darting beams,
Have oft driven back the horses of the Night,
Whenas they would have haled thee from my sight.
Sit on my knee, and call for thy content,
Control proud Fate, and cut the thread of Time:
Why, are not all the gods at thy command,   30
And heaven and earth the bounds of thy delight?
Vulcan[2] shall dance to make thee laughing-sport,

---

[1] "This expression is well illustrated by Titian's [?] picture (in the National Gallery) of the rape of Ganymede.—In Shakespeare's *Love's Labour's Lost,* act v. sc. 2, we have,—
'A lady *wall'd-about* with diamonds!' "—*Dyce.*

[2] This speech is undoubtedly by Marlow, but it is curious that Nashe, in *Summer's Last Will and Testament* speaks of the amusement caused, among the gods by the sight of Vulcan's dancing:—"To make the gods merry the celestial clown Vulcan tuned his polt foot to the measures of Apollo's lute, and danced a limping galliard in Jove's starry hall." (Hazlitt's *Dodsley,* viii. 91). In both passages there is perhaps an allusion to the lines in the first book of the *Iliad* (599–600), describing how "unquenchable laughter rose among the blessed gods when they saw Hephæstus limping through the hall."

And my nine daughters sing when thou art sad;
From Juno's bird I'll pluck her spotted pride,
To make thee fans wherewith to cool thy face;
And Venus' swans shall shed their silver down,
To sweeten out the slumbers of thy bed;
Hermes no more shall show the world his wings,
If that thy fancy in his feathers dwell,
But, as this one, I'll tear them all from him,   40
          [*Plucks a feather from* HERMES' *wings.*
Do thou but say, "their colour pleaseth me."
Hold here, my little love; these linkèd gems,
              [*Gives jewels.*
My Juno ware upon her marriage-day,
Put thou about thy neck, my own sweet heart,
And trick thy arms and shoulders with my theft.
  Gan. I would have a jewel for mine ear,
And a fine brooch to put in[to] my hat,
And then I'll hug with you an hundred times.
  Jup. And shall have, Ganymede, if thou wilt be my
    love.

Enter VENUS.

  Ven. I, this is it: you can sit toying there,   50
And playing with that female wanton boy,
Whiles my Æneas wanders on the seas,
And rests a prey to every billow's pride.
Juno, false Juno, in her chariot's pomp,
Drawn through the heavens by steeds of Boreas'
    brood,
Made Hebe to direct her airy wheels,
  VOL. II.   U

Into the windy country of the clouds;
Where, finding Æolus entrenched with storms,
And guarded with a thousand grisly ghosts,
She humbly did beseech him for our bane,   60
And charged him drown my son with all his train.
Then gan the winds break ope their brazen doors,
And all Æolia to be up in arms;
Poor Troy must now be sacked upon the sea,
And Neptune's waves be envious men of war:
Epeus' horse, to Ætna's hill transform'd,
Prepared stands to wreck their wooden walls;
And Æolus, like Agamemnon, sounds
The surges, his fierce soldiers, to the spoil:
See how the night, Ulysses-like, comes forth,   70
And intercepts the day, as Dolon erst!
Ay me! the stars supprised,[1] like Rhesus' steeds,
Are drawn by darkness forth Astræus' tents.[2]
What shall I do to save thee, my sweet boy?
Whenas the waves do threat our crystal world,
And Proteus, raising hills of floods on high,
Intends, ere long, to sport him in the sky.[3]
False Jupiter, reward'st thou virtue so?
What, is not piety exempt from woe?
Then die, Æneas, in thine innocence,   80
Since that religion hath no recompense.

    Jup. Content thee, Cytherea, in thy care,

---

[1] Surprised.

[2] The stars were the children of Astræus and Eos. See Hesiod, *Theogony*, ll. 381–2.

[3] These rhyming lines are suggestive of Nashe.

Since thy Æneas' wandering fate is firm,[1]
Whose weary limbs shall shortly make repose
In those fair walls I promised him of yore.
But, first, in blood must his good fortune bud,
Before he be the lord of Turnus' town,
Or force her smile that hitherto hath frowned :
Three winters shall he with the Rutiles war,
And, in the end, subdue them with his sword ;   90
And full three summers likewise shall he waste
In managing those fierce barbarian minds :
Which once performed, poor Troy, so long suppressed,
From forth her ashes shall advance her head,
And flourish once again, that erst was dead.
But bright Ascanius, beauty's better work,
Who with the sun divides one radiant shape,
Shall build his throne amidst those starry towers
That earth-born Atlas, groaning, underprops :
No bounds, but heaven, shall bound his empery,   100
Whose azured gates, enchasèd with his name,
Shall make the Morning haste her grey uprise,
To feed her eyes with his engraven fame.
Thus, in stout Hector's race, three hundred years [2]
The Roman sceptre royal shall remain,
Till that a princess-priest,[3] conceived by Mars,

---

[1] "Parce metu, Cytherea ; manént immota tuorum
   Fata tibi."   Virg. *Æn.* i. 257-8.
[2] "Hic jam ter centumt totos regnabitur annos
   Gente sub Hectorea."   Virg. *Æn.* i. 272-3.
[3] "Donec regina sacerdos
   Marte gravis geminam partu dabit Ilia prolem."
                                         Virg. *Æn.* i. 273.

Shall yield to dignity a double birth,
Who will eternish[1] Troy in their attempts.

   Ven. How may I credit these thy flattering terms,
When yet both sea and sands beset their ships,   110
And Phœbus, as in Stygian pools, refrains
To taint his tresses in the Tyrrhene main ?

   Jup. I will take order for that presently.——
Hermes, awake ! and haste to Neptune's realm,
Whereas the wind-god, warring now with fate,
Besiege[s] th' offspring of our kindly loins :
Charge him from me to turn his stormy powers,
And fetter them in Vulcan's sturdy brass,
That durst thus proudly wrong our kinsman's peace.

                        [*Exit* HERMES.

Venus, farewell : thy son shall be our care.——   120
Come, Ganymede, we must about this gear.[2]

           [*Exeunt* JUPITER *and* GANYMEDE.

   Ven.[3] Disquiet seas, lay down your swelling looks,
And court Æneas with your calmy cheer,
Whose beauteous burden well might make you proud,
Had not the heavens, conceiv'd with hell-born clouds,
Veil'd his resplendent glory from your view :
For my sake, pity him, Oceanus,
That erst-while issu'd from thy watery loins,
And had my being from thy bubbling froth.
Triton, I know, hath filled his trump with Troy,   130
And therefore will take pity on his toil,

---

   [1] Probably a misspelling of "eternise."
   [2] Business.
   [3] The scene shifts to a wood near the sea-shore.

And call both Thetis and Cymothoe [1]
To succour him in this extremity.

  Enter ÆNEAS, ASCANIUS, ACHATES, *and others.*
What do I see? my son now come on shore?
Venus, how art thou compassed with content,
The while thine eyes attract their sought-for joys!
Great Jupiter, still honoured mayst thou be
For this so friendly aid in time of need!
Here in this bush disguisèd will I stand,
Whiles my Æneas spends himself in plaints,   140
And heaven and earth with his unrest acquaints.

 Æn. You sons of care, companions of my course,
Priam's misfortune follows us [2] by sea,
And Helen's rape doth haunt us [2] at our heels.
How many dangers have we overpass'd!
Both barking Scylla, [3] and the sounding rocks,
The Cyclops' shelves, and grim Ceraunia's seat,
Have you o'ergone, and yet remain alive.
Pluck up your hearts, since Fate still rests our friend,
And changing heavens may those good days return, 150
Which Pergama did vaunt in all her pride.

 Ach. Brave prince of Troy, thou only art our god,
That by thy virtues free'st us from annoy,
And makes our hopes survive to coming [4] joys:

---

[1] Old ed. "Cimodoœ."—Cf. Virgil, *Æn.* i. 144.

[2] Old ed. "thee."

[3] "Vos et Scyllaeam rabiem penitusque sonantes
 Accestis scopulos, vos et Cyclopia saxa
 Experti: revocate animos, maestumque timorem Mittite."
       —Virgil, *Æn.* i. 200–203.

 Old ed. "cunning."

Do thou but smile, and cloudy heaven will clear,
Whose night and day descendeth from thy brows.
Though we be now in extreme misery,
And rest the map of weather-beaten woe,[1]
Yet shall the agèd sun shed forth his hair,[2]
To make us live unto our former heat,   160
And every beast the forest doth send forth
Bequeath her young ones to our scanted food.

   Asc. Father, I faint; good father, give me meat.

   Æn. Alas! sweet boy, thou must be still a while,
Till we have fire to dress the meat we killed!
Gentle Achates, reach the tinder-box,
That we may make a fire to warm us with,
And roast our new-found victuals on this shore.

   Ven. See, what strange arts necessity finds out!
How near, my sweet Æneas, art thou driven!   [*Aside.*

   Æn. Hold; take this candle, and go light a fire: 171
You shall have leaves and windfall boughs enow,
Near to these woods, to roast your meat withal.—
Ascanius, go and dry thy drenchèd limbs,
Whiles I with my Achates rove abroad,
To know what coast the wind hath driven us on,
Or whether men or beasts inhabit it.

             [*Exeunt* ASCANIUS *and others.*

   Ach. The air is pleasant, and the soil most fit
For cities and society's supports;

---

[1] Cf. *Titus Andronicus*, iii. 2 (a great part of which I attribute to Marlowe) :—

     "Thou *map of woe* that thus dost talk in signs" (l. 12).

  - Old ed. "aire."

Yet much I marvel that I cannot find   180
No steps of men imprinted in the earth.
   Ven. Now is the time for me to play my part.—
                                                  [Aside.

Ho, young men! saw you, as you came,[1]
Any of all my sisters wandering here,
Having a quiver girded to her side,
And clothèd in a spotted leopard's skin?
   Æn. I neither saw nor heard of any such.
But what may I, fair virgin, call your name,
Whose looks set forth no mortal form to view,
Nor speech bewrays aught human in thy birth?   190
Thou art a goddess that delud'st our eyes,
And shrouds thy beauty in this borrow'd shape;
But whether thou the Sun's bright sister be,
Or one of chaste Diana's fellow-nymphs,
Live happy in the height of all content,
And lighten our extremes with this one boon,
As to instruct us under what good heaven
We breathe as now, and what this world is called
On which by tempests' fury we are cast:
Tell us, O, tell us, that are ignorant!   200
And this right hand shall make thy altars crack
With mountain-heaps of milk-white sacrifice.
   Ven. Such honour, stranger, do I not affect:
It is the use for Tyrian[2] maids to wear
Their bow and quiver in this modest sort,

---

  [1] From this point to the end of the scene Marlowe follows Virgil very
closely.—Cf. *Æn.* i. 321-410.
  [2] Old ed. "Turen."

And suit themselves in purple for the nonce,
That they may trip more lightly o'er the lawnds,[1]
And overtake the tuskèd boar in chase.
But for the land whereof thou dost inquire,
It is the Punic kingdom, rich and strong,   210
Adjoining on Agenor's stately town,
The kingly seat of Southern Libya,
Whereas Sidonian Dido rules as queen.
But what are you that ask of me these things?
Whence may you come, or whither will you go?

Æ*n.* Of Troy am I, Æneas is my name;
Who, driven by war from forth my native world,
Put sails to sea to seek out Italy;
And my divine descent from sceptred Jove:
With twice twelve Phrygian ships I plough'd the deep, 220
And made that way my mother Venus led;
But of them all scarce seven do anchor safe,
And they so wrecked and weltered by the waves,
As every tide tilts 'twixt their oaken sides;
And all of them, unburdened of their load,
Are ballassèd with billows' watery weight.
But hapless I, God wot, poor and unknown,
Do trace these Libyan deserts, all despised,
Exiled forth Europe and wide Asia both,
And have not any coverture but heaven.   230

Ven. Fortune hath favour'd thee, whate'er thou be,

---

[1] Greene (in *Orlando Furioso*) uses the same form :—
    "Thou see'st that Mador and Angelica
      Are still so secret in their private walks,
      As that they trace the shady *lawnds.*"

In sending thee unto this courteous coast.
A' God's name, on ! and haste thee to the court,
Where Dido will receive ye with her smiles ;
And for thy ships, which thou supposest lost,
Not one of them hath perish'd in the storm,
But are arrivèd safe, not far from hence :
And so I leave thee to thy fortune's lot,
Wishing good luck unto thy wandering steps.   [*Exit.*

Æn. Achates, 'tis my mother that is fled ;   240
I know her by the movings of her feet.—
Stay, gentle Venus, fly not from thy son !
Too cruel, why wilt thou forsake me thus,
Or in these shades [1] deceiv'st mine eyes so oft ?
Why talk we not together hand in hand,
And tell our griefs in more familiar terms ?
But thou art gone, and leav'st me here alone,
To dull the air with my discoursive moan.

SCENE II.

Enter [2] IARBUS, *followed by* ILIONEUS, CLOANTHUS,[3]
SERGESTUS, *and others.*

Ili. Follow, ye Trojans, follow this brave lord,
And plain to him the sum of your distress.
Iar. Why, what are you, or wherefore do you sue ?

---

[1] " Quid natum totiens, crudelis tu quoque, falsis
    Ludis imaginibus."   Virg. *Æn.* i. 407-8.
[2] Scene : Carthage.
[3] Old ed. " Cloanthes."

Ili. Wretches [1] of Troy, envìed of the winds,
That crave such favour at your honour's feet
As poor distrèssed misery may plead :
Save, save, O, save our ships from cruel fire,
That do complain the wounds of thousand waves,
And spare our lives, whom every spite pursues !
We come not, we, to wrong your Libyan gods,   10
Or steal your household Lares from their shrines ;
Our hands are not prepared to lawless spoil,
Nor armèd to offend in any kind ;
Such force is far from our unweapon'd thoughts
Whose fading weal, of victory forsook,
Forbids all hope to harbour near our hearts.

Iar. But tell me, Trojans, Trojans if you be,
Unto what fruitful quarters were ye bound,
Before that Boreas buckled with [2] your sails ?

Clo. There is a place, Hesperia termed by us,   20
An ancient empire, famousèd for arms,
And fertile in fair Ceres' furrowed wealth,
Which now we call Italia, of his name
That in such peace long time did rule the same.
Thither made we ;
When, suddenly, gloomy Orion rose,
And led our ships into the shallow sands,
Whereas the southern wind with brackish breath
Dispersed them all amongst the wreckful rocks :

---

[1] For what follows cf. Virg. *Æn*. i. 524-78.
[2] The expression "buckle with" occurs twice in I *Henry VI.*, and once in 3 *Henry VI.;* nowhere in Shakespeare's undoubted plays.

From thence a few of us escaped to land;   30
The rest, we fear, are folded in the floods.

Iar. Brave men-at-arms, abandon fruitless fears,
Since Carthage knows to entertain distress.

Serg. I, but the barbarous sort do threat our ships,
And will not let us lodge upon the sands;
In multitudes they swarm unto the shore,
And from the first earth interdict our feet.

Iar. Myself will see they shall not trouble ye:
Your men and you shall banquet in our court,
And every Trojan be as welcome here   40
As Jupiter to silly Baucis'[1] house.
Come in with me; I'll bring ye to my queen,
Who shall confirm my words with further deeds.

Serg. Thanks, gentle lord, for such unlook'd-for grace:
Might we but once more see Æneas' face,
Then would we hope to quite such friendly turns,
As shall[2] surpass the wonder of our speech.

[Exeunt.

---

[1] Old ed. "Vausis."

[2] Dyce proposes "all" for "shall." Retaining "shall" the sense is
"we would hope to reunite your kindness in such a way as shall," &c.

ACT II.

SCENE I.

Enter[1] ÆNEAS, ACHATES, ASCANIUS, *and others.*

Æn. Where am I now? these should be Carthage-walls.

Ach. Why stands my sweet Æneas thus amaz'd?

Æn. O my Achates, Theban Niobe,
Who for her sons' death wept out life and breath,
And, dry with grief, was turned into a stone,
Had not such passions in her head as I!
Methinks,
That town there should be Troy, yon Ida's hill,
There Xanthus' stream, because here's Priamus:
And when I know it is not, then I die.   10

Ach. And in this humour is Achates too;
I cannot choose but fall upon my knees,
And kiss his hand.   O, where is Hecuba?
Here she was wont to sit; but, saving air,
Is nothing here; and what is this but stone?[2]

Æn. O, yet this stone doth make Æneas weep!
And would my prayers (as Pygmalion's did)
Could give it life, that under his condùct

---

[1] Scene: Juno's temple at Carthage.
[2] Virgil represents the tale of Troy depicted on a fresco in Juno's temple.

We might sail back to Troy, and be revenged
On these hard-hearted Grecians which rejoice   20
That nothing now is left of Priamus !
O, Priamus is left, and this is he !
Come, come aboard ; pursue the hateful Greeks.

    Ach. What means Æneas ?

    Æn. Achates, though mine eyes say this is stone,
Yet thinks my mind that this is Priamus ;
And when my grievèd heart sighs and says no,
Then would it leap out to give Priam life.—
O, were I not at all, so thou mightst be ;—
Achates, see, King Priam wags his hand !   30
He is alive ; Troy is not overcome !

    Ach. Thy mind, Æneas, that would have it so,
Deludes thy eye-sight ; Priamus is dead.

    Æn. Ah, Troy is sack'd, and Priamus is dead !
And why should poor Æneas be alive ?

    Asc. Sweet father, leave to weep ; this is not he,
For, were it Priam, he would smile on me.

    Ach. Æneas, see, here come the citizens :
Leave to lament, lest they laugh at our fears.[1]

    Enter CLOANTHUS, SERGESTUS, ILIONEUS, *and others.*

    Æn. Lords of this town, or whatsoever style   40
Belongs unto your name, vouchsafe of ruth
To tell us who inhabits this fair town,
What kind of people, and who governs them ;
For we are strangers driven on this shore,
And scarcely know within what clime we are.

---

[1] Perhaps a misprint for "tears."

Ili. I hear Æneas' voice, but see him not,[1]
For none of these can be our general.

    Ach. Like Ilioneus speaks this nobleman,
But Ilioneus goes not in such robes.

    Serg. You are Achates, or I [am] deceiv'd.   50

    Ach. Æneas, see, Sergestus, or his ghost!

    Ili. He names[2] Æneas; let us kiss his feet.

    Clo. It is our captain : see, Ascanius!

    Serg. Live long Æneas and Ascanius!

    Æn. Achates, speak, for I am overjoyed.

    Ach. O Ilioneus, art thou yet alive?

    Ili. Blest be the time I see Achates' face!

    Clo. Why turns Æneas from his trusty friends?

    Æn. Sergestus, Ilioneus, and the rest,
Your sight amazed me. O, what destinies   60
Have brought my sweet companions in such
        plight?
O, tell me, for I long to be resolved :

    Ili. Lovely Æneas, these are Carthage-walls;
And here Queen Dido wears th' imperial crown,
Who for Troy's sake hath entertained us all,
And clad us in these wealthy robes we wear.
Oft hath she asked us under whom we served;
And, when we told her, she would weep for grief,
Thinking the sea had swallowed up thy ships;
And, now she sees thee, how will she rejoice!   70

---

    [1] Æneas is not shrouded in a cloud, as the reader (remembering Virgil) might at first suppose. Ilioneus fails to recognise Æneas in his mean apparel.
    [2] Old ed. "meanes."

Serg. See, where her servitors pass through the hall,[1]
Bearing a banquet : Dido is not far.
Ili. Look, where she comes ; Æneas, view[2] her well.
Æn. Well may I view her ; but she sees not me.

Enter DIDO, ANNA, IARBAS, *and train.*

Dido. What stranger art thou, that dost eye me thus ?
Æn. Sometime I was a Trojan, mighty queen ;
But Troy is not :—what shall I say I am ?
Ili. Renowmèd Dido, 'tis our general,
Warlike Æneas.
Dido. Warlike Æneas, and in these base robes !   80
Go fetch the garment which Sichæus ware.—

[*Exit an* Attendant, *who brings in the garment, which*
ÆNEAS *puts on.*

Brave prince, welcome to Carthage and to me,
Both happy that Æneas is our guest.
Sit in this chair, and banquet with a queen :
Æneas is Æneas, were he clad
In weeds as bad as ever Irus ware.
Æn. This is no seat for one that's comfortless :
May it please your grace to let Æneas wait ;
For though my birth be great, my fortune's mean,
Too mean to be companion to a queen.   90
Dido. Thy fortune may be greater than thy birth :
Sit down, Æneas, sit in Dido's place ;

---

[1] We must suppose that the scene changes to Dido's palace.
[2] Old ed. " viewd."

And, if this be thy son, as I suppose,
Here let him sit.—Be merry, lovely child.

Æn. This place beseems me not ; O, pardon me !

Dido. I'll have it so : Æneas, be content.

Asc. Madam, you shall be my mother.

Dido. And so I will, sweet child.—Be merry, man :
Here's to thy better fortune and good stars.   [*Drinks.*

Æn. In all humility, I thank your grace.   100

Dido. Remember who thou art ; speak like thyself :
Humility belongs to common grooms.

Æn. And who so miserable as Æneas is ?

Dido. Lies it in Dido's hands to make thee blest ?
Then be assur'd thou art not miserable.

Æn. O Priamus, O Troy, O Hecuba !

Dido. May I entreat thee to discourse at large,
And truly too, how Troy was overcome ?
For many tales go of that city's fall,
And scarcely do agree upon one point :   110
Some say Antenor did betray the town ;
Others report 'twas Sinon's perjury ;
But all in this, that Troy is overcome,
And Priam dead : yet how, we hear no news.

Æn. A woful tale bids Dido to unfold,
Whose memory, like pale Death's stony mace,
Beats forth my senses from this troubled soul,
And makes Æneas sink at Dido's feet.

Dido. What, faints Æneas to remember Troy,
In whose defence he fought so valiantly ?   120
Look up, and speak.

Æn. Then speak Æneas, with Achilles' tongue :

And, Dido, and you Carthaginian peers,
Hear me; but yet with Myrmidons' harsh ears,
Daily inured to broils and massacres,
Lest you be mov'd too much with my sad tale.
The Grecian soldiers, tir'd with ten years' war,
Began to cry, "Let us unto our ships,
Troy is invincible, why stay we here?"
With whose outcries Atrides being appalled   130
Summon'd the captains to his princely tent;
Who, looking on the scars we Trojans gave,
Seeing the number of their men decreas'd,
And the remainder weak and out of heart,
Gave up their voices to dislodge the camp,
And so in troops all marched to Tenedos;[1]
Where when they came, Ulysses on the sand
Assayed with honey words to turn them back;
And, as he spoke, to further his intent,
The winds did drive huge billows to the shore,   140
And heaven was darkened with tempestuous clouds;
Then he alleg'd the gods would have them stay,

---

[1] "An odd mistake on the part of the poet; similar to that which is attributed to the Duke of Newcastle in Smollet's *Humphry Clinker* (vol. i. 236, ed. 1783), where his grace is made to talk about 'thirty thousand French *marching* from Acadia to Cape Breton.' (The following passage of Sir J. Harington's *Orlando Furioso* will hardly be thought sufficient to vindicate our author from the imputation of a blunder in geography:

'Now had they lost the sight of Holland shore,
    And *marcht* with gentle gale in comely ranke,' &c.
                                    B. x. st. 16.)"—*Dyce.*

The passage of Harington seems to amply vindicate Marlowe.

And prophesied Troy should be overcome:
And therewithal he call'd false Sinon forth,
A man compact of craft and perjury,
Whose ticing tongue was made of Hermes' pipe,
To force an hundred watchful eyes to sleep;
And him, Epeus having made the horse,
With sacrificing wreaths upon his head,
Ulysses sent to our unhappy town;   150
Who, grovelling in the mire of Xanthus' banks,
His hands bound at his back, and both his eyes
Turned up to heaven, as one resolved to die,
Our Phrygian shepherd[s] haled within the gates,
And brought unto the court of Priamus;
To whom he used action so pitiful,
Looks so remorseful, vows so forcible,
As therewithal the old man overcome,
Kissed him, embraced him, and unloosed his bands;
And then—O Dido, pardon me!   160
    Dido. Nay, leave not here; resolve me of the rest.
    Æn. O, th' enchanting words of that base slave
Made him to think Epeus' pine-tree horse
A sacrifice t' appease Minerva's wrath!
The rather, for that one Laocoon,
Breaking a spear upon his hollow breast,
Was with two wingèd serpents stung to death.
Whereat aghast, we were commanded straight
With reverence to draw it into Troy:
In which unhappy work was I employed;   170
These hands did help to hale it to the gates,
Through which it could not enter, 'twas so huge,—

O, had it never enter'd, Troy had stood !
But Priamus, impatient of delay,
Enforced a wide breach in that rampired wall
Which thousand battering-rams could never pierce,
And so came in this fatal instrument :
At whose accursèd feet, as overjoyed,
We banqueted, till, overcome with wine,
Some surfeited, and others soundly slept.   180
Which Sinon viewing, caus'd the Greekish spies
To haste to Tenedos, and tell the camp :
Then he unlocked the horse ; and suddenly,
From out his entrails, Neoptolemus,
Setting his spear upon the ground, leapt forth,
And, after him, a thousand Grecians more,
In whose stern faces shined the quenchless[1] fire
That after burnt the pride of Asia.
By this, the camp was come unto the walls,
And through the breach did march into the streets,   190
Where, meeting with the rest ; "Kill, kill !" they cried.
Frighted with this confusèd noise, I rose,
And, looking from a turret, might behold
Young infants swimming in their parents' blood,
Headless carcases pilèd up in heaps,
Virgins half-dead, dragged by their golden hair,
And with main force flung on a ring[2] of pikes,
Old men with swords thrust through their agèd sides,

---

[1] This epithet alone would show that the passage is Marlowe's.—Cf. *Edward II*, v. i. l. 44, "Heaven turn it to a blaze of *quenchless fire !*"

[2] We have had the expression "ring of pikes" in 2 *Tamburlaine*, iii. 2, l. 99.

Kneeling for mercy to a Greekish lad,   200
Who with steel pole-axes dash'd out their brains.
Then buckled I mine armour, drew my sword,
And thinking to go down, came Hector's ghost,[1]
With ashy visage, blueish sulphur eyes,
His arms torn from his shoulders, and his breast
Furrowed with wounds, and, that which made me weep,
Thongs at his heels, by which Achilles' horse
Drew him in triumph through the Greekish camp,
Burst from the earth, crying " Æneas, fly !
Troy is a-fire, the Grecians have the town ! "   210

Dido. O Hector, who weeps not to hear thy name ?

Æn. Yet flung I forth, and, desperate of my life,
Ran in the thickest throngs, and with this sword
Sent many of their savage ghosts to hell.
At last came Pyrrhus, fell and full of ire,
His harness [2] dropping blood, and on his spear
The mangled head of Priam's youngest son :
And, after him, his band of Myrmidons,
With balls of wild-fire in their murdering paws,
Which made the funeral flame that burnt fair Troy ;   220
All which hemmed me about, crying, "This is he ! "

Dido. Ah, how could poor Æneas scape their hands?

Æn. My mother Venus, jealous of my health,
Convey'd me from their crookèd nets and bands ;

---

[1] Mr. Symonds has an excellent criticism on this passage in *Shakespeare's Predecessors*, 664-5. He contrasts Virgil's reserve with Marlowe's exaggeration ; and remarks that "even Shakespeare, had he dealt with Hector's as he did with Hamlet's father's ghost, would have sought to intensify the terror of the apparition at the expense of artistic beauty."

[2] Armour.

So I escaped the furious Pyrrhus' wrath :
Who then ran to the palace of the king,
And at Jove's altar finding Priamus,
About whose withered neck hung Hecuba,
Folding his hand in hers, and jointly both
Beating their breasts, and falling on the ground,
He, with his falchion's point raised up at once,   230
And with Megæra's eyes, star'd in their face,
Threatening a thousand deaths at every glance :
To whom the agèd king thus, trembling, spoke ;
" Achilles' son, remember what I was,
Father of fifty sons, but they are slain ;
Lord of my fortune, but my fortune's turned :
King of this city, but my Troy is fired :
And now am neither father, lord, or king :
Yet who so wretched but desires to live ?
O, let me live, great Neoptolemus ! "   240
Not moved at all, but smiling at his tears,
This butcher, whilst his hands were yet held up,
Treading upon his breast, struck off his hands.
 Dido. O, end, Æneas ! I can hear no more.
 Æn. At which the frantic queen leaped on his face,
And in his eyelids hanging by the nails,
A little while prolonged her husband's life.
At last, the soldiers pull'd her by the heels,
And swung her howling in the empty air,
Which sent an echo to the wounded king :   250
Whereat he lifted up his bed-rid limbs,
And would have grappled with Achilles' son,
Forgetting both his want of strength and hands ;

Which he disdaining, whisk'd his sword about,
And with the wind thereof the king fell down;[1]
Then from the navel to the throat at once
He ripp'd old Priam; at whose latter gasp
Jove's marble statue gan to bend the brow,
As loathing Pyrrhus for this wicked act.
Yet he, undaunted, took his father's flag,   260
And dipped it in the old king's chill-cold blood,
And then in triumph ran into the streets,
Through which he could not pass for slaughter'd men :
So, leaning on his sword, he stood stone-still,
Viewing the fire wherewith rich Ilion burnt.
By this, I got my father on my back,
This young boy in mine arms, and by the hand
Led fair Creusa, my belovèd wife ;
When thou, Achates, with thy sword mad'st way,
And we were round environed with the Greeks :   270
O, there I lost my wife ! and, had not we
Fought manfully, I had not told this tale.
Yet manhood would not serve ; of force we fled ;
And, as we went unto our ships, thou know'st
We saw Cassandra sprawling in the streets,
Whom Ajax ravished in Diana's fane,[2]

---

[1] Old ed. "wound." The emendation was suggested by Collier.
Shakespeare certainly glanced at this passage when he wrote :—
           " Unequal match'd
        Pyrrhus and Priam drives, in rage strikes wide ;
        But with the whiff and wind of his fell sword
        The unnerved father falls."
Very slight heightening was required to give a burlesque turn to this
speech of Æneas.
[2] Old ed. "Fawne."

Her cheeks swollen with sighs, her hair all rent ;
Whom I took up to bear unto our ships ;
But suddenly the Grecians followed us,
And I, alas, was forced to let her lie !   280
Then got we to our ships, and, being aboard,
Polyxena cried out, "Æneas, stay !
The Greeks pursue me ; stay, and take me in !"
Moved with her voice, I leap'd into the sea,
Thinking to bear her on my back aboard,
For all our ships were launched into the deep,
And, as I swom, she, standing on the shore,
Was by the cruel Myrmidons surprised,
And, after that, by [1] Pyrrhus sacrificed.

Dido. I die with melting ruth ; Æneas, leave.[2]   290
Anna. O, what became of agèd Hecuba ?
Iar. How got Æneas to the fleet again ?
Dido. But how scaped Helen, she that caus'd this
       war ?
Æn. Achates, speak ; sorrow hath tir'd me quite.
Ach. What happen'd to the queen we cannot show ;
We hear they led her captive into Greece :
As for Æneas, he swom quickly back ;
And Helena betrayed Deiphobus,
Her lover, after Alexander died,
And so was reconciled to Menelaus.   300
Dido. O, had that ticing strumpet ne'er been born !—
Trojan, thy ruthful tale hath made me sad :

---

[1] Old ed. "And after by that."
[2] Cease speaking.

Come, let us think upon some pleasing sport,
To rid me from these melancholy thoughts.

> [*Exeunt all except* ASCANIUS, *whom* VENUS, *enter-
> ing with* CUPID *at another door, takes by the
> sleeve as he is going off.*

   Ven. Fair child, stay thou with Dido's waiting-
       maid :
I'll give thee sugar-almonds, sweet conserves,
A silver girdle, and a golden purse,
And this young prince shall be thy playfellow.

   Asc. Are you Queen Dido's son?

   Cup. I ; and my mother gave me this fine bow.   310

   Asc. Shall I have such a quiver and a bow?

   Ven. Such bow, such quiver, and such golden shafts,
Will Dido give to sweet Ascanius.
For Dido's sake I take thee in my arms,
And stick these spangled feathers in thy hat :
Eat comfits in mine arms, and I will sing.   [*Sings.*
Now is he fast asleep : and in his grove,[1]
Amongst green brakes, I'll lay Ascanius,
And strew him with sweet-smelling violets,
Blushing roses, purple hyacinth :   320
These milk-white doves shall be his centronels,[2]
Who, if that any seek to do him hurt,

---

[1] We must suppose that Venus had borne the sleeping Ascanius to
Cyprus.—Cf. Virg. *Æn.* i. 680–1 :—
> " Hunc ego sopitum somno super alta Cythera
> Aut super Idalium sacrata sede recondam."

[2] Sentinels. The form "centronel" (or "sentronel") occurs in the
Tryal of Chevalry (1605), i. 3 :—"Lieutenant, discharge Nod, and let
Cricket stand Sentronell till I come."

Will quickly fly to Cytherea's [1] fist.
Now, Cupid, turn thee to Ascanius' shape,
And go to Dido, who, instead of him,
Will set thee on her lap, and play with thee :
Then touch her white breast with this arrow-head,
That she may dote upon Æneas' love,
And by that means repair his broken ships,
Victual his soldiers, give him wealthy gifts,   330
And he, at last, depart to Italy,
Or else in Carthage make his kingly throne.
   Cup. I will, fair mother ; and so play my part
As every touch shall wound Queen Dido's heart. [*Exit.*
   Ven. Sleep, my sweet nephew,[2] in these cooling shades,
Free from the murmur of these running streams,
The cry of beasts, the rattling of the winds,
Or whisking of these leaves : all shall be still,
And nothing interrupt thy quiet sleep,
Till I return, and take thee hence again.   [*Exit.* 340

---

[1] Old ed. "Citheida's."
[2] Grandson (Lat. *nepos*).

ACT III.

SCENE I.

Enter [1] Cupid *as* Ascanius.

Cup. Now, Cupid, cause the Carthaginian queen
To be enamour'd of thy brother's looks :
Convey this golden arrow in thy sleeve,
Lest she imagine thou art Venus' son ;
And when she strokes thee softly on the head,
Then shall I touch her breast and conquer her.

Enter Dido, Anna, *and* Iarbas.

Iar. How long, fair Dido, shall I pine for thee ?
'Tis not enough that thou dost grant me love,
But that I may enjoy what I desire :
That love is childish which consists in words.   10
Dido. Iarbas, know, that thou, of all my wooers,—
And yet have I had many mightier kings,—
Hast had the greatest favours I could give.
I fear me, Dido hath been counted light
In being too familiar with Iarbas ;

---

1 Scene : a room in Dido's palace.

Albeit the gods do know, no wanton thought
Had ever residence in Dido's breast.
 Iar. But Dido is the favour I request.
 Dido. Fear not, Iarbas ; Dido may be thine.
 Anna. Look, sister, how Æneas' little son   20
Plays with your garments and embraceth you.
 Cup. No, Dido will not take me in her arms :
I shall not be her son, she loves me not.
 Dido. Weep not, sweet boy ; thou shalt be Dido's
   son :
Sit in my lap, and let me hear thee sing. [CUPID *sings.*
No more, my child : now talk another while,
And tell me where learn'dst thou this pretty song.
 Cup. My cousin Helen taught it me in Troy.
 Dido. How lovely is Ascanius when he smiles !
 Cup. Will Dido let me hang about her neck ? 30
 Dido. I, wag ; and give thee leave to kiss her too.
 Cup. What will you give me now ? I'll have this fan.
 Dido. Take it, Ascanius, for thy father's sake.
 Iar. Come, Dido, leave Ascanius ; let us walk.
 Dido. Go thou away : Ascanius shall stay.
 Iar. Ungentle queen, is this thy love to me ?
 Dido. O, stay, Iarbas, and I'll go with thee !
 Cup. An if my mother go, I'll follow her.
 Dido. Why stay'st thou here ? thou art no love of mine.
 Iar. Iarbas, die, seeing she abandons thee ! 40
 Dido. No ; live, Iarbas : What hast thou deserved,
That I should say thou art no love of mine ?
Something thou hast deserved.—Away, I say !
Depart from Carthage ; come not in my sight.

Iar. Am I not king of rich Gætulia?

Dido. Iarbas, pardon me, and stay a while.

Cup. Mother, look here.

Dido. What tell'st thou me of rich Gætulia?
Am not I queen of Libya? then depart.

Iar. I go to feed the humour of my love,   50
Yet not from Carthage for a thousand worlds.

Dido. Iarbas!

Iar. Doth Dido call me back?

Dido. No: but I charge thee never look on me.

Iar. Then pull out both mine eyes, or let me die.

[*Exit.*

Anna. Wherefore doth Dido bid Iarbas go?

Dido. Because his loathsome sight offends mine
    eye,
And in my thoughts is shrined another love.
O Anna, didst thou know how sweet love were,
Full soon wouldst thou abjure this single life!

Anna. Poor soul, I know too well the sour of love: 60
O, that Iarbas could but fancy me!   [*Aside.*

Dido. Is not Æneas fair and beautiful?

Anna. Yes; and Iarbas foul and favourless.

Dido. Is he not eloquent in all his speech?

Anna. Yes; and Iarbas rude and rustical.

Dido. Name not Iarbas: but, sweet Anna, say,
Is not Æneas worthy Dido's love?

Anna. O sister, were you empress of the world,
Æneas well deserves to be your love!
So lovely is he, that, where'er he goes,   70
The people swarm to gaze him in the face.

Dido. But tell them, none shall gaze on him but I,
Lest their gross eye-beams taint my lover's cheeks.
Anna, good sister Anna, go for him,
Lest with these sweet thoughts I melt clean away.
　　Anna. Then, sister, you'll abjure Iarbas' love?
　　Dido. Yet must I hear that loathsome name again?
Run for Æneas, or I'll fly to him.　　　　[*Exit* ANNA.
　　Cup. You shall not hurt my father when he comes.
　　Dido. No; for thy sake I'll love thy father well.— 80
O dull-conceited Dido, that till now
Didst never think Æneas beautiful!
But now, for quittance of this oversight,
I'll make me bracelets of his golden hair;
His glistering eyes shall be my looking-glass;
His lips an altar, where I'll offer up[1]
As many kisses as the sea hath sands;
Instead of music I will hear him speak;
His looks shall be my only library:
And thou, Æneas, Dido's treasury,　　　　　　　90
In whose fair bosom I will lock more wealth
Than twenty thousand Indias can afford.
O, here he comes! Love, love, give Dido leave
To be more modest than her thoughts admit,
Lest I be made a wonder to the world.

---

[1] The same form of expression occurs in the *Jew of Malta*, iii. ll.
32, 33 :—
　　　　" Upon which *altar I will offer up*
　　　　　My daily sacrifice of sighs and tears."

Enter ÆNEAS, ACHATES, SERGESTUS, ILIONEUS, *and*
CLOANTHUS.

Achates, how doth Carthage please your lord?

Ach. That will Æneas show your majesty.

Dido. Æneas, art thou there?

Æn. I understand your highness sent for me.

Dido. No; but, now thou art here, tell me, in sooth, 100
In what might Dido highly pleasure thee.

Æn. So much have I receiv'd at Dido's hands,
As, without blushing, I can ask no more:
Yet, queen of Afric, are my ships unrigg'd,
My sails all rent in sunder with the wind,
My oars broken, and my tackling lost,
Yea, all my navy split with rocks and shelves;
Nor stern nor anchor have our maimèd fleet;
Our masts the furious winds struck overboard:
Which piteous wants if Dido will supply,   110
We will account her author of our lives.

Dido. Æneas, I'll repair thy Trojan ships,
Conditionally that thou wilt stay with me,
And let Achates sail to Italy:
I'll give thee tackling made of rivelled[1] gold,
Wound on the barks of odoriferous trees;[2]
Oars of massy ivory, full of holes,
Through which the water shall delight to play;
Thy anchors shall be hewed from crystal rocks,

---

[1] "*I.e.* (I suppose) twisted."—*Dyce.*

[2] "The blank verse, falling in couplets, seems to cry aloud for
rhymes."—*Symonds.*

Which, if thou lose, shall shine above the waves;   120
The masts, whereon thy swelling sails shall hang,
Hollow pyramides of silver plate;
The sails of folded lawn, where shall be wrought
The wars of Troy,—but not Troy's overthrow;
For ballace,[1] empty Dido's treasury:
Take what ye will, but leave Æneas here.
Achates, thou shalt be so seemly[2] clad,
As sea-born nymphs shall swarm about thy ships,
And wanton mermaids court thee with sweet songs,
Flinging in favours of more sovereign worth   130
Than Thetis hangs about Apollo's neck,
So that Æneas may but stay with me.

    Æn. Wherefore would Dido have Æneas stay?

    Dido. To war against my bordering enemies.
Æneas, think not Dido is in love;
For, if that any man could conquer me,
I had been wedded ere Æneas came:
See, where the pictures of my suitors hang;
And are not these as fair as fair may be?

    Ach. I saw this man at Troy, ere Troy was sack'd.   140

    Æn.[3] I this in Greece, when Paris stole fair Helen.

    Ili. This man and I were at Olympia's[4] games,

---

  [1] Ballast.

  [2] I have adopted Dyce's emendation. The old ed. gives "meanly."
(Collier suggested "newly.")

  [3] Dyce gives this line to Sergestus, arguing that the prefix *Æn.* is
"proved to be wrong by the next speech of Dido." But we may suppose that Dido is there calling Æneas' attention to another set of pictures on the opposite side of the stage.

  [4] Old ed. "Olympus."

Serg. I know this face; he is a Persian born:
I travell'd with him to Ætolia.

Cloan. And I in Athens with this gentleman,
Unless I be deceived, disputed once.

Dido. But speak, Æneas: know you none of these?

Æn. No, madam; but it seems that these are kings.

Dido. All these, and others which I never saw,
Have been most urgent suitors for my love;   150
Some came in person, others sent their legates,
Yet none obtained me: I am free from all;
And yet, God knows, entangled unto one.
This was an orator, and thought by words
To compass me: but yet he was deceiv'd:
And this a Spartan courtier, vain and wild;
But his fantastic humours pleased not me:
This was Alcion, a musician;
But, play'd he ne'er so sweet, I let him go:
This was the wealthy king of Thessaly: 160
But I had gold enough, and cast him off:
This, Meleager's son, a warlike prince;
But weapons gree not with my tender years:
The rest are such as all the world well knows:
Yet now [1] I swear, by heaven and him I love,
I was as far from love as they from hate.

Æn. O, happy shall he be whom Dido loves!

Dido. Then never say that thou art miserable,
Because, it may be, thou shalt be my love,
Yet boast not of it, for I love thee not,—   170

---

[1] Old ed. "how."

And yet I hate thee not.—O, if I speak,
I shall betray myself! [*Aside.*]—Æneas, come : [1]
We too will go a-hunting in the woods;
But not so much for thee,—thou art but one,—
As for Achates and his followers.   [*Exeunt.*

SCENE II.

Enter [2] JUNO *to* ASCANIUS, *who lies asleep.*

Juno. Here lies my hate, Æneas' cursèd brat,
The boy wherein false Destiny delights,
The heir of Fury,[3] the favourite of the Fates,[4]
That ugly imp that shall outwear my wrath,
And wrong my deity with high disgrace.
But I will take another order now,
And raze th' eternal register of Time :
Troy shall no more call him her second hope,
Nor Venus triumph in his tender youth;
For here, in spite of Heaven, I'll murder him,   10
And feed infection with his let-out [5] life.
Say, Paris, now shall Venus have the ball?
Say, vengeance, now shall her Ascanius die?
O no! God wot, I cannot watch my time,

---

[1] Old ed. "speak" (repeated from the line above).
[2] Scene : a grove.
[3] "Heir of Fury" is certainly a strange expression, but I dare not
adopt Cunningham's emendation, "heir of Troy."
[4] Old ed. "face."
[5] Old ed. "left out."

Nor quit good turns with double fee down told :
Tut, I am simple, without mind[1] to hurt,
And have no gall at all to grieve my foes !
But lustful Jove and his adulterous child
Shall find it written on confusion's front,
That only Juno rules in Rhamnus town.[2]   20

Enter VENUS.

Ven. What should this mean? my doves are back
        return'd
Who warn me of such danger prest[3] at hand
To harm my sweet Ascanius' lovely life.—
Juno, my mortal foe, what make you here?
Avaunt, old witch ! and trouble not my wits.

Juno. Fie, Venus, that such causeless words of wrath
Should e'er defile so fair a mouth as thine !
Are not we both sprung of celestial race,
And banquet, as two sisters, with the gods ?
Why is it, then, displeasure should disjoin   30
Whom kindred and acquaintance co-unites ?

Ven. Out, hateful hag ! thou wouldst have slain my son,
Had not my doves discovered thy intent :
But I will tear thy eyes fro forth thy head,
And feast the birds with their blood-shotten balls,
If thou but lay thy fingers on my boy.

Juno. Is this, then, all the thanks that I shall have
For saving him from snakes' and serpents' stings,

---

[1] Old ed. "made."—The correction is *Dyce's.*
[2] See vol. i. p. 35, note 4.
[3] Ready.

That would have killed him, sleeping, as he lay?
What, though I was offended with thy son,   40
And wrought him mickle woe on sea and land,
When, for the hate of Trojan Ganymede,[1]
That was advancèd by my Hebe's shame,
And Paris' judgment of the heavenly ball,
I mustered all the winds unto his wreck,
And urg'd each element to his annoy?
Yet now I do repent me of his ruth,
And wish that I had never wrong'd him so.
Bootless, I saw, it was to war with fate
That hath so many unresisted[2] friends: 50
Wherefore I changed[3] my counsel with the time,
And planted love where envy erst had sprung.
   Ven. Sister of Jove, if that thy love be such
As these thy protestations do paint forth,
We two, as friends, one fortune will divide:
Cupid shall lay his arrows in thy lap,
And to a sceptre change his golden shafts;
Fancy[4] and modesty shall live as mates,
And thy fair peacocks by my pigeons perch:
Love, my Æneas, and desire is thine;   60
The day, the night, my swans, my sweets, are thine,
   Juno. More than melodious are these words to me,

---

[1] A Virgilian passage. Cf. *Æn.* i. 26-8 :—
        "Manet alta mente repostum
    Judicium, Paridis, spretæque injuria formæ,
    Et genus invisum, et rapti Ganimedis honores."
[2] Irresistible.
[3] Old ed. "change."
[4] Love.

That overcloy my soul with their content.
Venus, sweet Venus, how may I deserve
Such amorous favours at thy beauteous hand?
But, that thou mayst more easily perceive
How highly I do prize this amity,
Hark to a motion of eternal league,
Which I will make in quittance of thy love.
Thy son, thou know'st, with Dido now remains,   70
And feeds his eyes with favours of her court;
She, likewise, in admiring spends her time,
And cannot talk nor think of aught but him :
Why should not they, then, join in marriage,
And bring forth mighty kings to Carthage-town,
Whom casualty of sea hath made such friends?
And, Venus, let there be a match confirm'd
Betwixt these two, whose loves are so alike ;
And both our deities, conjoin'd in one,
Shall chain felicity unto their throne.   80
    Ven. Well could I like this reconcilement's means;
But much I fear my son will ne'er consent,
Whose armèd soul, already on the sea,
Darts forth her light [un]to Lavinia's shore.
    Juno. Fair queen of love, I will divorce these doubts,
And find my way to weary such fond thoughts.
This day they both a-hunting forth will ride
Into the [1] woods adjoining to these walls ;
When, in the midst of all their gamesome sports,
I'll make the clouds dissolve their watery works,   90

---

[1] Old ed. "these."

And drench Silvanus' dwellings with their showers;
Then in one cave the queen and he shall meet,
And interchangeably discourse their thoughts,
Whose short conclusion will seal up their hearts
Unto the purpose which we now propound.

   Ven. Sister, I see you savour of my wiles:
Be it as you will have [it] for this once.
Meantime Ascanius shall be my charge;
Whom I will bear to Ida in mine arms,
And couch him in Adonis' purple down.   100

                        [Exeunt.

SCENE III.

Enter[1] Dido, Æneas, Anna, Iarbas, Achates, Cupid
as Ascanius, *and* Followers.

   Dido. Æneas, think not but I honour thee,
That thus in person go with thee to hunt:
My princely robes, thou see'st, are laid aside,
Whose glittering pomp Diana's shroud[2] supplies;
All fellows now, disposed alike to sport:
The woods are wide, and we have store of game.
Fair Trojan, hold my golden bow a while,
Until I gird my quiver to my side.—
Lords, go before; we two must talk alone.

   Iar. Ungentle, can she wrong Iarbas so?   10

---

[1] Scene: a wood near Carthage.
[2] Old ed. "shrowdes."

I'll die before a stranger have that grace.
" We two will talk alone "—what words be these !

[*Aside.*

Dido. What makes Iarbas here of all the rest ?
We could have gone without your company.

Æn. But love and duty led him on perhaps
To press beyond acceptance to your sight.

Iar. Why ! man of Troy, do I offend thine eyes ?
Or art thou grieved thy betters press so nigh ?

Dido. How now, Gætulian ! are you grown so brave,
To challenge us with your comparisons ?   20
Peasant, go seek companions like thyself,
And meddle not with any that I love.—
Æneas, be not moved at what he says ;
For otherwhile he will be out of joint.

Iar. Women may wrong by privilege of love ;
But, should that man of men, Dido except,
Have taunted me in these opprobrious terms,
I would have either drunk his dying blood,
Or else I would have given my life in gage.   29

Dido. Huntsmen, why pitch you not your toils apace,
And rouse the light-foot deer from forth their lair ?

Anna. Sister, see, see Ascanius in his pomp,
Bearing his hunt-spear bravely in his hand !

Dido. Yea, little son, are you so forward now ?

Cup. I, mother ; I shall one day be a man,
And better able unto other arms ;
Meantime these wanton weapons serve my war,
Which I will break betwixt a lion's jaws.

Dido. What ? dar'st thou look a lion in the face ?

Cup. I; and outface him too, do what he can. 40

Anna. How like his father speaketh he in all!

Æn. And mought I live to see him sack rich Thebes,
And load his spear with Grecian princes' heads,
Then would I wish me with Anchises' tomb,
And dead to honour that hath brought me up.

Iar. And might I live to see thee shipp'd away,
And hoist aloft on Neptune's hideous hills,
Then would I wish me in fair Dido's arms,
And dead to scorn that hath pursu'd me so. [*Aside.*

Æn. Stout friend Achates, dost thou know this
    wood? 50

Ach. As I remember, here you shot the deer
That saved your famish'd soldiers' lives from death,
When first you set your foot upon the shore;
And here we met fair Venus, virgin-like,
Bearing her bow and quiver at her back.

Æn. O, how these irksome labours now delight,
And overjoy my thoughts with their escape!
Who would not undergo all kind of toil,
To be well stor'd with such a winter's tale?

Dido. Æneas, leave these dumps, and let's away. 60
Some to the mountains, some unto the soil,[1]
You to the valleys,—thou unto the house.

         [*Exeunt all except* IARBAS.

Iar. I, this it is which wounds me to the death,

---

[1] A deer or other animal was said to "take *soil*" when it fled from
its pursuers to the water. Dyce quotes from Cotgrave:—"*Souil de
sanglier.* The soile of a wild Boare; the slough or mire wherein he
hath wallowed."

To see a Phrygian, far-fet [1] o'er the sea,
Preferr'd before a man of majesty.
O love!   O hate!   O cruel women's hearts,
That imitate the moon in every change,
And, like the planets, ever love to range!
What shall I do, thus wrongèd with disdain?
Revenge me on Æneas or on her?   70
On her! fond man, that were to war 'gainst heaven,
And with one shaft provoke ten thousand darts.
This Trojan's end will be thy envy's aim,
Whose blood will reconcile thee to content,
And make love drunken with thy sweet desire.
But Dido, that now holdeth him so dear,
Will die with very tidings of his death:
But time will discontinue her content,
And mould her mind unto new fancy's shapes,
O God of heaven, turn the hand of Fate   80
Unto that happy day of my delight!
And then—what then?   Iarbas shall but love:
So doth he now, though not with equal gain;
That resteth in the rival of thy pain,
Who ne'er will cease to soar till he be slain.   [*Exit.*

SCENE IV.

The storm.   Enter ÆNEAS *and* DIDO *in the cave, at
several times.*

Dido. Æneas!

---

[1] Far-fetched.   There was a common proverb "*far-fet* and dear-
bought is good for ladies."—Old ed. "*far fet to* the sea."

Æn. Dido !

Dido. Tell me, dear love, how found you out this cave ?

Æn. By chance, sweet queen, as Mars and Venus met.

Dido. Why, that was in a net, where we are loose :
And yet I am not free,—O, would I were !

Æn. Why, what is it that Dido may desire
And not obtain, be it in human power ?

Dido. The thing that I will die before I ask,
And yet desire to have before I die.   10

Æn. It is not aught Æneas may achieve ?

Dido. Æneas ! no ; although his eyes do pierce.

Æn. What, hath Iarbas anger'd her in aught ?
And will she be avengèd on his life ?

Dido. Not anger'd me, except in angering thee.

Æn. Who, then, of all so cruel may he be
That should detain thy eye in his defects ?

Dido. The man that I do eye where'er I am :
Whose amorous face, like Pæan, sparkles fire,
Whenas he butts his beams on Flora's bed.   20
Prometheus hath put on Cupid's shape,
And I must perish in his burning arms :
Æneas, O Æneas, quench these flames :

Æn. What ails my queen ? is she faln sick of late ?

Dido. Not sick, my love : but sick I must conceal
The torment that it boots me not reveal :
And yet I'll speak,—and yet I'll hold my peace.
Do shame her worst, I will disclose my grief :
Æneas, thou art he—what did I say ?
Something it was that now I have forgot.   30

Æn. What means fair Dido by this doubtful speech ?

Dido. Nay, nothing; but Æneas loves me not.

Æn. Æneas' thoughts dare not ascend so high
As Dido's heart, which monarchs might not scale.

Dido. It was because I saw no king like thee,
Whose golden crown might balance my content;
But now that I have found what to affect,
I follow one that loveth fame 'fore [1] me,
And rather had seem fair [in] Sirens' eyes,
Than to the Carthage queen that dies for him.   40

Æn. If that your majesty can look so low
As my despisèd worths that shun all praise,
With this my hand I give to you my heart,
And vow, by all the gods of hospitality,
By heaven and earth, and my fair brother's bow,
By Paphos, Capys,[2] and the purple sea
From whence my radiant mother did ascend,[3]
And by this sword that sav'd me from the Greeks,
Never to leave these new-uprearèd walls,
Whiles Dido lives and rules in Juno's town,—   50
Never to like or love any but her!

Dido. What more than Delian music do I hear,
That calls my soul from forth his living seat
To move unto the measures of delight?
Kind clouds, that sent forth such a courteous storm
As made disdain to fly to fancy's lap!
Stout love, in mine arms make thy Italy,

---

[1] Old ed. "for."
[2] The father of Anchises.
[3] Old ed. "descend" (which Dyce and Cunningham strangely retain).

Whose crown and kingdom rests at thy command :
Sichæus, not Æneas, be thou call'd ;
The king of Carthage, not Anchises' son.   60
Hold, take these jewels at thy lover's hand,

       [*Giving jewels, &c.*

These golden bracelets, and this wedding-ring,
Wherewith my husband woo'd me yet a maid,
And be thou king of Libya by my gift.

       [*Exeunt to the cave.*

ACT IV.

SCENE I.

Enter[1] ACHATES, CUPID *as* ASCANIUS, IARBAS, *and* ANNA.

Ach. Did ever men see such a sudden storm
Or day so clear so suddenly o'ercast?

Iar. I think some fell enchantress dwelleth here,
That can call them[2] forth whenas she please,
And dive into black tempest's treasury,
Whenas she means to mask the world with clouds.

Anna. In all my life I never knew the like;
It hailed, it snowed, it lightened all at once.

Ach. I think, it was the devil's revelling night,
There was such hurly-burly in the heavens: 10
Doubtless Apollo's axle-tree is crack'd,
Or agèd Atlas' shoulder out of joint,
The motion was so over-violent.

---

[1] Scene: before the cave.
[2] The line is unrhythmical and corrupt. Qy. "That can *call forth the winds*"?

Iar. In all this coil, where have ye left the queen?

Asc. Nay, where's my warlike father, can you tell?

Anna. Behold, where both of them come forth the
  cave.

Iar. Come forth the cave! can heaven endure this
  sight?

Iarbas, curse that unrevenging Jove,

Whose flinty darts slept in Typhœus'[1] den,

Whiles these adulterers surfeited with sin.   20

Nature, why mad'st me not some poisonous beast,

That with the sharpness of my edgèd sting

I might have staked them both unto the earth,

Whilst they were sporting in this darksome cave!

              [*Aside.*

  Enter, from the cave, ÆNEAS *and* DIDO.

Æn. The air is clear, and southern winds are whist.[2]

Come, Dido, let us hasten to the town,

Since gloomy Æolus doth cease to frown.

 Dido. Achates and Ascanius, well met.

 Æn. Fair Anna, how escap'd you from the shower?

 Anna. As others did, by running to the wood. 30

 Dido. But where were you, Iarbas, all this while?

 Iar. Not with Æneas in the ugly cave.

 Dido. I see, Æneas sticketh in your mind;

But I will soon put by that stumbling-block,

And quell those hopes that thus employ your cares.[3]

              [*Exeunt.*

---

[1] Old ed. "Tiphous."   [2] Still, hushed.

[3] Old ed. "eares."

SCENE II.

Enter [1] IARBAS *to sacrifice.*

Iar. Come, servants, come; bring forth the sacrifice,
That I may pacify that gloomy Jove,
Whose empty altars have enlarg'd our ills.—
          [Servants *bring in the sacrifice, and then exeunt.*
Eternal Jove, great master of the clouds,
Father of gladness and all frolic thoughts,
That with thy gloomy [2] hand corrects the heaven,
When airy creatures war amongst themselves;
Hear, hear, O, hear Iarbas' plaining prayers,
Whose hideous echoes make the welkin howl,
And all the woods Eliza [3] to resound !   10
The woman that thou willed us entertain,
Where, straying in our borders up and down,
She crav'd a hide of ground to build a town,
With whom we did divide both laws and land,
And all the fruits that plenty else sends forth,
Scorning our loves and royal marriage-rites,
Yields up her beauty to a stranger's bed;
Who, having wrought her shame, is straightway fled :
Now, if thou be'st a pitying god of power,
On whom ruth and compassion ever waits,   20
Redress these wrongs, and warn him to his ships,
That now afflicts me with his flattering eyes.

---

[1] Scene : a room in Iarbas' house.

[2] The epithet "gloomy," here and in l. 2, contrasts oddly with "*Father of gladness and all frolic thoughts.*"

[3] Elissa (Dido).

Enter ANNA.

Anna. How now, Iarbas! at your prayers so hard?

Iar. I, Anna: is there aught you would with
    me?

Anna. Nay, no such weighty business of import
But may be slacked until another time:
Yet, if you would partake with me the cause
Of this devotion that detaineth you,
I would be thankful for such courtesy.

Iar. Anna, against this Trojan do I pray,   30
Who seeks to rob me of thy sister's love,
And dive into her heart by colour'd looks.

Anna. Alas, poor king, that labours so in vain
For her that so delighteth in thy pain!
Be rul'd by me, and seek some other love,
Whose yielding heart may yield thee more relief.

Iar. Mine eye is fixed where fancy cannot start:
O, leave me, leave me to my silent thoughts,
That register the numbers of my ruth,
And I will either move the thoughtless flint,   40
Or drop out both mine eyes in drizzling tears,
Before my sorrow's tide have any stint!

Anna. I will not leave Iarbas, whom I love,
In this delight of dying pensiveness.
Away with Dido! Anna be thy song;
Anna, that doth admire thee more than heaven.

Iar. I may nor will list to such loathsome change,
That intercepts the course of my desire.—
Servants, come fetch these empty vessels here;

For I will fly from these alluring eyes,　　　　　　　50
That do pursue my peace where'er it goes.

　　[*Exit.*—Servants *re-enter, and carry out the vessels, &c.*

　Anna. Iarbas, stay, loving Iarbas, stay !
For I have honey to present thee with.
Hard-hearted, wilt not deign to hear me speak ?
I'll follow thee with outcries ne'ertheless,
And strew thy walks with my dishevell'd hair.　　　[*Exit.*

SCENE III.

Enter ÆNEAS.[1]

Æn. Carthage, my friendly host, adieu !
Since Destiny doth call me from thy[2] shore :
Hermes this night, descending in a dream,
Hath summoned me to fruitful Italy ;
Jove wills it so : my mother wills it so :
Let my Phœnissa grant, and then I go.
Grant she or no, Æneas must away ;
Whose golden fortunes, clogg'd with courtly ease,
Cannot ascend to fame's immortal house,
Or banquet in bright Honour's burnished hall,　　　10
Till he hath furrowed Neptune's glassy fields,
And cut a passage through his topless[3] hills.—
Achates, come forth ! Sergestus, Ilioneus,
Cloanthus, haste away ! Æneas calls.

---

1 Scene : a room in Dido's palace.
2 Old ed. "the."
3 Cf. Faustus, scene xiv.—"And burnt the *topless* towers of Ilium."

Enter ACHATES, CLOANTHUS, SERGESTUS, *and* ILIONEUS.

Ach. What wills our lord, or wherefore did he call?

Æn. The dreams, brave mates, that did beset my bed,
When sleep but newly had embrac'd the night,
Commands me leave these unrenowmèd realms,[1]
Whereas nobility abhors to stay,
And none but base Æneas will abide.   20
Aboard, aboard! since Fates do bid aboard,
And slice the sea with sable-colour'd ships,
On whom the nimble winds may all day wait,
And follow them, as footmen, through the deep.
Yet Dido casts her eyes, like anchors, out,
To stay my fleet from loosing forth the bay:
" Come back, come back," I hear her cry a-far,
" And let me link thy [2] body to my lips,
That, tied together by the striving tongues,
We may, as one, sail into Italy."   30

Ach. Banish that ticing dame from forth your mouth,
And follow your fore-seeing stars in all:
This is no life for men-at-arms to live,
Where dalliance doth consume a soldier's strength,
And wanton motions of alluring eyes
Effeminate our minds, inur'd to war.

Ili. Why, let us build a city of our own,
And not stand lingering here for amorous looks.

---

[1] Old ed. "beames,"—a mistake, as Dyce observed, for "reames" (a common form of "realms)."

[2] Old ed. "my."

Will Dido raise old Priam forth his grave,
And build the town again the Greeks did burn? 　　40
No, no; she cares not how we sink or swim,
So she may have Æneas in her arms.

　　Clo. To Italy, sweet friends, to Italy!
We will not stay a minute longer here.

　　Æn. Trojans, aboard, and I will follow you.

　　　　　　　　　[Exeunt all except ÆNEAS.

I fain would go, yet beauty calls me back:
To leave her so, and not once say farewell,
Were to transgress against all laws of love.
But, if I use such ceremonious thanks
As parting friends accustom on the shore, 　　50
Her silver arms will coll[1] me round about,
And tears of pearl cry, "Stay, Æneas, stay!"
Each word she says will then contain a crown,
And every speech be ended with a kiss:
I may not dure this female drudgery:
To sea, Æneas! find out Italy! 　　　　　*[Exit.*

SCENE IV.

Enter[2] DIDO *and* ANNA.

　　Dido. O Anna, run unto the water-side!
They say Æneas' men are going aboard;
It may be, he will steal away with them:

---

[1] "Coll"=cling round the neck.
[2] Scene: a room in Dido's palace.

Stay not to answer me ; run, Anna, run !   [*Exit* ANNA.
O foolish Trojans, that would steal from hence,
And not let Dido understand their drift !
I would have given Achates store of gold,
And Ilioneus gum and Libyan spice ;
The common soldiers rich embroider'd coats,
And silver whistles to control the winds,   10
Which Circe [1] sent Sichæus when he lived :
Unworthy are they of a queen's reward.
See where they come : how might I do to chide ?

Re-enter ANNA, *with* ÆNEAS, ACHATES, CLOANTHUS,
    ILIONEUS, SERGESTUS, *and* Carthaginian Lords.

  Anna. 'Twas time to run ; Æneas had been gone ;
The sails were hoising up, and he aboard.
  Dido. Is this thy love to me ?
  Æn. O princely Dido, give me leave to speak !
I went to take my farewell of Achates.
  Dido. How haps Achates bid me not farewell ?
  Ach. Because I feared your grace would keep me
            here.   20
  Dido. To rid thee of that doubt, aboard again :
I charge thee put to sea, and stay not here.
  Ach. Then let Æneas go aboard with us.
  Dido. Get you aboard ; Æneas means to stay.
  Æn. The sea is rough, the winds blow to the shore.
  Dido. O false Æneas ! now the sea is rough ;

---

[1] Old ed. "Circes."

But, when you were aboard, 'twas calm enough:
Thou and Achates meant to sail away.

Æn. Hath not the Carthage queen mine only son?
Thinks Dido I will go and leave him here?   30

Dido. Æneas, pardon me; for I forgot
That young Ascanius lay with me this night;
Love made me jealous: but, to make amends,
Wear the imperial crown of Libya,

> [*Giving him her crown and sceptre.*

Sway thou the Punic sceptre in my stead,
And punish me, Æneas, for this crime.

Æn. This kiss shall be fair Dido's punishment.

Dido. O, how a crown becomes Æneas' head!
Stay here, Æneas, and command as king.

Æn. How vain am I to wear this diadem,   40
And bear this golden sceptre in my hand!
A burgonet of steel, and not a crown,
A sword, and not a sceptre, fits Æneas.

Dido. O, keep them still, and let me gaze my fill!
Now looks Æneas like immortal Jove:
O, where is Ganymede, to hold his cup,
And Mercury, to fly for what he calls?
Ten thousand Cupids hover in the air,
And fan it in Æneas' lovely face!
O, that the clouds were here wherein thou fled'st,[1]   50
That thou and I unseen might sport ourselves!
Heaven,[2] envious of our joys, is waxen pale;

---

[1] It is related in the fifth book of the Iliad how Aphrodite shrouded Æneas in a cloud when he was hard-pressed by Diomed.—Old ed. "fleest."

[2] Old ed. "Heavens."

And when we whisper, then the stars fall down,
To be partakers of our honey talk.

Æn. O Dido, patroness of all our lives,
When I leave thee, death be my punishment!
Swell, raging seas! frown, wayward Destinies!
Blow, winds! threaten, ye rocks and sandy shelves!
This is the harbour that Æneas seeks:
Let's see what tempests can annoy me now.   60

Dido. Not all the world can take thee from mine arms.
Æneas may command as many Moors
As in the sea are little water-drops:
And now, to make experience of my love,—
Fair sister Anna, lead my lover forth,
And, seated on my jennet, let him ride,
As Dido's husband, through the Punic streets;
And will [1] my guard, with Mauritanian darts
To wait upon him as their sovereign lord.

Anna. What if the citizens repine thereat?   70

Dido. Those that dislike what Dido gives in charge,
Command my guard to slay for their offence.
Shall vulgar peasants storm at what I do?
The ground is mine that gives them sustenance,
The air wherein they breathe, the water, fire,
All that they have, their lands, their goods, their lives!
And I, the goddess of all these, command
Æneas ride as Carthaginian king.

Ach. Æneas, for his parentage, deserves
As large a kingdom as is Libya.   80

---

[1] Desire, order.

Æn. I, and, unless the Destinies be false,
I shall be planted in as rich a land.
  Dido. Speak of no other land ; this land is thine :
Dido is thine, henceforth I'll thee lord.—
Do as I bid thee, sister ; lead the way :
And from a turret I'll behold my love.
  Æn. Then here in me shall flourish Priam's race ;
And thou and I, Achates, for revenge
For Troy, for Priam, for his fifty sons,
Our kinsmen's lives [1] and thousand guiltless souls,   90
Will lead an host against the hateful Greeks,
And fire proud Lacedæmon o'er their heads.
                    [*Exeunt all except* DIDO *and* Carthaginian Lords.
  Dido. Speaks not Æneas like a conqueror?
O blessèd tempests that did drive him in !
O happy sand that made him run aground !
Henceforth you shall be [of] our Carthage gods.
I, but it may be, he will leave my love,
And seek a foreign land called Italy :
O, that I had a charm to keep the winds
Within the closure of a golden ball ;   100
Or that the Tyrrhene sea were in mine arms,
That he might suffer shipwreck on my breast,
As oft as he attempts to hoist up sail !
I must prevent him : wishing will not serve.—
Go bid my nurse take young Ascanius,
And bear him in the country to her house ;
Æneas will not go without his son ;

---

1 Old ed. "loues."

Yet, lest he should, for I am full of fear,
Bring me his oars, his tackling, and his sails.

[Exit First Lord.

What if I sink his ships? O, he will frown !   110
Better he frown than I should die for grief.
I cannot see him frown ; it may not be :
Armies of foes resolv'd to win this town,
Or impious traitors vow'd to have my life,
Affright me not ; only Æneas' frown
Is that which terrifies poor Dido's heart ;
Not bloody spears, appearing in the air,
Presage the downfall of my empery,
Nor blazing comets threaten Dido's death ;
It is Æneas' frown that ends my days.   120
If he forsake me not, I never die ;
For in his looks I see eternity,
And he'll make me immortal [1] with a kiss.

Re-enter First Lord, *with* Attendants *carrying tackling,*
&c.

First Lord. Your nurse is gone with young Ascanius :
And here's Æneas' tackling, oars, and sails.

Dido. Are these the sails that, in despite of me,
Pack'd [2] with the winds to bear Æneas hence ?
I'll hang ye in the chamber where I lie ;
Drive, if you can, my house to Italy :
I'll set the casement open, that the winds   130

---

[1] Cf. *Faustus.*—
    "Sweet Helen, make me *immortal with a kiss.*"
[2] Intrigued.

May enter in, and once again conspire
Against the life of me, poor Carthage queen:
But, though ye[1] go, he stays in Carthage still;
And let rich Carthage fleet[2] upon the seas,
So I may have Æneas in mine arms.
Is this the wood that grew in Carthage plains,
And would be toiling in the watery billows,
To rob their mistress of her Trojan guest?
O cursèd tree, hadst thou but wit or sense,
To measure how I prize Æneas' love,   140
Thou wouldst have leapt from out the sailors' hands,
And told me that Æneas meant to go!
And yet I blame thee not; thou art but wood.
The water, which our poets term a nymph,[3]
Why did it suffer thee to touch her breast,
And shrunk not back, knowing my love was there?
The water is an element, no nymph.
Why should I blame Æneas for his flight?
O Dido, blame not him, but break his oars!
These were the instruments that launched him
     forth.   150
There's not so much as this base tackling too,
But dares to heap up sorrow to my heart:
Was it not you that hoisèd up these sails?
Why burst you not, and they fell in the seas?
For this will Dido tie ye full of knots,
And shear ye all asunder with her hands:

---

1 Old ed. "he."   2 Float.
3 Lat. *lympha* is the same word as *Nympha*.

Now serve to chastise shipboys for their faults :
Ye shall no more offend the Carthage queen.
Now, let him hang my favours on his masts,
And see if those will serve instead of sails ;   160
For tackling, let him take the chains of gold,
Which I bestow'd upon his followers ;
Instead of oars, let him use his hands,
And swim to Italy.   I'll keep these sure.—
Come, bear them in.   [*Exeunt.*

SCENE V.

Enter [1] Nurse, *with* CUPID *as* ASCANIUS.

Nurse. My Lord Ascanius, you must go with me.
Cup. Whither must I go?   I'll stay with my mother.
Nurse. No, thou shalt go with me unto my house.
I have an orchard that hath store of plums,
Brown almonds, services, ripe figs, and dates,
Dewberries, apples, yellow oranges :
A garden where are bee-hives full of honey,
Musk-roses, and a thousand sort of flowers ;
And in the midst doth run a silver stream,
Where thou shalt see the red-gill'd fishes leap,   10
White swans, and many lovely water-fowls.
Now speak, Ascanius, will you go or no?
Cup. Come, come, I'll go.   How far hence is your
          house?

---

[1] Scene : the open country near Carthage.

Nurse. But hereby, child; we shall get thither
    straight.

Cup. Nurse, I am weary; will you carry me?

Nurse. I, so you'll dwell with me, and call me mother.

Cup. So you'll love me, I care not if I do.

Nurse. That I might live to see this boy a man!
How prettily he laughs! Go, ye wag![1]
You'll be a twigger [2] when you come to age.—   20
Say Dido what she will, I am not old;
I'll be no more a widow; I am young;
I'll have a husband, or else a lover.

Cup. A husband, and no teeth!

Nurse. O, what mean I to have such foolish thoughts?
Foolish is love, a toy.—O sacred love!
If there be any heaven in earth, 'tis love,
Especially in women of your years.—
Blush, blush for shame! why shouldst thou think of
    love?
A grave, and not a lover, fits thy age.—   30
A grave! why, I may live a hundred years;
Fourscore is but a girl's age: love is sweet.—
My veins are withered, and my sinews dry:
Why do I think of love, now I should die?

Cup. Come, nurse.

Nurse. Well, if he come a-wooing, he shall speed:
O, how unwise was I to say him nay!   [*Exeunt.*

---

[1] The reader will be reminded of Juliet's Nurse.
[2] Wencher.

ACT V.

SCENE I.

Enter Æneas, [1] *with a paper in his hand, drawing the
   platform* [2] *of the city :* ACHATES, SERGESTUS, CLOAN-
   THUS, *and* ILIONEUS.

Æn. Triumph, my mates! our travels are at end :
Here will Æneas build a statelier Troy
Than that which grim Atrides overthrew.
Carthage shall vaunt her petty walls no more ;
For I will grace them with a fairer frame,
And clad her in a crystal livery,
Wherein the day may evermore delight ;
From golden India Ganges will I fetch,
Whose wealthy streams may wait upon her towers,
And triple-wise entrench her round about ;   10
The sun from Egypt shall rich odours bring,
Wherewith his burning beams (like labouring bees
That load their thighs with Hybla's honey-spoils) [3]

---

[1] Scene ; a room in Dido's palace.
[2] Plan.
[3] Old ed. " honeys spoyles."

Shall here unburden their exhalèd sweets,
And plant our pleasant suburbs with their[1] fumes.

Ach. What length or breadth shall this brave town
    contain?

Æn. Not past four thousand paces at the most.

Ili. But what shall it be call'd? Troy, as before?

Æn. That have I not determin'd with myself.

Clo. Let it be term'd Ænea, by your name.   20

Serg. Rather Ascania, by your little son.

Æn. Nay, I will have it callèd Anchisæon,
Of my old father's name.

        Enter HERMES *with* ASCANIUS.

Her. Æneas, stay; Jove's herald bids thee stay.

Æn. Whom do I see? Jove's wingèd messenger!
Welcome to Carthage new-erected town.

Her. Why, cousin, stand you building cities here,
And beautifying the empire of this queen,
While Italy is clean out of thy mind?
Too-too forgetful of thine own affairs,   30
Why wilt thou so betray thy son's good hap?
The king of gods sent me from highest heaven,
To sound this angry message in thine ears:
Vain man, what monarchy expect'st thou here?
Or with what thought sleep'st thou in Libya shore?
If that all glory hath forsaken thee,
And thou despise the praise of such attempts,
Yet think upon Ascanius' prophecy,

---

[1] Old ed. "her." In the *Athenæum* for 10th May 1884, Dr. Karl
Elze makes the plausible emendation, "And *scent* our pleasant suburbs
with *perfumes.*"

And young Iulus' more than thousand years,
Whom I have brought from Ida, where he slept,   40
And bore young Cupid unto Cyprus' isle.

Æn. This was my mother that beguil'd the queen.
And made me take my brother for my son :
No marvel, Dido, though thou be in love,
That daily dandlest Cupid in thy arms.—
Welcome, sweet child : where hast thou been this long ?

Asc. Eating sweet comfits with Queen Dido's maid,
Who ever since hath lull'd me in her arms.

Æn. Sergestus, bear him hence unto our ships,
Lest Dido, spying him, keep him for a pledge.   50
                    [*Exit* SERGESTUS *with* ASCANIUS.

Her. Spend'st thou thy time about this little boy,
And giv'st not ear unto the charge I bring ?
I tell thee, thou must straight to Italy,
Or else abide the wrath of frowning Jove.   [*Exit.*

Æn. How should I put into the raging deep.
Who have no sails nor tackling for my ships ?
What ? would the gods have me, Deucalion-like,
Float up and down where'er the billows drive ?
Though she repair'd my fleet and gave me ships,
Yet hath she ta'en away my oars and masts,   60
And left me neither sail nor stern [1] aboard.

Enter IARBAS.

Iar. How now, Æneas ! sad ! what means these dumps ?

---

[1] Rudder. Cf. 1 *Henry VI.* i. 1 :—
    " The king from Eltham I intend to send,
      And sit at chiefest *stern* of public weal."

Æn. Iarbas, I am clean besides myself;
Jove hath heaped on me such a desperate charge,
Which neither art nor reason may achieve,
Nor I devise by what means to contrive.

Iar. As how, I pray? may I entreat you tell?

Æn. With speed he bids me sail to Italy,
Whenas I want both rigging for my fleet,
And also furniture for these my men.　　　　70

Iar. If that be all, then cheer thy drooping looks,
For I will furnish thee with such supplies,
Let some of those thy followers go with me,
And they shall have what thing soe'er thou need'st.

Æn. Thanks, good Iarbas, for thy friendly aid:
Achates and the rest shall wait on thee,
Whilst I rest thankful for this courtesy.

　　　　　　　　　[Exeunt all except ÆNEAS.

Now will I haste unto Lavinian shore,
And raise a new foundation to old Troy.
Witness the gods, and witness heaven and earth,　　80
How loath I am to leave these Libyan bounds,
But that eternal Jupiter commands!

Enter DIDO.

Dido. I fear I saw Æneas' little son
Led by Achates [1] to the Trojan fleet.
If it be so, his father means to fly:—
But here he is; now, Dido, try thy wit.—　　　　*[Aside.*
Æneas, wherefore go thy men abroad?

---

[1] At l. 50 the stage-direction was "Exit *Sergestus* with Ascanius."

Why are thy ships new-rigged? or to what end,
Launched from the haven, lie they in the road?
Pardon me, though I ask; love makes me ask.   90

Æn. O, pardon me, if I resolve thee why!
Æneas will not feign with his dear love.
I must from hence: this day, swift Mercury,
When I was laying a platform[1] for these walls,
Sent from his father Jove, appear'd to me,
And in his name rebuk'd me bitterly
For lingering here, neglecting Italy.

Dido. But yet Æneas will not leave his love.

Æn. I am commanded by immortal Jove
To leave this town and pass to Italy;   100
And therefore must of force.

Dido. These words proceed not from Æneas' heart.

Æn. Not from my heart, for I can hardly go;
And yet I may not stay.   Dido, farewell.

Dido. Farewell! is this the 'mends for Dido's love?
Do Trojans use to quit[2] their lovers thus?
Fare well may Dido, so Æneas stay;
I die, if my Æneas say farewell.

Æn. Then let me go, and never say farewell:
Let me go; farewell:[3] I must from hence.   110

Dido. These words are poison to poor Dido's soul:
O, speak like my Æneas, like my love!

---

[1] Plan.

[2] Requite.

[3] A word which it is not easy to supply has been omitted.   Dyce's
"farewell [none]" and Cunninghan's "Let me go *is* farewell" are
equally unsatisfactory.

Why look'st thou toward the sea? the time hath been
When Dido's beauty chain'd[1] thine eyes to her.
Am I less fair than when thou saw'st me first?
O, then, Æneas, 'tis for grief of thee !
Say thou wilt stay in Carthage with thy[2] queen,
And Dido's beauty will return again.
Æneas, say, how can'st thou take thy leave?
Wilt thou kiss Dido?   O, thy lips have sworn   120
To stay with Dido ! canst thou take her hand ?
Thy hand and mine have plighted mutual faith ;
Therefore, unkind Æneas, must thou say,
" Then let me go, and never say farewell ? "

   Æn. O queen of Carthage, wert thou ugly-black,
Æneas could not choose but hold thee dear !
Yet must he not gainsay the gods' behest.

   Dido. The gods ! what gods be those that seek my
      death ?
Wherein have I offended Jupiter,
That he should take Æneas from mine arms ?   130
O no ! the gods weigh not what lovers do :
It is Æneas calls Æneas hence ;
And woful Dido, by these blubber'd[3] cheeks,
By this right hand, and by our spousal rites,
Desires Æneas to remain with her ;
Si[4] *bene quid de te merui, fuit aut tibi quidquam*

---

1 Old ed. "chaunged."
2 Old ed. "my"
3 Cf. i *Tamburlaine*, v. i. l. 21.
4 Virgil, *Æn.* iv. 317.

Dulce meum, miserere domus labentis, et istam,
Oro, si quis adhuc[1] *precibus locus, exue mentem.*

   Æn. Desine[2] *meque tuis incendere teque querelis ;*
Italiam non sponte sequor.   140

   Dido. Hast thou forgot how many neighbour kings
Were up in arms, for making thee my love?
How Carthage did rebel, Iarbas storm,
And all the world calls me a second Helen,
For being entangled by a stranger's looks?
So thou wouldst prove as true as Paris did,
Would, as fair Troy was, Carthage might be sack'd,
And I be called a second Helena!
Had I a son by thee, the grief were less,
That I might see Æneas in his face :   150
Now if thou go'st, what canst thou leave behind,
But rather will augment than ease my woe?

   Æn. In vain, my love, thou spend'st thy fainting
        breath :
If words might move me, I were overcome.

   Dido. And wilt thou not be mov'd with Dido's words?
Thy[3] mother was no goddess, perjured man,
Nor Dardanus the author of thy stock ;
But thou art sprung from Scythian Caucasus,
And tigers of Hyrcania gave thee suck.—
Ah, foolish Dido, to forbear this long!—   160

---

[1] Old ed. "ad hæc."
[2] Virgil, *Æn.* iv. 360.
[3] Cf. Virgil, *Æn.* iv. 365-7 :—
   "Nec tibi diva parens, generis nec Dardanus auctor,
      Perfide ; sed duris genuit te cautibus horrens
      Caucasus, Hycanæque admorunt ubera tigres."

Wast thou not wrecked upon this Libyan shore,
And cam'st to Dido like a fisher swain?
Repaired not I thy ships, made thee a king,
And all thy needy followers noblemen?
O serpent, that came creeping from the shore,
And I for pity harbour'd in my bosom,
Wilt thou now slay me with thy venomed sting,
And hiss at Dido for preserving thee?
Go, go, and spare not; seek out Italy:
I hope that that which love forbids me do,   170
The rocks and sea-gulfs will perform at large,
And thou shalt perish in the billows' ways
To whom poor Dido doth bequeath revenge:
I, traitor! and the waves shall cast thee up,
Where thou and false Achates first set foot;
Which if it chance, I'll give ye burial,
And weep upon your lifeless carcasses,
Though thou nor he will pity me a whit.
Why starest thou in my face?   If thou wilt stay,
Leap in mine arms: mine arms are open wide;   180
If not, turn from me, and I'll turn from thee;
For though thou hast the heart to say farewell,
I have not power to stay thee.   [*Exit* ÆNEAS.
                                                Is he gone?

I, but he'll come again; he cannot go;
He loves me too-too well to serve me so:
Yet he that in my sight would not relent,
Will, being absent, be obdurate[1] still.
By this, is he got to the water-side;

---

[1] Old ed. "abdurate."

And, see, the sailors take him by the hand ;
But he shrinks back ; and now remembering me,   190
Returns amain : welcome, welcome, my love !
But where's Æneas ? ah, he's gone, he's gone !

Enter ANNA.

Anna. What means my sister, thus to rave and cry?
Dido. O Anna, my Æneas is abroad,
And, leaving me, will sail to Italy !
Once didst thou go, and he came back again :
Now bring him back, and thou shalt be a queen,
And I will live a private life with him.
Anna. Wicked Æneas !
Dido. Call him not wicked, sister : speak him fair,   200
And look upon him with a mermaid's eye ;
Tell him, I never vow'd at Aulis' gulf
The desolation of his native Troy,
Nor sent a thousand ships unto the walls,
Nor ever violated faith to him :
Request him gently, Anna, to return :
I crave but this,—he stay a tide or two,
That I may learn to bear it patiently :
If he depart thus suddenly, I die.
Run, Anna, run ; stay not to answer me.   210
Anna. I go, fair sister : heavens grant good success !
[*Exit.*

Enter Nurse.

Nurse. O Dido, your little son Ascanius
Is gone ! he lay with me last night,
And in the morning he was stoln from me :
I think, some fairies have beguilèd me.

Dido. O cursèd hag and false dissembling wretch,
That slay'st me with thy harsh and hellish tale !
Thou for some petty gift hast let him go,
And I am thus deluded of my boy.—
Away with her to prison presently,		220

Enter Attendants.

Trait'ress too kenned [1] and cursèd sorceress !
Nurse. I know not what you mean by treason, I ;
I am as true as any one of yours.
Dido. Away with her ! suffer her not to speak.
		[*Exit* Nurse *with* Attendants.
My sister comes : I like not her sad looks.

Re-enter ANNA.

Anna. Before I came, Æneas was aboard,
And, spying me, hoist up the sails amain :
But I cried out, "Æneas, false Æneas, stay !"
Then gan he wag his hand, which, yet held up,
Made me suppose he would have heard me speak ;		230
Then gan they drive into the ocean :
Which when I view'd, I cried, " Æneas, stay !
Dido, fair Dido wills Æneas stay !"
Yet he, whose heart['s] of adamant or flint,
My tears nor plaints could mollify a whit.
Then carelessly I rent my hair for grief :
Which seen to all, though he beheld me not,
They gan to move him to redress my ruth,

---

[1] Old ed. "keend." If "kenned" is the right reading, we must
suppose the meaning to be "too clearly perceived."

And stay a while to hear what I could say ;
But he, clapp'd under hatches, sail'd away.   240
 Dido. O Anna, Anna, I will follow him !
 Anna. How can you go, when he hath all your fleet ?
 Dido. I'll frame me wings of wax, like Icarus,
And, o'er his ships, will soar unto the sun,
That they may melt, and I fall in his arms ;
Or else I'll make a prayer unto the waves,
That I may swim to him, like Triton's niece.
O Anna, [Anna,[1]] fetch Arion's [2] harp,
That I may tice a dolphin to the shore,
And ride upon his back unto my love !   250
Look, sister, look ! lovely Æneas' ships !
See, see, the billows heave him [3] up to heaven,
And now down falls the keels into the deep !
O sister, sister, take away the rocks !
They'll break his ships.   O Proteus, Neptune, Jove,
Save, save, Æneas, Dido's liefest [4] love !
Now is he come on shore, safe without hurt :
But, see, Achates wills him put to sea,
And all the sailors merry-make for joy ;
But he, remembering me, shrinks back again :   260
See, where he comes ! welcome, welcome, my love !
 Anna. Ah, sister, leave these idle fantasies !
Sweet sister, cease ; remember who you are.

---

[1] I have repeated "Anna" for the sake of the metre.   Cf. l. 241.
[2] Old ed. "Orions."
[3] Dyce's correction "'em" seems unnecessary.
[4] Dearest.   Cf. 2 *Henry VI.* iii. 1 :—
   "And with your best endeavours have stirred up
   My *liefest* liege to be mine enemy."

Dido. Dido I am, unless I be deceiv'd :
And must I rave thus for a runagate ?
Must I make ships for him to sail away ?
Nothing can bear me to him but a ship,
And he hath all my [1] fleet.—What shall I do,
But die in fury of this oversight ?
I ; I must be the murderer of myself :   270
No, but I am not ; yet I will be straight.—   [*Aside.*
Anna, be glad ; now have I found a mean
To rid me from these thoughts of lunacy :
Not far from hence
There is a woman famousèd for arts,
Daughter [2] unto the nymphs Hesperides,
Who will'd me sacrifice his ticing relics :
Go, Anna, bid my servants bring me fire.   [*Exit* ANNA.

              Enter IARBAS.

Iar. How long will Dido mourn a stranger's flight
That hath dishonoured her and Carthage both ?   280
How long shall I with grief consume my days,
And reap no guerdon for my truest love ?

        Enter Attendants *with wood and torches.*

Dido. Iarbas, talk not of Æneas ; let him go :
Lay to thy hands, and help me make a fire,
That shall consume all that this stranger left ;
For I intend a private sacrifice,
To cure my mind, that melts for unkind love.

---

[1] Old ed. "thy."

[2] "Daughter" is nonsense. Should we read "Guardian to" (or
"unto") ? Cf. Virg., *Æn.* iv. 484 :—
              " Hesperidum templi *custos.*"

Iar. But afterwards, will Dido grant me love?
Dido. I, I, Iarbas; after this is done,
None in the world shall have my love but thou. 290
                    [*They make a fire.*
So leave me now; let none approach this place.
                    [*Exeunt* IARBAS *and* Attendants.
Now, Dido, with these relics burn thyself,
And make Æneas famous through the world
For perjury and slaughter of a queen.
Here lie [1] the sword that in the darksome cave
He drew, and swore by, to be true to me:
Thou shalt burn first; thy crime is worse than his.
Here lie the garment which I cloth'd him in
When first he came on shore; perish thou too.
These letters, lines, and perjur'd papers, all 300
Shall burn to cinders in this precious flame.
And now, ye gods, that guide the starry frame,
And order all things at your high dispose,
Grant, though the traitors land in Italy,
They may be still tormented with unrest:
And from mine ashes let a conqueror rise,
That may revenge this treason to a queen
By ploughing up his countries with the sword!
Betwixt this land and that be never league;
Litora [2] *litoribus contraria, fluctibus undas* 310
Imprecor, arma armis; pugnent ipsique nepotes! [3]

---

[1] Here and in l. 298 Dyce needlessly reads " lies."
[2] Virg., *Æn.* iv. 628.
[3] The best editions o Virgil read "*ipsique nepotesque.*"

Live, false Æneas; truest Dido dies;
Sic,[1] *sic iuvat ire sub umbras.*

> [*Throws herself into the flames.*

Re-enter ANNA.

Anna. O, help, Iarbas! Dido in these flames
Hath burnt herself! ay me, unhappy me!

> *Re-enter* IARBAS, *running.*

Iar. Cursèd Iarbas, die to expiate
The grief that tires [2] upon thine inward soul!—
Dido, I come to thee.—Ay me, Æneas!

> [*Stabs himself and dies.*

Anna. What can my tears or cries prevail [3] me now
Dido is dead!   320
Iarbas slain, Iarbas my dear love!
O sweet Iarbas, Anna's sole delight!
What fatal destiny envies me thus,
To see my sweet Iarbas slay himself?
But Anna now shall honour thee in death,
And mix her blood with thine; this shall I do,
That gods and men may pity this my death,
And rue our ends, senseless of life or breath:
Now, sweet Iarbas, stay! I come to thee.

> [*Stabs herself, and dies.*

---

[1] Virg., *Æn.* iv. 660.   [2] Preys.   [3] Avail.

END OF VOL II.